G000123959

TREMEDDA DAYS

A View of Zennor, 1900–1940

ALISON SYMONS

TABB HOUSE

First published 1992
Tabb House, 7 Church Street, Padstow, Cornwall, PL28 8BG

British Library Cataloguing in Publication Data
Symons, Alison
A portrait of Zennor, 1900–1940.
1. Cornwall. Penwith (District), history
I. Title
942.375
ISBN 0-907018-83-1

Every endeavour has been made to contact copyright holders of illustrations appearing in this book. The publishers apologise to any artist, photographer or agency who has not been traced and whose work has been used.

Typeset by Exe Valley Dataset, Exeter, Devon
Printed and bound by Short Run Press Ltd, Exeter, Devon

CONTENTS

ACKNOWLEDGEMENTS

AT the time of writing this book I was greatly indebted to my father Maurice Griggs, Dick Berryman, Sydney Berryman, John Berryman, Hilda Jelbert and Clara and Harold Semmens for the wealth of information they gave me. I should also like to thank William Garnett for his encouragement and editing, Judy Symons for her drawings, Graeme Norways for his cover design and photography, and many other people for their help, including the loan of or permission to use photographs, in particular Mary Uren, Hazel Oliver, Charles Jelbert, Renee and Rex Whelan, Enid Tummon, Sonia Berryman, James Osborne, Willie Osborne, Ellen Fleming, Robina Craze, Flora Berryman, K Laughton, Denys Rooke, Reg Watkiss, Ander Gunn, Edwin Way Teale, Roger Symons, Mr S. Bennetts of St Ives, the Zennor Women's Institute for photos and items from their 'Changing Farm' competition, the Wayside Museum at Zennor, the St Ives Museum, the County Museum, the County Reference Library at Truro, the Hulton Picture Company, and the Ordnance Survey Office for use of the OS map on the cover. Special thanks to Mr Williamson and Mr Stanley Cock for their patience with the photography. Also thanks to Christopher Symons for photocopying and the plan of Tremedda buildings, and all my typist friends, particularly Anne Spencer, who gave great encouragement and help with the text.

Zennor Churchtown

TO TREMEDDA

KEY TO ZENNOR CHURCHTOWN

1. Blacksmith
2. Chy an Eglos
3. Church
4. School
5. Bos Cres (Granny Grigg's house)
6. Round Reading Room
7. Tinners' Arms
8. The Row
9. Glebe farm buildings
10. The Vicarage
11. Treveglos Farm House
12. Treveglos Farm Yard
13. The Chapel
14. Bridge Cottage

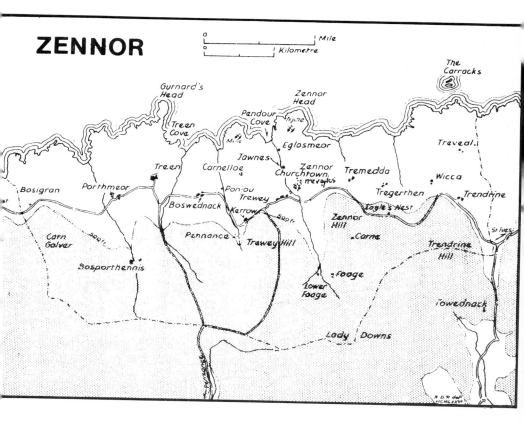

LIST OF ILLUSTRATIONS

ix

1. Elsie Pilcher and cow at Talland House, St Ives. p. 3

2. Maurice Griggs, p. 6, and Elsie with Ellen, their first child.

3. Plateau between cliff and hill, 1920s. p. 1. Foreground, L-R: Trewey, Zennor Chapel, Zennor Churchtown. Middle distance, L-R: Boswednack farms, Poniou, Carnellow Farm. Far distance, L-R: Porthmeor farms, Gurnard's Head Hotel, Treen farms, Chy Barnett, Gurnard Head jutting out to sea.

4. Trewey Farm with Zennor Churchtown in the background, 1870.

PART ONE: INTRODUCTORY

Zennor and its Farms in 1900

THE tiny hamlet of Tremedda, or Tremeadow as spelt by our neighbours, situated half a mile east of Zennor village on the plateau between Tremedda Carn and the cliff, and the surrounding parish of Zennor, is the setting for the following account of farming and rural life between 1900 and 1940. The hamlet consisted of three small farms, of which the Osborns farmed the westerly Tremeadow and my mother later farmed the remainder. Much of the information in this book comes from elderly Zennor farming friends. The rest comes from my early recollections of farming at Tremedda, greatly aided by my late father.

A glimpse into the parish of Zennor in 1900 would reveal many small groups of farms and cottages scattered along the narrow plateau between cliff and hill and in the valleys running inland. Around the church stood a larger group of buildings, including the Wesleyan chapel, vicarage, pub, shop, post office, blacksmith and school, making up Zennor Churchtown. All the buildings were low and built of granite, with walls often three or four feet thick. They seemed glued to the ground and impervious to the fierce winter gales that roared in from the Atlantic.

The small hamlets amidst the patchwork of tiny, irregular, rock-strewn fields were scarcely distinguishable from neighbouring outcrops of rock. On closer inspection, each hamlet could be seen to be made up of two or three farms and cottages. Each farm had a farmhouse, a barn with cowshouse, stable and hay house on the ground floor and loft above, a long, low piggery and cart-house. These buildings usually encircled a

1

central farmyard. Various little 'crows', or sheds, for pigs, hens and yearlings were dotted about. Some of the buildings were slate-roofed, many
still wore a covering of thatch. Each farm had neatly thatched hay- and
cornricks in a nearby mowhay, a fern (bracken) rick adjacent to the
piggery, and furze (gorse) and turf ricks handy to each dwelling.

Small herds of dairy cattle, horses and occasional flocks of sheep
grazed the tiny fields, crofts, moors and cliffs. Pigs wandered at large
in fields and around the farmstead and flocks of poultry cackled,
quacked, hissed and gobbled all over the place. People on foot and on
horseback traversed the winding footpaths, lanes and roads, on which
many horsedrawn vehicles might also be seen. The roads were surfaced
with 'rab', the yellowish clay formed from decomposed granite, found
locally under the soil. Travelling for the Zennor farmer was usually
limited to the distance there and back that a horse could manage in a day.
Many of the parishioners walked many miles to work, to school and to
market.

Many workers toiled in the fields; often the whole family would be
there digging, ditching, hedge trimming, 'leasing' (picking up) stones,
and generally tilling the soil and reaping the harvests. Neighbourly chat
and commands to the horses could be heard. During busy times such as
harvest, 'croust' was carried out to the field in the middle of the morning
and in the afternoon. The whole work force gathered under a hedge and
ate splits and cream, saffron cake and heavy cake washed down with
cups of tea, having a sociable, well-earned break.

Sounds of industry came from Foage and Trevail Valleys where the last
of the tin mines were still working. A few small fishing boats worked
from two rocky coves, catching fish when weather permitted.

The Zennor farmer of 1900 derived his income from many sources; the
sale of cream, butter, eggs, poultry, pigs, cattle, horses, lambs, and fleece
(wool) mainly. Some of them hired out their horses and carts to work on
the roads or help at the mines, while others worked in the mines or went
fishing, as well as farming a few acres.

The Zennor inhabitants were a hardy, close-knit, self-sufficient farming
community, presided over by the vicar. Many were descended from
families who had lived in this neighbourhood for hundreds of years. They
walked to the village for most of their social activities. They attended
church and chapel services, choir practices, socials, dances, meetings,
teas and cricket matches. A social was an entertainment put on by some
of the villagers. They produced plays, tap-danced, sang and recited
poetry, all on a tiny stage erected at one end of the schoolroom, always
finishing the programme with all standing for *God Save the King*. Only
the men went to the two local pubs, the Tinners' Arms and Gurnard's
Head Hotel.

This hardy, weather-beaten tribe of Zennor farming folk worked hard and long hours, scraping a living with little to spare from the wild rocky terrain. Farm life, however hard, was greatly enriched by independence and variety.

How Tremedda became my Home

DURING the early 1900s my mother Elsie Pilcher, then a girl in her twenties, found herself living in St Ives, the daughter of well-to-do Scottish parents. Her stepfather, Millie Dow, was an artist and had come to join the early art colony of that town. Talland House had been bought in 1897 from the *litterateur* Leslie (Sir Leslie) Stephen. The Stephen children, including the painter Vanessa (Bell) and the writer Virginia (Woolf), had regularly spent their summer holidays there; indeed, the house and bay form the thinly-disguised setting of Virginia's novel *To The Lighthouse*. Here the family always kept a cow, often a calf, a couple of horses and goats. My mother had a great affection for these animals and spent much of her time caring for them. They sparked off her burning desire to start farming in her own right. The idea grew and grew; she read books on farming and was an avid gleaner of information from every farmer she met. Mr Uren, who farmed at Porthminster Point and provided milk for the household, gave her many a long lecture on the local farming methods.

Her parents were dead against this madcap scheme, as they thought it. It took my mother a long time to bring them round. They even took the drastic measure of shipping her off to relations in India for a year to try to eradicate all thoughts of farming from her mind, but to no avail. On returning home she was as determined as ever and finally won them over. By 1910 her stepfather had bought the three small Tremedda farms. The largest one, bought in 1905 for £1,905, was rented out to the Osborns for many years, so my mother settled on the two smaller farms and started to make her dream come true. It must have caused quite a stir and given much scope for gossip in the parish of Zennor to find a single, well-brought-up young lady of means farming in their midst, a thing quite unheard of in those days.

After settling in at Tremedda, complete with an Italian chaperone, Alma Amicci Grossi, my mother proceeded to turn the two adjoining thatched cottages into one decent-sized house. These two little farms combined had forty acres arable and a hundred acres of hill, croft and cliff land. The old farm buildings were very rickety and run down and my mother had most of them rebuilt.

Only goats were kept for a short while as the fields were rented out. These goats were very friendly and knowing and grazed the hill and cliff. Alma was a tiny, dark lady who talked and gesticulated with great verve, although Uncle George Kennedy said "Alma looks as though she has been buried for a hundred years and then dug up." She was given the job of managing the goats. They were sent up the hill or down the cliff to graze, the leader of the little herd was staked and the rest stayed nearby. They were brought in to be fed and milked and would prance up the flight of stone steps to their smart little goat parlour at one end of the loft where each one had a little wooden stall, manger and hayrack. One day poor Alma was leading a very exuberant goat who pulled her over and dragged her all the way down the lane on the end of a rope. Rikki Garstin (Alethea Garstin the artist) told me of another occasion when she and Aunt Mary arrived at Tremedda driven by Roberts – "a great bully", says Rikki, who made the horse very nervous – bringing the provisions from St Ives, which they unloaded onto the kitchen table. They were all struggling to get the fire going in the open chimney with damp furze and turf, when the goats stepped in and ate the lot. Sometimes the goats pretended they couldn't get up the cliff while grazing the steep lower slopes. When people went down with ropes to rescue them they laughed, and leapt up and away.

Some of the goats were well bred and were shown at the Dairy Show in London. They went up by train accompanied by Alma and were taken from Paddington to Islington by taxi. One year a goat called Seleni was chosen champion of the show. My mother refused an offer of £1,000 for her: the following year she died. My mother had her skin as a bedside mat for many years. After three years Alma had trouble with interbreeding and some of the goats became hermaphrodite.

Anne Eddy, the old sewing woman from Bosporthennis, made coats for these goats. I am not sure whether they were smart ones for crossing London by taxi or rough ones to keep them warm in winter. The goats' milk was made into cheese, some of which, during the First World War, found its way into officers' Messes, paid for by the government.

When the fields became vacant my mother bought Kervis, her first cow, a Jersey-Guernsey cross, from Sam Nankervis of Trewey. All the descendants of this cow were called Nan or Kervis with the prefix old or young before it. As more cattle, horses and pigs came onto the farm, so the goat episode came to an end. My mother had begun farming in earnest.

Many people worked on Tremedda Farm: Maurice Griggs, a farming man from Zennor Churchtown, worked there for a short period before the First World War. Later he joined the army and served in France. Aunt Mary Kennedy, my mother's younger half-sister, who married at an early age and now had two small boys, John and Horas, came down to

5. Talland House. Standing in the group, L-R, Elsie Pilcher, Mary, Florence and the artist Millie Dow.

6. Goats mounting the barn steps, with Elsie Pilcher and Alma Amicci Grossi.

Cornwall, as her husband Uncle George was serving overseas. She left the children and their nanny with her mother in St Ives and came to Tremedda to help on the farm, visiting her family at weekends.

On returning home when the war ended, Maurice Griggs went to work for my mother once again and started courting her. Alma was terribly jealous: every time Maurice walked into the room, she rose and went out. My mother now had another battle royal on her hands to persuade her parents to agree to her marriage to Maurice. The couple all but eloped to Canada to farm. However, Millie Dow was finally won over by Great Aunt Katy. He stipulated that they should wait a year before the wedding took place: if they were still of the same mind then, he would say no more. In 1920, a year later to the day, they were married in Zennor parish church. Little did everyone know what a successful union this was to be. Mrs Arnold Foster from Eagle's Nest was heard to let out a sigh of relief, saying "Now sanity will return to the farming practices at Tremedda". The following impression of the newly married couple by Hamada, the famous Japanese potter and contemporary of Bernard Leach of St Ives, although not entirely accurate, is nonetheless interesting:

There was a family near St Ives whose daughter graduated from university and then went to Switzerland and Italy to learn the art of cheese-making. She married a tenant farmer, who had been educated in one of the local schools. Grig[g] their name was. Everybody was surprised at this marriage. They were so happy, and there was a wonderful barn he had made. They were living in this barn, and there were no drawings or paintings on the walls. A quilt spread on the bed was the highlight of the bedroom. In the kitchen were very fine tiles on the wall, old-fashioned pots and pans, and they had slipware for dishes. They burnt turf in a huge stone fireplace.

We were invited to a dinner there. The other guests included an architect, a painter, a writer and other good friends in the neighbourhood. Her husband had very little schooling, just grade school, so he did not participate very much in the conversation, which had turned to the new station built in London, Charing Cross Station, where there were decorations by Mestrovic and Eric Gill. The works of about four artists were exhibited there. When the guests discussed whose work was better and so forth there was no pleasure for the husband. I was very impressed with the wife, who was neither ashamed of him for not knowing much, nor did she try to shut him up when he said something. She just understood him and embraced him with great loving thoughts. The young wife modestly joined in the conversation and agreed with what her husband said – a very pleasant scene indeed. When the young wife talked, the husband kept quiet and ate the food. But when someone admired the butter served, the husband's eyes sparkled, and he began to explain how the butter was made. He proudly said that he regularly supplied the butter exclusively to a first class hotel in London. When someone mentioned how tender the rabbit meat was in the pie, he came to life and began to describe how he caught the rabbit, why it was tender – the entire chase with his hunting dog, jumping over fences and running across fields. If the rabbit is killed immediately, the flesh will be tender. Such knowledge he had. We were all extremely interested and suddenly learned to respect him for what he was. It was marvellous to see this happen.

The rabbit meat pie was simply delicious. The meat was stewed together with onions and potatoes and was placed in a slipware baking dish before getting too soft. Then the piecrust dough was unrolled over the dish. Holes were put in the crust to allow steam to escape while baking. I realised then that the holes were made into the initials S.H. – my initials.

In the large granite fireplace a turf fire was burning on the stone hearth. The chimney rising up the wall was equally impressive. It was all extremely imposing. After the stone flooring of the hearth was heated by the burning turf, they pushed aside the turf and placed the slipware dish containing the pie directly on the hot granite. They then covered the dish with a large steel pot and covered this pot with the burning turf. Unpeeled potatoes had been placed around the dish to fill the space inside the iron pot. When the pie was cooked the potatoes were done too. The potatoes were served with plenty of home-made butter together with the rabbit pie.

It was quite a feast at the farmer's house. The people, the way the slipware was used, and the way the food was cooked still remain vividly in my memory.

Six years later, I visited St Ives and I had an impatient desire to see the Grig[g] family. On my way, I met a sturdy young lady riding bareback. She was on her way to the blacksmith. I thought she came from the direction of the farmhouse so I called and asked her. She said she came from the very house I was to visit and that she was living with the family to learn how to make butter. She also told me that the house no longer could accommodate all those who gathered there, and many were renting rooms in houses nearby. I pictured then how the family had flourished since my last visit there six years before.

The kitchen floor was tiled, and the wooden handle of the door was hand-made. The quilts on the bed were brilliant in the chalky bedroom. The students made cheese, Cornish clotted cream and tea. When I was about to leave the house, accompanied to the door by the wife, I noticed an old stone mason silently chipping new concrete window frames. She told me she used concrete to fill in the frames to save time, instead of stones, to repair the mullion windows. Giving the concrete frames a finish like stone, she said, would make them blend with the house better.

In due course four little girls arrived on the scene, in the space of five years: Ellen, Robina, Alison (myself) and Flora. Annie Christopher was most indignant when Flora, the youngest, was born, saying "Not another lil' ol' maid!" When small, we were looked after by nannies, as my mother much preferred the outdoor work on the farm.

Thus Tremedda became my home.

Buildings

AT the beginning of this century all the Zennor buildings were built with local granite. They were low and snug, with very thick walls. Some of the better houses were ashlar-fronted, that is, built with cut stone. Roofs were now beginning to change from thatch to slate and later corrugated iron appeared on many little outhouses, often rusted to a bright reddish brown in hue. The church tower rose majestically above its low neighbours. The lovely warm tones of the stone, when reflected in the evening sunlight, made a very pretty picture.

A typical cottage in Zennor consisted of two rooms down, three up and maybe a lean-to as a back-kitchen or dairy at the rear. The front door was off-centre, as the much lived-in kitchen with its open chimney was considerably larger than the little parlour, which was only used on special occasions. The staircase between these two rooms confronted you as you entered the front door. There was one bedroom at either end of the cottage and a tiny one over the stair well.

The granite was built with a mixture of rab and lime; no cement was used. A pit at the bottom of Foage Lane produced a type of clay known locally as 'lias' which, when mixed with lime, made a hard and more cement-like surface. This had its special uses, such as paving the school yard and probably some floors.

At Tremedda, the only original buildings I can remember still standing in 1930 were the farmhouse, the old stables, an ancient barn and a little old pigs' 'crow' (sty). When my mother moved in, the farmhouse roof was thatched; however after the thatch caught fire, the roof was slated. Alterations to the buildings (begun in 1913, soon after she had settled in), were interrupted during the First World War owing to the labour shortage, and were finished after the war ended. Most of the farm buildings were rebuilt. My mother's brother-in-law George Kennedy, an architect, designed the buildings, giving a slightly Italian flavour with many arches, round windows and a loggia with a curved ceiling. My mother, having lived in Italy for a year during her adolescence, loved all things Italian and spoke the language fluently. The new buildings followed the conventional farming pattern, but were very handsome in design. George Kennedy had a great eye for proportion and included much detail in cut granite. These buildings were, and still are, quite remarkable.

The following is my aunt Mary's account of the rebuilding at Tremedda carried out under the direction of her husband.

The first part [to be rebuilt] round the old cider trough, was converted from a cow shed and opened up by two arches. The work was done by a local man, Bamfield.

The main building was built under contract with the Country Gentleman's Association, who supplied a foreman and used local labour. It consisted of a large cowshouse, dairy, separating and cheese-making room, loggia, outside bedroom, and two storage lofts. Part of one of these was fitted as a goat house, the goats finding no difficulty in mounting the steep flight of granite steps from the back yard.

Most of the stone used came from The Rocky Field on the farm, but the dressed stone came from a small quarry in the carn and was worked by Jimmy Thomas under direction of the architect. Jimmy Thomas was a wonderful craftsman and could handle granite in a truly remarkable way. He used one of his finger nails, which he had allowed to grow and become horny, to mark the required mouldings on the granite as dictated to him by the architect, by word of mouth or rough sketches. He always seemed to lose his pencil.

The huge lintels on top of the pillars of the main building (the cowshouse) were dragged in from the field by horses and erected and put in place with the aid of an endless chain. On the declaration of the First World War, the finishing of the building stopped as most of the labour force were naval reservists and were immediately called up. The scaffolding was taken down and no pointing completed, and one can still see the holes in the face of the building where supports had been temporarily inserted between the cut stones on the front of the building.

During the war (1914-1918) the building continued in a modest way whenever local labour (generally untrained) and materials were available. A heifers' house and space for a bull were built, with a flat concrete roof at the east end of the building. This was quite a low building with no architectural features but made use of the fall of the ground for the animals to enter from the yard at the back, which was on a lower level.

The wood used was chiefly wreckwood, obtained from the rocks below the farm and carried up to the top of the cliff by hand (very hard work), and then pulled up from there by a horse and drag [locally known as a draw] to the farm, about one mile away. A good deal of the wood was useless, having been too long in the sea and attacked by barnacles. But the heavy wooden hatches made excellent stall divisions for the animals, and other wood was used for shuttering and supports for the concrete flat roof. Jimmy Thomas and all on the farm enjoyed wrecking and a kind current brought the wood onto our rocks from the remains of the many ships (usually wooden in those days) sunk by the u-boats off the Cornish coast.

About this time, internal alterations and improvements were made to the dwelling house. Granite fireplaces were worked by Jimmy Thomas. Water was obtained from a stream. Later, water from this stream was piped down to a turbine, installed low down on the cliff path to supply electric light, though it proved to be in some jeopardy from the sea when spring tides and heavy seas combined together.

When peace was declared – and the architect returned from the trenches – a further building was designed at right-angles to the flat-roofed part as a fodder house and stable for horses.

This was followed by a Dutch barn with a precast Cassettone roof, supported by massive granite pillars. This building, though very handsome, has given some trouble as it seemed impossible to make the Cassettone roof completely waterproof in this climate; though now with the choice of many waterproofing products on the market I think the slight leaks have been overcome. The advantage of this type of roof construction was that it required very little timber, which was in short supply at the end of the war. Rough wood obtained from the sea was used for temporary supports and could be used over again, when the cement sections had set. The architect himself made the moulds for the sections to be cast, one mould serving for many square sections.

Before ending this account I would like to add a few words about the building of granite houses. Most of the old farmhouses used cut stone for their front elevation. The walls were very thick and on the inside smaller, uneven stones were used. This double wall was tied at intervals with granite or iron ties. The centre of the wall was often filled with rab or rab and clay, which crumbled away as it dried out, so that the wall became hollow and a natural cavity wall with good insulation. This meant that the houses were dry and warm; and as no cement was used on the interior walls, there was no condensation. Before the mixture of quicklime and clay was used, it had to be turned several times and mixed very well, and left for several days until the lime had ceased to heat.

To a certain extent, G.L. Kennedy used this method for the buildings at Tremedda, much to the astonishment and trepidation of the Country Gentleman's Association's foreman, who had been used to building with cement. The granite had to be very carefully vetted before being used, as some of it with a brownish tinge was very porous and let the rain straight through.

I will endeavour to describe the Tremedda Farm buildings of the 1930s and their uses, starting with the wash-house adjoining the dwelling and following the buildings around the rectangular yard.

It was the local custom to call each separate part of the building the such-and-such house, even if it were only a tiny room, such as the calves' house, the furnace house, the flour house, etc.

The wash-house was a tiny room containing a large white china sink, two wooden draining-boards and some wooden shelves. The shelves held large wooden egg boxes, the egg-collecting baskets and a motley collection of strong-smelling animal medicines, drenching bottles, flit for flies, hens' rings, pigs' rings and mousetraps, etc. The egg chart and a small mirror hung from convenient nails and a roller towel hung on the back of the door. All the dairy utensils were washed here, including the separator, buckets and butter-making utensils and later the large unwieldy milk churns; also the eggs and the laundry. All the buckets of water needed for so many jobs on the farm were collected in the wash-house and the workmen cleaned themselves up here. A covered walk ran from the wash-house to the outer dairy. On one side was an open

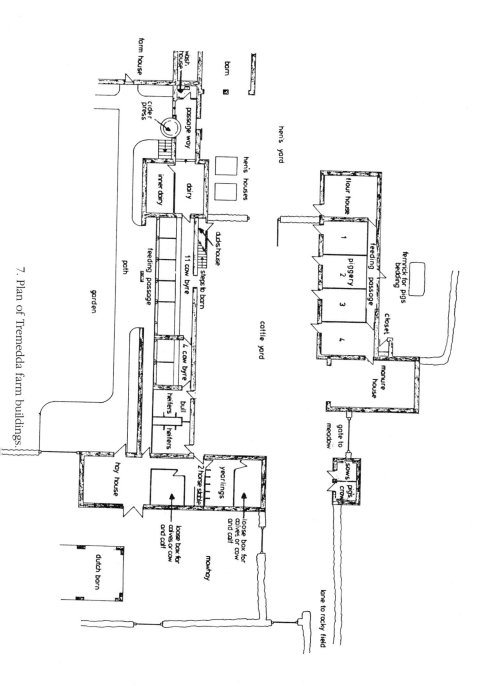

7. Plan of Tremedda farm buildings.

8. 'Some of the better houses were ashlar-fronted', p. 8. Treveglos Farmhouse and the Berryman family, late 19th century.

9. Tremedda barn, at left, covered walk to outer dairy and loggia above inner dairy; with house and garden. p. 10

archway into the garden and a large granite cider trough long since disused, hewn out of one enormous rock, about six feet across, two and a half feet deep and with an outlet at the bottom. A bucket rack, the sliding door into the outer yard, hooks for old coats and scythes, a much-used mangle, a hand-driven washing machine and a red cheese press all lined this passageway. Next came the outer dairy, a square room, red-brick floored and furnished with the butterworker, churn, separator and a blue cupboard. A copper boiler, under which a fire could be lit, was built into one corner. A door on the right led into the small, cold and rather dark inner dairy that was lined with thick slate shelves on which stood pans of cream awaiting buttermaking day. Large 'bussas' (earthenware crocks) containing potted eggs and potted butter stood on the floor and a jumble of cardboard boxes, paper and string for butter packing, littered a wooden rack. A door at the further end of the outer dairy led into the long cowshouse, known at Tremedda as the byre, my mother having introduced certain words from her Scottish vocabulary. This byre had eleven cow stalls with chain tie-ups and a cement division between each two cows. The floor was divided into three parts running lengthways: the stalls, the gutter and the walk. Three large wooden bins stood against the wall on the walk. The first one held sand for the floors and the other two held cow-cake, crushed oats, etc. Various stools were scattered about; a grease tin, flit gun and a pussy dish stood on the sandbin and a large crook hung from the ceiling, on which to hang the spring balance for weighing the milk. A large broom and a Cornish shovel and 'eval' (fork) leant against the wall for cleaning purposes and for arranging bedding. A raised feeding passage, in front of the cows, ran the whole length of the byres to the hay house at the far end. In front of the large byre, this passage was open to the garden with big granite arches, but during the winter months all but one of these were closed up with boarding. A long ladder and strings of onions hung over this passageway. We used to try to walk the length of the ladder hanging upside down by our feet, crooking our toes over each rung as we went. The mangold chopper was housed here and it was the dogs' favourite sleeping quarters, as the floor was strewn with bits of hay and straw, while in April and May when the feeding of hay and corn had finished, brooders and chicken coops jostled for room.

On into the next byre, known as the four byre, because it had four stalls. This was one of my mother's extravaganzas and was equipped with very modern tubular metal fittings. A metal rail divided off each stall, and yokes were tubular metal, clipped together at the top. A long deep trough ran the length of the byre with metal divisions all on one bar, which could be raised up for easy cleaning of the trough. Each cow had a water bowl with a piped water supply. As the cow pressed her nose on a little plate at the base of the bowl, so the water flowed in.

Over the dairies and byres were the loggia, the loggia bedroom, the loft and the far loft. The loggia was reached by a wide flight of granite steps leading up from the garden by the cider trough. A door on the left opened into the loggia bedroom while another flight at the further end led into the large loft and far loft. During the summer months, when our house overflowed with London relations, the loggia, with its large arched doorway and windows open to the elements, was the bedroom of us four girls.

The loft and far loft were grain and potato stores during the winter and wet- weather playroom and overflow bedrooms during the summer. One end of the loft was equipped for goats; however, these animals had all departed by the 1930s. It was cement floored, with drainage, and was divided from the rest of the loft by a tall chequered frame, the length and breadth of which we clambered over like monkeys. My mother's old side-saddle hung in one of the squares.

On ground level once more, the four byre led into the one-storied bull and heifers' house; this had two rows of five stalls head-to-head with a small feeding passage in the middle. All the partitions were wooden and made an excellent gymnasium for us children. One always felt very daring walking on top of the partition past the bull's nose. The hay house at the end of the feeding passage formed one corner of the rectangle. During the winter months it was filled with soft, loose, sweet-smelling hay and sheaves of corn. Various bits of horse tackle and oddments hung from wooden pegs on one wall and a large, arched double door opened into the mowhay. The hay house was the cats' paradise; they played, slept and had their nurseries here. There always seemed to be a nest of kittens hidden away. Sometimes a hen might steal in when the doors were open and lay her egg in a hidden nest. We climbed, bounced and rolled in this hay pile, always searching for kittens and eggs. Sometimes a tramp also slept here.

Next to the hay house was the loose box for young calves or a cow and calf, and the cobbled stable for horses. On down to the end of this building were small tie-up stalls for about seven yearlings, and a second loose box above which was a little open-ended loft reached by a ladder. Potatoes were put to shoot up here and it was used as a store for potato baskets, 'mawns' (large two-handled baskets), broccoli crates and other 'ric rac'.

Across the yard stood the little ancient pigs' crow with two small sties. Rats ran freely through the old walls, and we often watched them join in the meal when the sows were fed inside. An iron gate opening into the meadow hung between this crow and the manure house, a large deep open shed. The piggery, adjoining this, was a long low building divided inside by low, thick slate partitions. There were four pens with a feeding passage at the back and a flour house at the far end. A door in the passageway gave onto a small mowhay where the fern rick was, and another one gave access to the manure house. Each pen had a 'heps' door into the yard; the top half could be left open in fine weather.

The flour house was a favourite haunt for us children. It was crammed full of all sorts of things and a rich smell came from the different meals. A large wooden bin stood the length of one wall, divided into several compartments for barley meal, bran, thirds, flaked maize and whole maize. Thirds and sharps were different grades of wheat flour. A metal dustbin contained a dark brown, very strong smelling fish meal. The delicious porridgy mixture of skim milk and flour for pigs and poultry was made here, stirred in large buckets with a big stick. Full sacks, empty sacks – all hessian – boxes and string were all found in the flour house. It was also used for poultry plucking and was full of feathers and cobwebs; it had a coating of fine white flour dust on everything and so was a haven for mice. Occasionally, during a long rainy spell, we were allowed to play shops in the flour house; a great treat. We took weighing scales, paper bags and wooden and horn spoons and spent hours weighing up little bits of this and that, putting it in paper bags and selling it to each other.

The last building at the wash-house end of the rectangle was the rickety old barn with very precarious flooring, taken over mostly by poultry. Up the lane a few steps and behind this barn, were the old stables now filled with wreck wood, chicken coops, junk and sitting hens during the hatching season.

The yard was divided in two by a stone wall and gate, making the inner and outer yards. The inner and larger one was the true farm yard, where the cattle, horses and pigs collected. An outside flight of stone steps led up to the loft, under which ducks lived in a small house. The yard was bare and rab paved except for a drinking-trough and two granite pigs' troughs. Poultry flocked in the outer yard where they were fed and two wooden hen-houses with sliding rooves stood here. All the comings and goings took place in the outer yard; horses and carts, ponies and traps, a few motor vehicles and, of course, people, as this was the entrance, from here through the sliding door into the garden and so to the front door.

Tremedda had two mowhays. The large one situated behind the hay house and stables was for the corn- and hayricks. An open Dutch barn stood here and it was home to another flock of hens. A small mowhay behind the piggery contained the fern rick, a hen-house, the cart-house built by Aunt Mary and Jimmy Thomas and a tiny earth closet for the men tucked into one corner.

A large garden both in front and behind the house was bordered by the byres, the mowhay and the Shoot Field.

These sturdy, low, stone-built and slate-roofed buildings blended in well with the rugged countryside and stood up to the many storms that battered them.

The House

INSIDE the house all was simple and homely. Walls and ceilings were whitewashed with lime, doors and partitions were made of scrubbed wood, and floors were cement or polished wood, with rugs for some covering. There were few curtains, and all latches were wooden or brass. Inside the front door, which had no lock on it, was a small hall furnished with a row of coat hooks, a small chair to rest the postman, fishman or tramp, and a table for letters received and letters to post, above which hung a curly horn that could only be blown by the few with plenty of puff. To the right of the hall was the busy kitchen, full of draughts. The main feature here was the open chimney with its huge granite lintel, down which winds often howled and rain pitter-pattered onto the stone slabs below. When my mother first went to Tremedda the open chimney was the only means of cooking and entailed much labour. She soon had an American coal-burning stove installed, on which black pots and kettles simmered away and the ever-present teapot stood warmed and at the ready. The iron stove was cleaned and polished with black lead in a similar fashion to cleaning shoes. The rest of the kitchen was furnished with a long scrubbed wood table, a form and a few chairs to sit on, a kitchen cabinet, a large porcelain sink with wooden drainer and a row of hooks for old coats, oilers and milking aprons, under which stood wellington boots and hobnailers. A door by the sink led into a large airy larder.

To the left of the hall was the little sitting-room. Cupboard doors painted in two shades of sunny yellow gave added colour to this room. An old white painted dresser displayed many beautiful Italian and French plates and dishes and the much-used tea-set, creamy-yellow in colour and bordered with a green and yellow floral pattern. In front of the window stood a table with a blue linen tablecloth, where the family often had their meals. An attractive little granite fireplace, designed by Uncle George, with its bright fire of driftwood, furze 'stogs' (sticks) and coal warmed the room and many feet and hands during the winter months. Above it was a wooden mantelpiece supported by two granite corbels, over which hung a blue and white china Della Robbia plaque, one of my mother's Italian treasures. The rest of the sitting-room furnishings were my father's wingbacked armchair, an old blue linen-covered sofa, a writing desk, and a small table. The walls were hung with flower and landscape paintings by Millie Dow, my mother's stepfather. A passage from the hall led to the glasshouse through which one reached the nursery, a large room with various toy cupboards, a grand piano, a wooden-backed settle, table and chairs, a dolls' house, a handsome gramo-phone given to us by Great Aunt Annie that was encased in polished wood and stood on a matching stand with a rack for records underneath, and another Uncle George-designed granite fireplace.

Many of our most treasured toys were hand-me-downs and were rather shabby and battered, having been cherished by former little girls. Great Aunt Rosie sent us a large upholstered box containing dolls and dolls' clothes. My favourite, Elizabeth, was a cloth doll with a hard head; the only hair she possessed was painted on. She was certainly not a beauty, and her saving grace was the set of clothes she wore, beautifully made by Katherine Laughton. Another doll called Nellie had beautiful real hair, bobbed and with a fringe, giving one scope with brush and comb. Eileen, a small baby doll, was sent to me by Aunt Eileen when we all had scarlet fever. She could only be gazed upon through a window, until we were free from infection. Eileen had a most peculiar shaped body but when dressed in long baby clothes was quite presentable. Flora had a beautiful, smart, new doll bought in Nurnberg, with long plaits and dressed in a dirndl and blouse. Robina had a really old bridal doll with china head and jointed legs and arms complete with a long white satin dress and veil. One Christmas Katherine Laughton gave Ellen a baby doll called Lucy Snow, much the same size as a real baby, with a china head. K had made the stuffed body and all the dainty baby clothes, and had fitted out its little basket crib in the same fashion as those used in the Truby King nurseries for babies where K had worked. We all thought Lucy Snow a wondrous doll indeed.

This motley collection of dolls occupied various cradles and prams, the largest of which were also used by kittens and Shetland collies.

Uncle Hope sent us a large box of bricks made at his works in Dundee. These afforded us hours of pleasure. We built farms and houses, furnishing them with battered farm animals and dolls' house furniture. There were just enough bricks to build a tower reaching to the ceiling. We built an enclosed passage for kittens to walk through and a long winding snake of bricks standing on their edge, one in front of the other. Pushing the first one over started off a continuous run of falling bricks down to the tail end, like one long rippling wave.

The red-brick painted Victorian dolls' house standing on legs, which had been my mother's when small, opened in front with double doors revealing four rooms, one for each of us. Ellen had the drawing-room, Robina the dining-room, and Flora the bedroom, while I had the kitchen. All the rooms were carpeted and wallpapered in old-fashioned designs and curtained with spotted muslin. The rather grand drawing-room contained a set of furniture: sofa, chair, sideboard and stool, all upholstered in purple silk and decorated with tiny seashells, a wee polished wood piano that played a few tinny notes, and a little old-fashioned black fireplace, the grate filled with red crinkly paper, by which stood a minute, black, helmet-shaped coal-scuttle. The dining-room, equally grand, was furnished with matching sideboards, dresser, corner cupboard, a long oval table and six chairs. The set was beautifully carved with tiny cupboards and drawers. The chairs were high-backed and upholstered in red plush with a fringe round the edge. Tiny landscape paintings, executed by Millie Dow, hung on the walls of these two rooms. In the bedroom were various beds and cupboards, a neat little wooden bed, cradle and chair from Switzerland. The kitchen was a hotchpotch of tables, chairs, dresser, an old-fashioned cooking stove, pots and pans and crockery. The inmates were four cloth dolls with heads, arms and legs from the elbows and knees down, made from china. Agnes, definitely the lady of the house, wore a long, very full, pink silk dress with rows of lace round the skirt and a necklace of tiny beads. Lewis, a gentleman, due to his rather stiff, neat grey suit, had to stand around, leaning on table or chair. Mary, slightly more of a background figure or maiden aunt, not as grand as Agnes, was dressed in lacy pink and white, and cook was dressed in a dark plum velvet dress and white apron. Various other little dolls appeared for a while and then disappeared.

Returning to the dwelling house, next came the back kitchen, a small room smelling of paraffin and dog biscuits, with a back door leading to the old stables and the lane. Its contents were a *mêlée* of cleaning materials, lamps of all descriptions, the paraffin container and a large metal bin full of square dog biscuits. These had to be hammered into pieces on newspaper on the floor when the dogs were fed. The downstairs toilet was entered from the back kitchen. The top cottage consisted of two rooms with its own front door and a door leading into the nursery. Here was another open chimney seldom used. These rooms were mainly used for storage and the hatching of baby chicks in the incubator, except during the summer months when hordes of visitors necessitated other uses.

Scrubbed wooden stairs went up in three stages to the landing, off which were my mother's bedroom, the bathroom, Granny Dow's bedroom and the toilet. Up two steps and along a polished passage were a small bedroom, the spare room and the night nursery. Cupboards fitted with slides lined one side of this passage. My mother bought many bits and pieces from the shipbreaking yard at Hayle, including the slides, the bathroom chest of drawers and brass lamps.

There were two balconies, one outside my mother's bedroom, where in fine weather she aired the bedclothes and often sat on the low surrounding wall to brush and plait her hair. The other balcony at the top end of the house had access from the night nursery and the spare bedroom, through double doors with sliding shutters. It was surrounded by iron railings and had granite steps leading down into the back orchard. From here we played dares, sneaking into the garden in bare feet and nighties when we were supposed to be in bed and climbing the old ash tree or seeing how near we could approach the grown-ups without being seen.

Although turned into one house, both cottages kept some of their own characteristics such as different window styles.

The Garden

My Mother spent many hours in her garden, which she loved. It was not tilled with any sort of scientific method nor were the plants and shrubs planted in neat tidy rows. It was a large and varied garden, well fed with farmyard manure, and full of surprises. In the front of the house were flower beds, rab paths, small lawns, vegetable and fruit patches, a washing green, a shrubbery and a bee garden. The postman's path ran up the length of the house, under a cut granite archway and on, up to a stile into the Shoot field. At the top end of the house was The Top Orchard and behind it the Back Orchard. In the flower bed immediately in front of the house my mother waged a long war with ground elder, until one year she really got to grips with it, removing every plant and digging deep, thus gaining the upper hand at last. Every year, in their turn, pansies, pinks, polyanthus, catmint, cowslips, flag iris, ranunculi, tulips and London pride flowered, with here and there patches of cornflower, candytuft and night scented stocks, sown at random. Woven through this profusion was a sea of bright blue forget-me-nots and golden marigolds.

On the bottom end fence, near the front door, rambled an old-fashioned, large, double pink rose. When in bloom its delicious scent reached all who went in and out. The rear fence supported a dark green, glossy leafed, creamy white rose, with delicate, almost yellow, buds. A square lawn, stepped up on three sides, lay in front of the byre. In another flower bed grew the tall pink and white sweet rocket, and blue and purple Michaelmas daisies tumbling over each other in a wild mass.

All sorts of bushes grew in odd corners – rosemary, French lavender, flowering currant, wygelia, fuschia and many hydrangeas, including the delicate flat-headed lacy type with a circlet of single flowers surrounding a centre of little bobbles in delicate pinks, blues and white. Fruit trees and bushes were scattered everywhere. Currants and gooseberries filled a square in the front garden; a loganberry and two pear trees climbed the walls at the end of the path leading to the mowhay. One of the pear trees bore delicious fruit, which was always picked and eaten before becoming really ripe; the other produced no more than two or three very wooden pears which were quite inedible. A cherry tree grew up the wall of the house, bearing no fruit at all. A crab apple grew in the back orchard; a most decorative tree, both in spring with its frilly white blossom and in late summer, when covered with the dear little bright yellow and red oval fruits used for making crab apple jelly. Rather stunted apple trees, mostly covered in lichen, were dotted round the top orchard and the bee garden, and edged the washing green. Some seasons these trees bore a certain amount of scrunchy apples, but only too often when in bloom a strong wind blew the flowers off, before the apples had set, resulting in a very meagre crop.

The bee garden, a little place enclosed by a stone hedge and leaning sycamores and thorns, sheltered in one corner the large white bee house containing three hives of bees. In general, the bees gave us no trouble. During the summer months, when a continual droning came from the hive, one watched them from a safe distance, busily coming out, flying away to some distant patch of gorse, clover or heather, and returning heavily laden with their spoils to alight on the doorstep and crawl in to their very highly organised domestic life, which included the making of delicious honeycombs. At times when they decided to swarm, following a new young queen in one black mass, when the beeman came to take off the honey, or when there was any disturbance to the hives, they all, but especially the Italian bees, became vicious, stinging little brutes. Then we stayed indoors with windows shut, until all was serene in the bee quarter. During one such disturbance John Crockett, who was helping with the bees, received one or two nasty stings. He raced down the postman's path and dived into the cider trough, which happened to be full of water, to rid himself of the vicious creatures.

The rest of the bee garden was grassed, with a few apple trees here and there. A single red rambler rose wandered about, entwined with honeysuckle, to cover much of one wall, while sheltered beneath the hedges and apple trees were numerous polyanthus, primroses and violets. Another wall was blanketed with snowy-white arabis during early spring.

The washing green was a most important part of the garden, not only as a drying ground but also for bleaching.

To one side of the washing green were four tiny gardens, one for each of us girls, and at the back of each stood a baby beech tree, dug up in Trevaylor Woods. We filled our plots with the smaller daisies, pansies, primroses, alyssum, pinks and London pride. Little paths ran between each garden, with a neat border of French lavender, neat or not so neat as our enthusiasms waxed and waned.

The shrubbery was somewhat of a mystery; the bushes grew so large and close together that it was hard to penetrate this secret mass.

In the Top Orchard along the end wall of the house, there was a flower bed surveyed by the torso of a fascinating little china man in bright colours, cemented into the wall. It was a small orchard, carpeted with daffodils in spring, one end completely taken up by an amazing old ash tree. It must have grown upwards, as is the wont of normal trees, until, reaching the top of the high hedge behind which it sheltered and then feeling the tremendous blasts of the Atlantic gales, it decided to arch over and grow downwards behind its snug hedge once more. On reaching the ground it wandered along under the lea of the hedge, looking for all the world like a large boa constrictor. This old tree lent itself well for climbing, and the top of the archway formed by the trunk often supported a row of small children viewing their surroundings from this excellent vantage point, like birds on a bough.

The Back Orchard grew no apple trees apart from the crab apple; it also had a flowering cherry that was a wedding present to my parents. In a fork of the flowering cherry branches a thrush nested each spring. We could look down from my mother's balcony and see her sitting on her eggs; it was a mystery to us how she escaped being robbed or caught by the cats.

The grass here was full of gems. In February and March it was a white sheet of snowdrops nodding their little heads in the cold winter winds. These were interspersed with bright patches of orange and mauve crocuses, quickly followed by blue grape-hyacinths, bluebells in pale blue and white that were slightly larger and grander than the wild ones, a tiny patch of pink cyclamen carefully guarded by a large stone, and, earlier in the year, another of Christmas roses. The path was edged with a rockery and by the glasshouse a rambling rose with little pink pompom-like flowers climbed the wall, doing its best to enter through minute cracks, and often succeeding. A fly-proof meat safe stood on wooden legs in the shade of the trees, a forerunner of the modern fridge. From the back orchard a little gate led out into the lane.

Cecil or simple Ernie undertook the more arduous tasks in the garden, digging, clearing out overgrown corners, mowing the grass and weeding the paths. Ernie was very much in tune with nature and small children. He greeted anyone who might happen to pass by with a word about the weather, and loved to tease small children about their dollies. My mother would race into the garden between jobs to weed a patch of flower bed, plant some precious seedlings given her by the Talland gardener, or divide a clump of snowdrops, replanting them in empty corners.

The garden was a joy, to folk and animals alike.

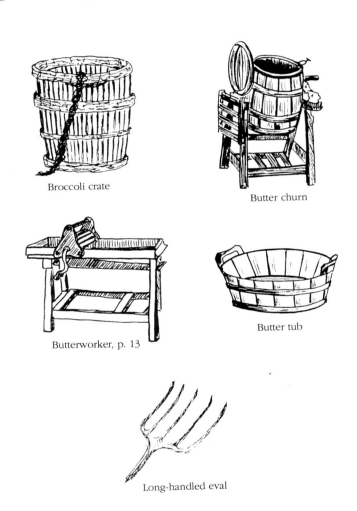

Broccoli crate

Butter churn

Butterworker, p. 13

Butter tub

Long-handled eval

PART TWO: ANIMAL HUSBANDRY

THERE is something special about working with animals; they all have their little idiosyncracies, some maddening, others endearing, but they don't argue with you and if treated kindly are usually most willing to please.

Animal husbandry was the main work of the Zennor farmer, the rough terrain and Atlantic gales making crop growing, other than feed for the animals, impracticable. Animals rubbed shoulders in yards and grazed the tiny fields and roughlands and even invaded the kitchens when sick. As time went on and motor traffic increased, roads became a hazard to animals and *vice versa*, causing their confinement to enclosed grazing.

The number of cattle per acre gradually increased, due to the introduction of new labour-saving machinery and the availability of relatively cheap cattle feeds and artificial manures. Farmers were becoming more aware of the chemical properties of the soil and were able to grow more and better quality grass. They were also given subsidies to break in rough land.

Horses

HORSES were by far the most important animals on the farm during the early part of this century. The working horses were housed in comfortable stables and fed on the choicest food the farm could produce. Hay was made solely for horse fodder. On the rare occasions when the vet was called in, it would be for a sick horse; the other animals were treated by the farmer or quack vet. Grooming was a very important part of working-horse management.

The larger farms of seventy acres or more kept two carthorses, a general purpose cob and one or two ponies. The cob helped the two carthorses when required and was used in the jingle or trap. The smaller farms of about forty acres kept one carthorse, a general purpose cob and a pony.

One or two farmers kept a stallion but many used the services of well-bred stallions from further afield. George Richards, in 1981 aged eighty-six and still active, walked these stallions from farm to farm, visiting Zennor on his rounds. He started this job at the age of sixteen and carried on for thirty-eight years. He first visited Tremedda in 1910. The stallions belonged to a Mr Semmens and came from near St Hilary.

Most farmers reared and broke in their own colts. The more able horsemen such as old Dick Berryman and his sons of Treveglos Farm, broke in colts for neighbours and reared young stock on the cliffs and hills for sale. Dicka's Dick, one of his sons, could do anything with a horse. To teach a young horse to work he was made to pull implements with a quiet old mare, which meant he was unable to break loose and soon learnt what was wanted of him.

The working horses were stabled all winter. Work was their exercise. As well as toiling in the fields, the horse had many regular tasks: pulling the water barrel to and from the pump, fetching coal from St Ives, carting pigs to market, fetching goods from town, and walking around and around on the 'whim round' to power the barn thresher. Many of these tasks were a day's work in themselves.

The horses were fed twice a day on a mixture of crushed oats, bran and chaff, i.e. chopped-up straw. Their diet also included hay and chopped mangolds. The horses were taken out to drink twice a day and the stables mucked out and the horses' legs washed down once a day. Horses with neglectful owners often got 'Monday morning leg', a stiffness caused by stopping in the stable over the weekend and not being cleaned. It was said that a good cleaning was as good as a gallon of corn. The horses were kept trace-clipped from October to February – clipped below the traces only.

During the summer months the working horses were left out to graze in the fields. A sackful of crushed oats was kept by, to give them a handful during haymaking and harvest. Some common old carthorse names were Blossom, Doll, Bess, Rose, Duke, Captain, Lady and Darling.

The young colts and ponies grazed the cliffs during the summer and the hills and moors in winter. A constant watch had to be kept on the animals grazing the cliff as it was not unusual for an unfortunate pony or heifer, on reaching over the cliff edge for one more succulent bite, to be nudged

10. 'By far the most important animals on the farm', p. 23. Robert Osborn with Madame at Embla Farm, Towednack.

11. A horsy scene in the Court, Zennor Churchtown. The horses, L-R, Topsy, Victor and, on the Town Plat, Blossom, and people Old Dicka, John, Willie and Dick Berryman, Rex Whelan. The horses are 'trace clipped'. p. 24

12. 'Animals rubbed shoulders in yards', p. 23. Tremedda yard, subsequently turned into the garden.

13. Young Kervis. p. 4

by its neighbour and go toppling over, usually to its death on the rocks below; sometimes, if lucky, it was salvaged. The old men tell a story of a white horse lost on Zennor cliffs. They searched for it for days. One night Eddy Trudgeon's father dreamed it was up an 'adit' and, sure enough, this was where it was found alive and well. It had walked up a long dark mining tunnel too narrow for turning and had not got the sense to back out.

Just west of Zennor Head there was a narrow spit of land called the Horseback with a wide patch of grass at the far end, jutting out into the sea. A narrow path two foot wide, with almost sheer drops of a hundred feet or so on either side to rocks and the surging sea, led out to the grassy patch. This was a very dangerous spot: many animals had fallen to their deaths here; also a lad bird-nesting. One day, Dick Berryman went down the cliff to find four of his ponies quietly grazing out on this patch of grass. He decided the only course to take was to leave them alone. They all came back without mishap. The Horseback was a challenge to the youths of Zennor. To have walked to the end and back was considered a great achievement. My father managed it once, but never again, he said.

In view of these dangers, young lads were sent off on ponies to account for all the animals grazing far afield, a job they enjoyed immensely. When the horses were roaming the hills in the winter they were a 'weather spot': if they came home and stood by the Chapel, bad weather was coming; when the storm subsided off they would go again.

Blacksmiths' shops abounded in the countryside and there was one in Zennor village. All the working horses were shod, and some farmers performed this task themselves.

A few Shetland ponies were reared to be used in the mines. Sucking colts, always black ones, were bought at Marazion Fair for fifty shillings (£2.50) each. They grazed on cliff and moorland until they reached the age of three or four, then were broken in and worked a bit before being sold for twenty pounds each to work in the pits. They were sturdy and hard-working little ponies, most of whom went to the coal mines in South Wales.

Fairs abounded around the countryside: at Marazion, Lowerquater, Lelant, and Halsetown, to mention but a few. The buying and selling of horses and ponies was the main business at these fairs, where often a field-full changed hands.

The cobs and ponies played a second and minor role in that they were also used for pleasure. Some farmers rode many miles to follow the Western Hunt, while others took part in races. Everyone who could, attended the St Buryan Races on Easter Monday, and all the Zennor parishioners flocked to Towednack Races on Towednack Feast Monday.

Hordes of people walked and rode over the downs while others drove in jingles and traps along the rab roadway.

At each race meeting there were about five races, with six or seven horses in each. Bill Jack, a Berryman from Trewey Farm, was a great one for the races; he rode Greybird, a little hard nut of a pony. All sorts of things went on at the meetings, the big attraction being the gambling. Bets were placed on horses, and a gipsy tribe came and set up their own gambling pitch. They had fifteen sticks, each one marked with three numbers, one to forty-five. These were sold to the crowd for a few pence each. A dice was thrown and the person with that number on his stick was the winner. He won the price of twelve sticks, and the gipsies kept the price of three. Local races finished in the 1920s when the National Hunt and its many regulations came in.

Saturday evening was the time for visiting relations, when usually the young visited the elderly. The farmer, his wife and all the children were packed into the jingle or trap, in winter time well tucked in with rugs and trap lights ablaze, then off to see Mother and Father or Grandpa and Grandma. It took a sturdy pony or cob to pull large families five or six miles.

One or two of the less sober parishioners often drove to pubs further afield; by the end of the evening, the driver, hardly able to stand, was hoisted into the bottom of the trap by the publican, the reins were tied up and the pony sent on his way, usually trotting the seven or eight miles home faultlessly. On one such occasion, Will Berryman from the Row, in Churchtown, was returning from the Radjel in Pendeen: as he neared home the pony trotted down the Gurnick, made a slight misjudgement and caught the trap wheel in the iron railings on the bridge, tipping up the trap and throwing the slumbering Will into the river to a rude awakening in cold water.

Horses were not just working machines. Each one had its own characteristics, some good, some bad. Accidents quite often occurred. Sidney Berryman's uncle, while tooth-harrowing one day, turned the harrow too sharply. It turned over, pulling the mare right back onto the harrow teeth where she bled to death. On another occasion Charlie Jelbert from Carnellow Farm was carting stone in the valley below Zennor village, for the building of Carn Cobba. A violent hailstorm blew in from the Atlantic, frightening his mare Rose; she started backing the cart up a steep, muddy gapway, one cartwheel went up on the hedge causing the mare and cart to overturn. A horse cannot move if he is unable to move his head so Charlie made Henry Symons, who was helping, sit on Rose's head while he carefully unhitched all the harness. Rose jumped up rather nervous but unhurt and was put to work once more.

During the First World War my mother had a very flighty cob called Sarah. She asked Tom Berryman to sow and harrow-in some grass seed up at Carn on top of the hill, using Sarah. She told him to go quietly and not drive her too hard. When halfway through with his harrowing, Tom decided to give her a rest as she was sweating a bit. No sooner had he sat on the hedge than Sarah bolted, pulling the harrow behind her. He just managed to reach the gap before Sarah and caught her. On returning to Tremedda he told my mother in no uncertain terms that Sarah was a devil and never to trust her. However, my mother could manage most horses. One day she and Aunt Amy were driving to Nance Farm to a dairy school, with Sarah in the shafts. On reaching Boscubban Hill the horse shied, upsetting the trap. The rattle of cream cans as they were thrown out onto the road did not improve matters. My mother was thrown out and Aunt Amy dragged down the hill. Finally, the shafts broke and Sarah bolted, shafts and all. My father arrived at the scene and having attended to my mother and Aunt Amy, went in search of Sarah. He asked a man walking on the road if he had seen her. His reply was "If she's still going at the pace she was when she passed me, she's up Camborne by now." She was finally caught at Towednack. My mother and Amy survived with only cuts and bruises and having to miss that day's butter and cheese making classes.

There was some fun in Zennor when the mobile thresher was on its rounds, and it caused the greatest commotion among the horse fraternity. It took four or five horses to pull the thresher and a couple more to pull the engine. As no one farmer owned that many horses, strange horses had to work side by side, often hating each other on sight, kicking and biting and squealing; they had to have their heads held sideways to prevent them from seeing their neighbouring workmate.

The horses on Tremedda Farm, as I recall them, are described in other chapters. Lion the carthorse seemed ever present, a beautiful quiet, hard-working horse, black with a white star on his face and white feathers on his feet. Sarah helped Lion bring sand for building from Porthmeor beach in St Ives; with him in the shafts and Sarah in traces, she could do no harm.

There was a great shortage of horses during the First World War, as the Army commandeered many thousands to move men, equipment, guns and stores, both in England and in France.

The decline in the horse population began about 1930. The transport side of their work was gradually taken over by the public bus, the charabanc, the car, the van, and the lorry. The Zennor blacksmith had disappeared and horses had to be taken further afield to be shod. There were very few horses in Zennor when the tractor finally took over. Fortunately, today, the horse population has greatly increased: mainly hunters and ponies and a few Shires. The Western Hunt, pony clubs and a growing interest in Shires all help to keep a thriving population of these grand animals.

Cattle and Dairying

AT the turn of the century, dairy cattle and pigs were interdependent, the pigs being fed on skim milk, and were of almost equal importance as a source of income on the smaller Zennor farms. Gradually, over the years, the cattle population per acre increased as farming methods improved and dairy cattle became the mainstay of the farm. The cows kept in these parts were always the Channel Island breeds, mostly Guernseys with the occasional Jersey or Jersey/Guernsey cross. Most Zennor farms kept their own bull, often bought in from pedigree stock as a calf and reared on the farm. On some of the very small farms with only five or six cows, the farmer would drive his cows to a neighbour's bull.

During the spring and summer all the cattle were turned out and grass was their only food. The cows were milked outside in the yard, as it was less work; and each one knew her own place there. A young heifer newly calved might be held up against a gate for the first couple of milkings, but after that she knew her place.

The land of adjoining farms was often very mixed up, as was the case with the Glebe and Treveglos in Churchtown. Will Berryman of the Glebe had a right of way through Treveglos yard. He often brought his cattle through when Treveglos cows were being milked. However, cattle on the whole are rather placid creatures and no commotion ensued. The cowshouses, during the spring and summer, were used as extra housing for the porkers. Come Michaelmas, the pigs were moved; many were killed at this time in order to help the farmer pay his rent. The cows were brought in to be fed and milked inside during the winter. The Zennor farmer started feeding cattle cake to his cows in the 1920s. It was known as cotton cake. Women always did the milking; young boys might help, but seldom the men. If the men were away at a fair or funeral, women did the lot: milking and feeding.

During the summer the heifers and yearlings were sent down the cliff to graze where there was plenty of grass. The grass near the sea was always a bit sweeter. Someone went down every evening with the dog to bring them all up to the top of the cliff, and again in the morning. There was always plenty of labour in those days. When winter came, the yearlings were brought up and housed and the heifers sent to graze the hills and moors: the cliff then became too dangerous as the animals edged ever nearer the brink in search of a bite of grass.

Marketing cattle during the early part of this century was a long hard grind for the farmer. The animal was driven on foot the seven miles to Penzance cattle market (held every Thursday) and, if it wasn't sold, it had to make the double journey. Cattle bought in the market were brought home in a similar fashion. When driving a cow and calf to market, often the little calf of only seven to ten days old would 'go to lie' and wouldn't move. Then it either had to be hoisted onto the farmer's shoulders and carried, or he had to walk home and fetch the trap in which to give it a lift. When taking a grown bull to market a couple of cows had to go with it to get it there; then the cows were brought home again. Taking cattle from the St Ives area took two days. The cattle were driven five miles to Trenowin Farm near Castle-an-Dinas, where they spent the night. The farmer walked home, returning next day by pony and trap to drive them the last four miles to Penzance market. Sometimes he put the calf in the trap and the cow would follow.

There was no auction in those days, and all the business was done by dealers, by word of mouth. The dealers went out of Penzance to meet the cattle. The further out of town you met the dealer, the higher the market price. If a Zennor man met the dealer at the blacksmith's shop, between Trythal and Heamoor, he knew the prices were up; if he met him only at Heamoor, there was not much doing. The dealers followed the cattle into Penzance and business was rarely done on the way.

Most farmers went to Penzance on market day; when not driving cattle they or their womenfolk went by pony and trap, taking their butter and eggs for sale. There were various stables in Penzance where the pony and trap could be left while the farmers went about their business. They went to the different markets, noting the prices of the day, and bought provisions for the farm and household, always including *The Cornishman*. This weekly newspaper was the only source of outside news to the country folk. Frequently the last port of call was one of the pubs for a well-earned pint of ale and a good 'coose' (chat).

In 1900 a cow and calf sold for around £5, a calf on its own brought 15s. and a good bull cost £12.10s.0d.

During the 1920s and '30s taking cattle to market became much easier; a motor bus service from Zennor to Penzance provided carriage for the tiny calves and the rest went by lorry, thus putting an end to cattle droving.

Another big change in dairying methods, easing the workload of the Zennor farmer, came in 1933 when the Milk Marketing Board was formed. It protected and later guaranteed milk prices and arranged for the collection of raw milk in ten gallon churns. All the Zennor farmers changed over to selling raw milk, and separating and buttermaking became a thing of the past. My father started selling raw milk in 1935. At first the skim milk was sent back to the farms for feeding to pigs, and the women had the job of washing the heavy, unwieldy churns before they were filled with fresh milk once more. But soon skim milk was no longer available, and this started a decline in pig-keeping. The milk lorry came once a day, picking up the milk and returning the empty churns clean and sterilised. All the milk went to the factory at St Erth. Tremedda milk was collected at 8 a.m. This meant early rising, in order to have all the cows milked and the churns taken to the top of the lane on time.

During the late 1930s my father's mother, Granny Griggs, came to live in the top house at Tremedda. She helped with the milking, mended all my father's clothes, and often cooked for us, as outside labour had lessened considerably. She was a stickler for early rising. At 6 a.m. she was up and about; and after her first cup of tea she would come down and rouse our household by banging on all the wooden ceilings with a broom handle, shouting "Come on, come on". She gave my father a cup of tea and had often begun the milking when the rest of us arrived bleary-eyed.

As time went on, the number of dairy cows in Zennor increased. They were better fed with the addition of more concentrates and hay, and were housed for feeding and milking all the year round.

Milk Recording

FOR some years the milk at Tremedda was recorded. This was organised by the English Guernsey Society, of which my father was a member.

Every five or six weeks Mr Laity, the milk recorder, paid us a visit. He was present at the morning and evening milking, noting the weight of milk given by each cow and taking samples to be tested for butterfat. After breakfast Mr Laity wrote up his books, checking the large blue ledger in which my father wrote down weekly the amount of milk given by each cow. This provided a useful record of each cow's yield and its butterfat content. Thus my father could rear heifer calves from the best milkers to add to his milking herd. Some of the best milkers gave five gallons a day when at their peak.

The highlight of Mr Laity's visit for us children was the rides he gave us up and down the lane on the back of his motorbike, often two at a time.

Buttermaking

THE sale of butter from 1900 to the mid 1930s was one of the Zennor farmers' weekly incomes. Milk from the Guernsey cattle grazed on the strip of land between St Ives and Land's End is some of the richest in the world, having a very high butterfat content. The butter is bright yellow in colour and is most delicious. It sold at four to six old pence a pound at the beginning of this period.

During the very early part of the century, the following buttermaking methods were used. Every farmhouse had a dairy – a cool room lined with thick, slate shelves. The rich, yellow Guernsey milk was poured into wide, shallow tin pans, which stood in the dairy overnight to allow the cream to rise. The pans had a handle on each side and were made locally by a man in New Street, Penzance, who also made buckets. On the larger farms there might be seven or eight panfuls. The following day, each pan in turn was scalded. It was placed on a 'brandis' (a three-legged, triangular iron stand or trivet) in the open chimney over a fire of red-hot turfy embers and heated to a few degrees below boiling point. The pans were then returned to the dairy for a further twenty-four hours when the cream, which formed a thick crust on the surface, was skimmed off with a skimmer or plate into cream pans to await buttermaking.

Butter was made twice a week, or even three times during hot, sultry weather. By 1900, most of the Zennor farms had a butter churn, with the exception of a few who made butter on a very small scale and simply beat the cream in a large bowl with the bare hand. The early barrel-shaped churn had fixed beaters inside and was slung horizontally across a stand with a handle at one end. A bigger version, such as they had at Kerrow Farm, had a handle at both ends. When the butter 'came' it was transferred to a large oak tub (18 inches deep by 36 inches across) where it was thoroughly washed by pouring bucketfuls of cold well water onto it and tipping it out repeatedly. Then the butter was pressed with a damp muslin cloth, ensuring all the buttermilk was washed away. Salt was added during the pressing and when thoroughly clean the butter was placed on a large slate and made up into one pound and half pound pats with butter pats or scotch hands. Some of the pats had beautiful designs of roses, thistles or maybe a cow pressed on them with wooden moulds. During hot sultry weather the butter often had to be lowered into the 'peath', or well, in a bucket to cool, or the buttermaker would rise at 4 a.m. in the cool of the early morning, to pat it up, as otherwise it would be too soft to be printed. The pats were neatly wrapped in greaseproof paper and stored in the dairy, until the weekly market day, when they were packed into a large square wicker basket with a lid, taken by pony and trap to St Ives or Penzance and sold to the local shops.

Before Dick Berryman's mother had a trap she took the butter to market on horseback. She placed the butter basket on the 'hipping stock' (horse mounting block), mounted the horse, then transferred it onto the horse's back in front of her, and so off to town.

In May and June when the cows were at the peak of lactation, there was more butter produced than could be sold, so the surplus was potted – stored in brine. Layers of butter, then salt, were put into large earthenware bussas that stood in the dairy. 'Pot' butter made delicious saffron cake.

By the 1920s, the Zennor farmer had progressed to using a mechanical cream separator, an end-over-end churn with no beaters and a butter-worker.

Buttermaking classes were held on various farms in the district. The Cornwall Education Committee provided a teacher and the equipment. I remember one such school that was held in the Tremedda barn. It lasted three weeks and was attended mainly by young girls. Ten or twelve small churns and butterworkers were set up in the large barn. A very important part of this operation was a strong lad to keep the buttermakers supplied with plenty of hot and cold water. After collecting a stack of furze stogs and lighting a fire under a large iron boiler standing on legs in the yard, he spent the rest of the day attending to the fire and marching up and down the barn steps carrying heavy bucketfuls of water. There was no water supply or drainage system in the barn. Bill Nankervis carried out this strenuous task at the Tremedda classes.

Miss Nicholas was the instructress at these classes for many years. She had presided over classes held at Nance Farm, which my mother attended when she was first learning the art of butter and cheese making. She was a stickler for cleanliness. The pupils wore long, spotless white aprons and all the equipment had to be well scrubbed with soap and water and scalded before and after each lesson. The pupils arrived on foot each morning, bringing their own cream with them. All day the barn hummed with noises of churning and chatting, laughing and patting, the swish of water and the clanking of pails. This busy barn was a great attraction for us children. We crept up the granite steps, through the loggia and up into the barn, peering wide-eyed through the door at all the fascinating people and their works, or ran out to the yard where Bill was always ready to tease and make fun of us. At the end of the day Miss Nicholas made up a dishful of butter for each pupil; beautiful little artistic arrangements of roses, leaves, and other devices. The pupils took their own butter home with them, carrying their little dish of roses with care to show to the rest of the family.

A small amount of cheese was made in the parish at the beginning of the century. Olive Nichols from Kerrow Farm could make cheese. Some

14. A dairy class. p. 34

15. Ready for milking. K Laughton with pail, Maggie Carlyon.

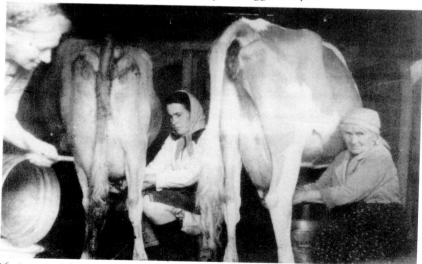

16. A warm job on a cold day. Elsie Griggs filling the cats' dish, Flora and Granny Griggs milking. p. 64

of the locals carried their milk to Kerrow and Olive made cheese with it for them.

I often helped my mother with the task of buttermaking at Tremedda Farm during the 1930s. At one period we were allowed Wednesdays off from our small school in St Ives in order to help with the buttermaking. We all wore overalls and wellington boots, water being much in evidence for most of the processes. The work took up most of the day and was carried out in the outer dairy, where the churn and butterworker stood.

The churn was well rinsed with cold water and the week's cream poured into it. The cream was churned by hand until it separated into butter and buttermilk. This was a fairly arduous task and took anything from a half to one hour. If the weather was warm and thundery the cream became 'sleepy' and the churning took ages. Every so often a valve in the lid was pressed to allow air to escape as presssure built up inside the churn. A small glass disk in the lid became clear as the butter formed, also a thud and a splash were heard instead of the regular beat. The churn was hooked into position, the bung taken out and the buttermilk allowed to run out into large buckets through a sieve, which caught any odd lumps of butter. These were then returned to the churn. The buttermilk was fed to the pigs. Two or three buckets of cold water were added to the butter, the churn closed and rotated several times, then the water let out through a sieve onto the floor. This process was repeated three or four times in order to wash the butter well and get rid of all traces of buttermilk. It was then ready to transfer to the buttermaking table, or worker. The butterworker was tilted to one corner, where all excess water ran out through a hole onto the floor, and the butter was placed in front of a corrugated, wooden roller at one end of the table. This was rolled over the butter by means of winding the roller handle and pushing the bar running above the roller. It pressed the butter into a flat corrugated sheet, and thus squeezed out the water. It was then dabbed with a large, damp muslin cloth. The flat sheet of butter was rolled up like a Swiss roll by turning the roller backwards and pushing it along behind the butter. This roll of butter was once again placed end on in front of the roller and the process repeated several times, to make sure all the water was extracted. It was then ready to salt. The butter was divided into two portions; so much for fresh and so much for salt butter. The portion to be salted was rolled out once again and sprinkled with handfuls of coarse salt taken from a large earthenware jar. It was rolled up and flattened several times to mix in the salt.

The butter was now ready to be weighed into one pound and half-pound quantities and made up into pats. This was when one really began to enjoy the work. A regular rhythm of bang (on the worker) pat pat (on the butter) could be heard as the work progressed. Two separate patterns were printed on the salt and the fresh butter to tell them apart. We really went to town in showing our artistic skills when making up the little dishes for the house – smaller round pats with diamond-shaped patterns, squares with zig-zags, butter men, dishes full of butter balls the size of marbles, and whirls which were butter balls squared flat and then rolled up. All these and many more were presented at the dining-table.

Next came the packing. Each pat was placed on a square of grease-proof paper and carefully wrapped. All those for posting were packed in cardboard boxes, which in turn were wrapped in brown paper and tied up with string. I can still to this day make up a tidy brown paper parcel, knowing exactly how to tie each knot. Some of the butter was sold to various relations in Scotland and the rest went to Hoskings, a family grocer in Tregenna Place, St Ives.

At half past three, the calm of the dairy was shattered; Charlie Roberts had arrived. He was my grandmother's first coachman, and came out from St Ives driving Ariel, a very showy horse, in the baroccino, a light Italian trap. He brought out our groceries and took back the butter and eggs for market, and used to come through the sliding door like a gale of wind, his leggings and red face shining. He shouted at everyone "Is everything ready? Come on, come on, you're late!" as though his very life depended on returning to St Ives immediately and was furious if asked to wash the eggs himself, or help pack the butter. When all the produce was neatly stacked in the large wicker basket under the seat, Roberts jumped in, cracked the whip over poor Ariel, making him very nervous, and raced up the lane.

The final job was to scrub thoroughly all the equipment, first with hot water and soap, then with cold, finally brooming the last of the water into the drain.

What a satisfactory way to spend the day! Especially when school was the alternative.

The Milk Lorry and Cream

UNTIL the commencement of the milk lorry era, farming in Zennor had continued on the same lines for many a decade. As previously mentioned, the formation of the Milk Marketing Board, which bought the raw milk, brought about a big change.

Milk was collected daily by lorry in ten gallon churns or twice daily in very hot weather. For a short period some farmers sold raw cream to a dairy where it was made into butter. The Jelberts at Carnellow Farm sent cream in one or two gallon cans to Mr Jenkin of Catchall Dairies in Sancreed; it was collected twice a week.

At Tremedda, raw milk selling started in 1935. For a while, a small amount of milk was separated each week and the cream made into butter for the household, but eventually home-made butter became a thing of the past. Scalded cream was still made every day. Now, a large enamel pan holding six to eight pints of fresh raw milk was left to stand overnight in the cool dairy, and in the morning it was put on the stove to scald. When nearly boiling, the pan was removed and left in the larder until the following morning. A thick, bright yellow crust formed and was skimmed off into bowls.

The skim milk was used for cooking and was fed to dogs, baby chicks and calves. The cats were much too fastidious to drink it.

After the mornings' milking, the full churns were taken up the lane by horse and cart and dumped on the milk-stand to await the arrival of the milk lorry at 8 a.m. There was always a great rush to get the milk up on time. Sometimes Ploughboy the horse didn't want to be caught and caused great consternation. My father always took our neighbour Johnnie's (often called Jackie) churns with our own, as we had the greater number. Every morning Johnnie came peering into the yard in a great state, waving his arms and shouting "Come on, come on, you're late". Often we were late, and the milk lorry waited, hooting at the top of the lane. However, the milk always went.

It was a great thrill for me when I was allowed to harness Ploughboy, hitch him into the cart and take the milk up the lane on my own. In winter, Ploughboy was usually waiting in the stables for me to harness him. First, a heavy padded leather collar was pushed up over his neck and buckled on top, then the 'hames' (two long, curved, metal pieces, joined together near the top by a chain), were fixed over the collar, neatly fitting into grooves down each side and fastened underneath. Then the breeching was hoisted onto the horse's back. This consisted of a small saddle-like piece, made of wood and leather, to which were attached large leather straps that ran along the horse's back, down each side and around his hind-quarters. The breeching was held firmly in place by a girth or belly band. Finally the halter was removed and the 'mops' (bridle) put on. Ploughboy was now ready to be hitched into the cart. The various crooks and chains were hooked in place, and the long rope reins tied onto the mops, and all was ready. The churns were loaded into the cart and I drove up the lane, lifted them onto the milk stand, loaded the empties in their place, and went back to the farm. Ploughboy was unharnessed and given a welcome feed or turned out to grass.

Pigs

IN the early 1900s all the Zennor farmers kept pigs, as the sale of porkers brought in an important part of their small incomes. The top price for a porker at this time was about five old pence a pound. Favoured breeds were the Cornish Lop-Eared and the Large White. The Lop-Ears were very important, for if the pigs had too wide a vision, they were liable to climb hedges or break into forbidden territory, causing untold damage to crops and gardens.

Five or six sows were kept for breeding purposes on the larger farms. A few farmers kept a boar, which was used by those who had none. The sows and young pigs or 'runners' – on average ten to twelve pigs were reared twice a year – were allowed to run in the fields, and a convenient pigs' crow, near the farmyard or in a field, provided shelter for them by night. The job of ringing the sows and neutering the young boars had to be done by the farmer. When weaned at about eight weeks old, the young pigs were brought in and housed to be fattened, a few weeks prior to selling. All farms had a piggery, a long low building divided into four or five pens with a feeding passage along the back and a flour house, which might also be a furnace house, at one end.

The pigs and sows were fed on a sloppy mixture of skim milk and buttermilk mixed with various bought foodstuffs, such as sharps (hard parts of ground wheat, barley meal, thirds (wheat flour), flaked maize, bran, and sometimes a strong-smelling fish meal. They were also given mangolds. Household scraps of such delicacies as vegetable parings, eggshells, tea leaves and the odd piece of paper were all thrown into the yard and enjoyed with relish. One or two sows in Churchtown had the added bonus of beer drippings from the pub, a drink they were very partial to. On one occasion, when William Nankervis was landlord of the Tinners' Arms, someone left the tap running on one of the beer barrels and a couple of sows from Trewey were given bucketfuls of beer. On making for home, they were quite unable to get up the steep Gurnick and only just managed to reach the chapel, where they collapsed. One of them was in the bog for two days 'as drunk as a pig'.

Before 1930 pigs were killed on the farm as porkers, weighing out at nine or ten score (180 to 200 lbs), and were carted to the butchers or pig markets in Penzance and St Ives. There was some life on the farm on pig-killing day, when five or six pigs were killed. Both men and women took part. Fires had to be stoked, water boiled, knives sharpened and rope and boards put ready. Then of course the pigs had to be caught, with much shouting and cursing and blood-curdling squeals from the unfortunate animals. A rope was tied around the pig's top jaw and it was hoisted up on a beam in a convenient shed with its hind feet just touching the ground. Often pig, rope and all escaped and the process had to be repeated. Finally, when the pig was in position, often held steady by the farmer's wife, the farmer with his small 'sticking knife' pierced the jugular vein in the throat. The rule was 'put the knife in a bit and aim for his tail then give him the full knife' – he bled better that way. If his windpipe was cut, he dropped like a stone. At Treveglos Farm in Zennor Churchtown, Mrs Harvey the parson's wife always appeared at pig-killing time, carrying a pail in which to catch the blood for her vine. She would run up with the blood from one pig and back down again for the next bucketful. That vine was fed all right! After the pig had bled it was put on a strong board and cleaned and scraped. Boiling water with a drop of cold added to make it just the right temperature was poured over the pig, which was then scraped with a large pig knife and 'candlestick' until it was spotless and smooth. The candlestick was similar to a saucepan lid, with a handle on one side and a sharp scraping rim on the other. It was so called because it resembled a miner's candlestick. The great quantity of boiling water used was either heated in large black kettles on the brandis in the open chimney, or if the farmer had a furnace house, a fire was lit under the copper boiler, in which the water was brought to the boil and bucketfuls were drawn off. After scraping, the pig was hung up by two ropes, one attached to each hind leg, keeping them well apart; it was slit down the centre of the stomach and the entrails taken out; then the pig was washed clean and left to dry.

Pigs were killed on Wednesday for the Thursday market. When perfectly clean and ready for the butcher's shelf, with various cloths pushed in to mop up drainings, they were loaded into a trap or cart lined with a clean sheet and driven to Penzance or St Ives. There was murder if a drop of blood was showing anywhere. If a farmer hadn't a full load, he would take pigs from neighbouring farmers as well. Christmas time and Michaelmas, when rents were due, were very busy pig-killing times.

Pigs were cured for home consumption. The meat was put into large bussas with layers of salt, and hams were hung in the old open chimney and smoked. The Thomases of Carnellow Farm smoked hams for the Westlakes, gentry who owned Eagle's Nest and often came there for holidays.

During the 1920s, farmers started selling pigs live to Redruth factory. They carted them to the station and put them on the train to Redruth. Around 1930 the first lorries made their appearance, and live pigs were sent direct by lorry to the factory. This change brought about the end of pig-killing in Zennor for market.

These intelligent, comical animals were an integral part of the farmyard scene. The sows wandered here and there, rooting in rubbish, eating the coal or waiting at the back door, giving out conversational grunts as they went. They were not averse to a snooze on the manure pile or a wallow in a muddy pool. The matronly mothers, followed closely by their tiny pink babies, wandered about, airing their offspring and teaching them to root around for titbits. The young fatteners in the piggery could be heard scuffling and quarrelling and at feeding time they set up such a commotion and squealing you would imagine each one was having his throat cut.

The men undertook most of the pig husbandry. Pigs were no respecters of persons; they had no fear, and pushed and shoved, knocking one over or upsetting the buckets of feed.

Pigs were also no respecters of property, much to the consternation of many campers. The old sows were drawn like magnets to tents, and if the occupants were out they would push their way in and have a gay old time, eating all the provisions and tasting anything that looked remotely like food, such as toothpaste, soap, and sponges. What a sight met the eyes of the unsuspecting campers when they returned!

During the great flood of 1894, several pigs belonging to Tom Berryman were drowned in Tremedda yard. It must have been a deluge indeed.

The decline in pig-keeping began in the late 1930s when raw milk instead of butter was sold, making skim milk no longer available as pig feed. Owing mainly to economics, pigs are now reared on the more specialised pig farms where they are herded by the hundred in pens, and machines take over much of the feeding, watering and cleaning. I fear most of the fun is taken out of farming today.

Sheep

SHEEP were not a popular animal in this district: they used up precious grazing needed for the cattle and caused untold aggravation, as they were well able to clamber over the Cornish hedges, eating crops and sometimes devastating vegetable gardens. Nevertheless, small flocks were kept on and off on different farms. Farmers with plenty of grazing, including suitable croft and cliff land, often kept sheep. I can remember sheep at Tregerthen, Wicca, and Trendrine. Many of them were hobbled with a piece of rope tied to one front and one back leg on the same side to try to prevent them from jumping hedges. Despite these precautions, hobbled sheep from Tregerthen, our neighbouring farm, were often to be found grazing the Tremedda fields; no doubt the grass was sweeter.

I have little knowledge of sheep husbandry, as they were never kept at Tremedda.

Poultry

IN the early part of this century poultry was an important source of income to the Zennor farmer. The feathered flock ran free, and were found all over the farmyard and the nearby fields, scratching and scraping and finding much of their own food – grass, insects, and corn around the ricks. As a general rule no special breeds were kept; simply the ordinary farmyard fowl dressed in white, brown, black or speckled feathers. The farmer's wife and daughters attended to the poultry, feeding, hatching, rearing and dressing table birds for market. Hens, ducks, geese and sometimes turkeys were kept. All the hatching was done at home. Broody hens were much sought after during the months of March and April, those with a surplus often lending to those who had but few.

During April, May and June the farmyard and areas near the house were alive with baby chicks, ducklings and goslings, with mothers on the alert, ready to attack at the first sign of danger. The week before Christmas, many long hours were spent plucking and trussing poultry for the table. They were sold privately and to butchers in Penzance and St Ives.

Eggs were taken to town once or twice a week and sold to the grocers' shops. One Annie Polmeor, who lived at Tregerthen cottages, made a meagre living by collecting eggs in the parish and walking the five miles to St Ives, carrying them in a large basket. She walked around town selling the eggs and then returned home once more on foot, having made a very small profit. At peak laying times eggs were 'potted': pickled in waterglass in bussas; these were used for cooking when eggs were scarce during the winter months.

A large number of poultry was kept on Tremedda Farm during the 1930s: about eighty white Leghorns and twenty Light Sussex hens, three breeding cockerels and thirty to forty cockerels for the table; up to forty runner ducks, a few Aylesbury ducks, two geese and a gander, and some years up to twenty turkeys reared for the Christmas market.

My mother took a great interest in poultry as did her brother, Hope Pilcher, who lived in Scotland. Every year, about Easter time, Uncle Hope sent us 100 day-old white Leghorn chicks. He bred extremely good layers through the method of trap-nesting. Each hen wore a numbered ring on her leg and on entering the nest box was trapped there until someone came to release her, writing her number on the egg. By this method only the best layers were chosen for breeding. These chicks travelled by train from Scotland, packed in cardboard boxes full of hay, with holes around the sides, about twenty-five to a box. On arrival they were put into two brooders with sliding roofs. These usually stood in the open feeding passage in front of the cows. They were either given oil lamps to keep

17. Young runners exploring the Town Plat. p. 39

18. Flora feeding the Invergowrie Leghorns. p. 42

19. Collecting the eggs. Elsie Griggs and Little Dan.

20. Aggravating the ducks on the Tremedda duckpond. p. 58

them warm, or preferably two quiet broody hens were found for each brooder; I say quiet, as two in one house were inclined to fight. Hens made better mothers than oil lamps! When the chicks started running around in the garden they protected them against such enemies as cats, carrion crows, magpies and Nethy the spaniel – and of course they look much nicer. And I recall one terrible catastrophe when one of the oil lamps smoked during the night, suffocating all the chicks.

As well as this yearly batch of chickens from Scotland, a fair amount of hatching took place on the farm. Around Easter time the back kitchen and old stables were full of large, covered, wooden, hay-lined boxes, each containing a broody hen sitting on a clutch of eggs of one sort or another: thirteen hen's or duck's eggs or maybe eight goose or turkey eggs. These hens were put out once a day. They were tethered by the leg with various lengths of string onto some firm object outside the back kitchen door and given grain and water; after ten minutes they were returned to their nests, which were covered with a lid and a heavy stone. Some of the more flighty 'mothers-to-be' struggled, pecked and cackled as they were being handled while others of a quieter nature simply clucked contentedly and ruffled up their feathers. The latter type of hen could often be left free of fetters to eat and drink, and would return to her nest of her own accord. She made the best mother, sitting quietly while the chicks or ducklings hatched, and keeping them warm. The more flighty mother might dash about in the face of any disturbance, often treading on and harming her offspring.

Some of the eggs were hatched in an incubator. The incubator drawer, lined with a piece of soft material, held fifty eggs. Each egg was marked with a cross on one side and a nought on the other. A small oil lamp kept them at an even temperature, and a tray of water kept the atmosphere moist. All the eggs were turned over, the crosses showing one day and naughts the next, ensuring that no eggs were overlooked. The oil lamp was filled with paraffin and the water topped up. After a week, the eggs were tested for fertility. A hole the shape of an egg was cut in the centre of a piece of cardboard, and the egg held up to this hole against a strong light. If most of it appeared dark the egg contained a chick, but if a lot of light showed through, and on shaking, the egg sounded full of liquid, it was addled and had to be thrown away. At last came the day when cheeping could be heard and small cracks in the eggs appeared. As they hatched, the chicks were moved to a special compartment and the empty egg-shells were taken out. The chicks changed rapidly from little wet feathered weaklings to tough alert balls of yellow fluff running hither and thither. Finally, when all the hatching was complete, the chicks were taken out to the brooder. The poultry hatched by broody hens in boxes were moved to various coops in front of the cows and on the lawn. From then on, the garden became alive with cheeping and clucking, chicks and ducklings under one's feet, and hens tied to strings or poking their heads out of coops. An array of dishes lay scattered about: saucers and long, covered feeding dishes with little round holes down each side just big enough for a chick's head, and an odd assortment of drinking dishes including a Frenchman's wooden sabot, each one containing a stone for the chicks to scramble up on, to prevent them from drowning.

The garden gradually took on a look of disarray as the chicks and ducks grew more and more active, scrabbling and scratching in flower beds, messing up the lawn and scraping hay from the feeding passage out onto the path. Every so often these activities ceased and they ran exhausted to their mothers for a short rest, creeping under her feathers for warmth and safety. One hen could cover twenty chicks. She sat with her feathers fluffed out like an old dame with voluminous skirts, with often a chick perched on her back and tiny faces peeping out between her feathers. Finally they had to be banished to a house in the yard or mowhay, or maybe the Hosier house in the field. The Hosier house was a very up-to-date chicken pen with sleeping compartments and wire-netting pen in one unit. When the chicks fouled the ground, it could be moved across the field onto fresh patches of grass by means of a lever. It had the advantage of providing fresh grass whenever necessary and cut out the risk of losing chicks to the fox or carrion crow.

Ducklings were to me the most endearing of them all, with their smiling faces, beady black eyes and dark yellow, velvety fluff, which they kept for some time. They were always reared by hens, who were deemed better mothers and easier to handle than ducks. The ducklings waddled around the garden in single file, searching for slugs, 'grammersows' (woodlice) and 'eariwigs'. Every now and then they would march to a large baking tin full of water to have a little swim – they enjoyed exploring the bottom with their little tails up in the air. As they grew older, they were transferred to the outer yard and large duckpond. Their poor foster mother would tear about distracted, as her brood swam away where she could not follow.

Turkeys, when reared, were segregated in the back orchard, needing special care and feeding; even so, they often died for no apparent reason. They ate such delicacies as baked custard and chopped onion, the whole brood then giving off an oniony aroma.

My mother often bought a setting of eggs of some special breed she fancied. One year it was the large, glossy Jersey Black Giants, another the quiet, pale brown Buff Orpingtons. The colourful Rhode Island Reds were popular as they were both good layers and table birds. Ellen and I were given some heavy, brown speckled Indian game birds. They had to be penned in because they were so fierce, fighting everything and everyone! They laid rich little dark brown eggs and were excellent roasted.

Just before Christmas a busy time ensued, killing, plucking and trussing many of these birds. My father or Cecil was the executioner, pulling the necks of the hens and cockerels and chopping off heads of ducks, geese and turkeys. We kept well and truly out of the way but were called upon to help with the plucking. All available hands assembled in the flour house, where the birds were hung up by their legs and the feathers plucked into two separate boxes: one for feathers and one for down. Nothing was wasted in those frugal days. The down was stuffed into large paper bags and baked in a slow oven to kill all the lice and 'beasties' before being used for filling 'feather tics' (mattresses), pillows, and quilts. The best of the wing feathers were collected in bundles, tied together at the quill end and were used for dusting difficult corners and other cleaning purposes. The birds were trussed or cleaned on the kitchen table by my mother and Sylvia.

All these feathered birds, although noisy and messy, added gaiety and colour to the farmyard scene. They are often missing on farms today and would find little to tempt them in many of the hosed-down, concrete yards.

Enemies of the Poultry

THE poultry had their enemies, and of these, the fox was by far the worst. Very occasionally a badger acquired a taste for poultry. The carrion crow, the magpie and the occasional domestic cat or dog that way inclined, all kept an eye on the young, ready to snatch one away if unprotected. Crows and magpies were shot and hung up nearby to remind their fellows that the same fate might overtake them if they came too near. When magpies became too numerous my mother raided their nests in the shrubbery, hoping to lessen their numbers.

The dear old badger was seldom hunted or killed and he rarely ate poultry; only the odd rogue might do so. He was useful to the farmer in that his diet consisted of slugs, grubs and other pests, but also of roots and shoots. He could be quite a nuisance just before harvest time, when he liked a good roll in the corn field, laying it flat and making it difficult to reap. On one occasion my father heard a commotion in one of the hen-houses and sent Trotter the spaniel in. Instead of the suspected fox, a badger was after the hens. Badgers are very fierce fighters when cornered and Trotter had to retreat, unable to overcome his foe.

Foxes were shot and hunted by the Western Hunt. They were a real menace. Every evening someone had to shut all the hen-house doors, making sure the poultry were safe for the night. If one little door was forgotten a fox was sure to find it. When a fox managed to enter one of the hen-houses during the night, the destruction was carnal. A fox does not kill just one fowl and carry it off for a meal, he has a real go, killing dozens if not disturbed, leaving them lying dead or half dead. The cackling of the terrified hens used to rouse the dogs, who rushed to the scene barking. They, in turn, usually woke my father who would dash out in his pyjamas, snatching up the shotgun as he went. Sometimes he managed to shoot the fox, but more often than not the fox glided away into the darkness, with a squawking hen in its mouth. The scene in the hen-house would be horrific, with feathers everywhere, hens lying around decapitated and many more having to be put out of their misery. The next day a tell-tale trail of feathers would show us the fox's escape route. One night a fox broke into our neighbour Johnnie Osborn's hen-house. Walter Palfrey appeared with his gun, took aim and fired, but missed the fox and killed a hen. During springtime when the vixens had young cubs to feed, they became very daring and would slink up to the farmyard during broad daylight, catch an unwary bird from under our noses and off and away to feed the cubs. Despite the havoc caused by foxes, it was still a pleasure, while walking on the cliffs on a summer's evening, to come across fox cubs gambolling on the grass.

The country would be a poorer place without these 'enemies'.

Sick Animals

IN 1900 there were only seven vets in Cornwall. At that time vets were rarely called on by the Zennor farmers, except occasionally to tend a valuable horse. In 1907 a visit from the vet cost five shillings. The old people said "It's better to lose a bullock than keep calling out the vet." There were very few regulations concerning animal health. The animals were hard and tough, and the survival of the fittest was the rule.

If a vet was needed, the farmer had to ride the seven miles to Penzance, find him and ride back again. The vet came on horseback or by pony and trap. Mr Motton, a Penzance vet, tall, gaunt and rather forbidding with a large hooked nose, tended the sick animals in Zennor for many years between the wars. He came by pony and trap until he bought his first motor car in the 1930s. He always wore a top hat, and put on a white coat for close inspection of animals.

In 1900, anthrax was about the only notifiable disease. By 1935 the following gruesome-sounding ailments had been added: foot and mouth, sheep scab, swine fever, glanders, farcy, rinderpest (cattle plague), epizootic lymphangitis, sheep pox, parasitic mange, rabies, tuberculosis of the udder in bovines, pleuro-pneumonia and bovine contagious abortion. However, the ordinary farmer knew little about this dreaded list: his animal took sick and either died or was cured.

Farmers had their own cures for most animal ailments. Quacks came round selling coloured water for chills. Sometimes a farmer, more knowledgeable on cures, was called in. Dick Jenkin came to Zennor to 'cut' (castrate) the young colts. He would do three or four at a time, bringing his own special stuff with him. His father was a quack: it was said he once cured foot and mouth disease by making the cattle walk through lime. Sam Nankervis from Trewey was often called in. Two of his favourite cures were stockholm tar for 'claw ill' (foul of the foot), used on the tongue for 'husk' (lung worm) and for foot rot in sheep, and Devonshire oil for massaging into udders for mastitis and for sores on teats. The following medicines have delicious-sounding names whatever their taste: sweet spirits of nitre and ginger, for horses who had been worked too hard – a real pick-you-up, I imagine; black treacle and molasses for digestive disorders in cattle; and cataline for everything.

Dicka's Dick (Dick Berryman Junior) from Churchtown could do most things as well as a vet, as far as horses were concerned. He had a mare with a poisoned foot. He cleaned it out, put turpentine on it – "That's a searcher" says Dick – then wrapped it up. By the time he had finished, there was a knock at the door: the vet had come. He couldn't do any more for the horse. Dick looked at the vet's kit and told him he didn't keep it clean enough to do jobs like that, it was rusty and dirty. Dick's tools were sterilised, sharp as a razor and clean as a pin. The following week the mare was working and perfectly all right.

Tom Berryman from the Row bought a sucking colt for ten guineas. She turned into a hansom mare, but at four years old was frightened one night by lightning. She ran into a gate-post and knocked her shoulder out. Stevens the vet was called in. He said the only way he could see to cure her was to put her in a flat-bottomed boat, take her out to sea and throw her overboard: she might put her shoulder back trying to swim! Needless to say, this cure was never tried and the mare was kept for breeding instead of work.

The remedies I remember being used by my father were many and varied. A whole new-laid egg, shell and all, was stuffed down the throat of a young calf ailing with the scour. A cow down with the 'reel' (milk fever) after calving, had her udder blown up and each teat tied with white tape to prevent the air escaping. If the cow failed to get up on her own, the neighours were called in, slings were fixed under her body and she was hoisted to her feet manually, rather like a sunken ship being pumped up with air to refloat her. Many's the time I have seen my father 'drenching' cattle and sometimes horses. A large, dark green glass bottle with a long neck, containing some evil-smelling medicine, was thrust down the cow's gullet. My father firmly grasped her with finger and thumb between the nostrils to keep her head nose-upwards while the liquid ran down her throat. The animal struggled and rolled its eyes with disapproval. A cow with stomach trouble was given new ivy shoots to eat. Cattle were always eager to eat the new, rich grass in springtime. It was most important to keep them out of the 'seeds' as it was called. The new grass was rationed out to them in small doses of perhaps one or two hours' grazing at a spell. However, sometimes a gate was left open by mistake, or they managed to climb over the hedge and eat their fill of the rich new clover and verdant grasses. This often resulted in the cattle 'bloating', and severe cases could end in death. A powerful gas would form inside the stomach, blowing the animal up to an enormous size. An old remedy was to drench the affected animal with butter melted in warm water. Any sort of edible oil would suffice, as this floated on the surface of the stomach contents helping to prevent more gas forming. A good rub, making the cow belch, often did the trick. In severe cases a stick was sharpened to a point, dipped in stockholm tar and stuck into the side of the cow between the pin and the rib, piercing the stomach and releasing the gas.

A careful eye was kept on all births. In the main, they were quite natural and trouble free. If a calf happened to be twisted the wrong way round or rather large, it needed careful manipulation or pulling before the little creature saw daylight. Before the advent of anaesthetics and antibiotics, which made the caesarean section a relatively easy operation, cows unable to calve had to be slaughtered. Sometimes a nervous sow would stamp around while pigging, nearly treading the life out of her newly born babies; as each one arrived it was quietly removed, then all were returned to her when she finally settled down to feed them. The kitchen slab often had an old box alongside it containing a baby pig, lamb, or chick needing special care and warmth for a few hours.

Dogs occasionally returned from a hunting foray, having been bitten by an adder. If bitten on the face, they looked almost unrecognisable, the swelling would be so great. This might be lanced with a sharp razor blade, releasing a cupful of pink fluid. The dog was then given cold coffee grounds, to make a speedy recovery.

If one of the larger animals died or had to be put 'out of time' (with a shotgun, before the arrival of the humane killer), owing perhaps to broken bones or an incurable illness, the carcase was hoisted onto the draw and pulled by Lion to the clifftop where it was dumped down an old mineshaft.

I suppose, often unbeknown to the farmer, the cattle spread tuberculosis and brucella to humans. Today, these two diseases have been almost stamped out. On the whole it was the survival of the fittest; the Guernsey cattle were a very hardy breed.

Showing

THE Royal Cornwall Show was one of the big yearly events attended by most Zennor farmers. During the first part of the century it had no fixed showground and alternated between east and west Cornwall. It was held in the beginning of June and lasted two days.

My father loved shows of every description; he had a very sociable disposition and delighted in getting out and about, having a drink and meeting all his old friends and making new ones. He was also a great Guernsey man and took much pride in his cattle.

My father kept many pedigree cows and usually showed some of these at the Royal Cornwall Show each year. Every spring maybe one, two or three animals were picked out for showing. These were given extra special treatment in the way of food and, later on, grooming. Much time was spent leading them about the yard to get them used to the halter. Just before the show, in early June, their coats were washed and brushed until the last vestige of their winter fur had disappeared and they shone like silk. Their tails were well shampooed and hung down in snowy white curls, and their hooves and horns were sand-papered and polished with wax from their ears until they were as smooth as old ivory. Their stalls were kept scrupulously clean until they were finally loaded into the lorry and sent to the show. My father went with the cattle, the day before the show, looking very smart in his best suit and hard hat, which was not quite a topper. He stayed until the evening of the last day, when they were brought home again. He took with him a couple of perfectly-laundered white coats, and his mack and wellington boots as a precaution against wet weather. If it rained, the showground could become quite a quagmire. While at the show, all the cattle had to be fed, watered and the cows milked. It was the practice to leave the milking on the morning of judging until this was over, thus showing off their bags (udders), now bursting with milk, to the best advantage.

Senora was the first cow my father showed. He took her to the Royal Cornwall Show where he and Sam Semmens, each with a good cow, stood in the pouring rain waiting for Lord Poltimore to pronounce judgement on them. Senora won the first prize and many more in subsequent years. She was a beautiful cow: a rich yellowy brown in colour with white underparts. Her back was as straight as a ramrod, her udder even and well-shaped, and she had two lovely slightly curved horns. It was a great moment to watch our own cattle led around the ring in the grand parade, wearing one of the coloured rosettes denoting first, second or third prize or highly commended. Long rows of rosettes and prize certificates were nailed up on the beams in the cowshouse.

When showing a bull it often took two men to lead him around the show ring. Two staffs were hooked onto his nose ring, one on either side. As a general rule the smaller the breed, the fiercer the bull. The enormous North and South Devons plodded placidly around the ring giving their leader no trouble while the smaller, more agile Guernseys and Jerseys pranced along with a wicked look in their eyes, trying to make a dash for it.

My father often attended the dairy and fatstock shows in London and many other smaller shows in Cornwall. As well as showing cattle, he was also a Guernsey steward at the Royal Cornwall for many years, up until the year he died aged eighty. In his later years he became a Guernsey judge, using his expert knowledge and keen eye for cattle at many a small and large show, including the Bath and West and the Royal Show of England. One year, he was asked to judge the female Guernseys at the Royal Show. Another man was to judge the bulls. As the other judge did not arrive on time owing to a slight car accident, my father judged both classes. When the other judge finally turned up he was well satisfied with my father's choice of prize winners. When the champion cow and bull of the whole show were judged, the two first prize Guernseys, picked out by my father, were chosen, much gratifying him.

Animal Characters

ALL the farm animals were known individually to everyone on the farm, their names and their characters. One always had to respect their temperaments and act accordingly.

The horses, a varied lot, were a necessity to the farmer, not a luxury as they mainly are today. Handsome Lion, the large black carthorse with a white blaze on his face and white feathers on his feet, undertook all the heavy work on the farm. Tony, given to us by Great Aunt Rosie, was a very game, half Arab pony with a light brown coat and black tail

21. Maurice Griggs in later years, talking to Prince Charles at the Royal Cornwall Agricultural Show. p. 45

22. 'Showing off'. Maurice Griggs and Senora. p. 51

and mane. Although broken-winded and prone to much coughing and wheezing, he was well able to help Lion with the field work when two horses were needed, carry my father to hounds, and give us children rides. He had a nasty habit of turning around and trying to nip you while you were trying to mount. Polly was a little brown Exmoor pony bought from Uncle Thomas, who previously drove her in a trap on his milk round in St Ives. She was kept mainly as a pet for children to ride. We rode her around the fields, making little jumps here and there, and generally making a great fuss of her. She was like a homing pigeon: with difficulty we made her trot to the farthest field but as soon as we turned in a homeward direction she galloped like the wind right back to the yard. We spent many hours grooming Polly and Tony with brushes and currycombs – giving their manes and tails exotic hairstyles. Merrylegs, an even smaller brown pony of a great age, was sent to Tremedda, also by Aunt Rosie, to spend her retirement on the cliffs. Occasionally we tried to ride her but were always thrown off by her bucking and rearing; she had quite decided that her retirement was to be complete.

We had a short Shetland pony episode when Beetle arrived, bought in Penzance market – a dear little black pony. We were quite small at the time and rode her around the garden. She loved whizzing around the square gooseberry patch and often the rider would fall if she took the corners too quickly, or she would knock our legs on the fence. Eventually Beetle gave birth to Spider, a tiny black and white foal. As he grew up, my father tried to break him in but he always remained very wild and unsuitable for children. Spider was eventually sold and the last news we had of him was that he was performing on the stage in Plymouth.

The pretty little, light brown and white Guernseys were all horned and much more handsome than their de-horned offspring of today. On the whole the cattle were a placid lot, living a quiet life out in the fields. There were the odd butters and kickers, and a cow could become very fierce when protecting her new-born calf. The smell of a ferret sent them frantic. The bulls were often not so placid and were not to be trifled with.

The most notable of the Tremedda herd was Old Kervis, a descendant of my mother's first cow. She was a Jersey-Guernsey cross and browny black in colour. She might well be called the matron of the herd. Owing to her quiet disposition and the fact that she was extremely easy to milk, we all learned the art of hand-milking on her from about the age of three upwards.

As a rule the Tremedda cows were named after wild flowers and ferns. Ones I well recall were Buttercup, Daisy, Bluebell, Potentilla, Speedwell, Holly, Cowslip, Primrose, Olive, Ladyfern, Maidenhair, Senora, Leading Lady, and always a Nan or a Kervis – descendants of Old Kervis. Leading

Lady, a senior for many years, led the herd through gaps and into the cowshouse. Cowslip was a vicious kicker. Many's the time her milker was kicked over backwards and a bucketful of creamy milk upset. The first person out to milk always chose Olive as she had nice long even teats and gave masses of milk very freely: the bucket filled up with warm frothy milk in next to no time. Senora was the star of the herd with many rosettes and prize certificates to her credit. The name Senora was derived from St Senara, the patron saint of Zennor.

During the months of September and October the cows, while in the cowshouse, were aggravated by the onslaught of hundreds of biting flies. They were continually a-dance while being milked, their tails thrashing to and fro. Shouting and swearing rang out, more or less forcibly according to who the milker was, as manurey tails were whipped across faces. If excessively bad, the whole cowshouse and the cows were sprayed with a yellow flit gun and the cows' tails were tied with binder twine to one of their hind legs.

The Guernsey bulls kept at Tremedda were certainly not to be trifled with. They had grand names such as Tregonning Myrtle Boy, Tremedda Granite, and Tregye Aircraft. The latter had horns sticking straight out, and, my father told me, "was bought for fifteen guineas when Lady Margaret sold up at Boscowan near Truro". The bull was often led out to drink by a chain clipped onto his nose ring. I always had rather a fear while chaining up the bull and tried to perform this task as quickly as possible. If the bull happened to be out with the cows, and their field had to be crossed, one very wary eye was kept on him and one on the nearest hedge. Great consternation was caused if the bull managed to escape into the outer yard and so get near the house. One day while looking out of the kitchen window, I saw a large black face appear around the corner. The bull had been digging in the coal pile with his horns and looked most fearsome, with only the whites of his eyes showing. Another time a fierce bull escaped into the garden and was found looking into Flora's pram, much to the horror of my mother. My father had a narrow escape one day: he was bringing the bull in from the Shoot Field and stopped to take off his pullover. While he was pulling it up over his head, and unable to see, the bull made a charge at him. Uncle Thomas who happened to be nearby started off in pursuit waving a foxglove! However the bull, on nearing my father, was so nonplussed by the reaction or lack of it to his charge that he stopped in his tracks. Many's the time the hundred yard sprint and the high jump records were broken when fleeing over the nearest hedge away from this large creature, who could run at great speed. Occasionally one of the neighbouring bulls managed to jump a wall and meet up with ours, resulting in a terrifying bullfight with much snorting and clods of earth flying. If perchance it was the

Tregerthen bull, he was returned to his home by the following method: Arthur Ost, the Tregerthen workman, was sent for and the bull, who had a great dislike of Arthur, chased him all the way back to Tregerthen!

The baby calves were a great favourite among us children. As soon as a new arrival appeared on the scene, we would rush out to admire the little fellow, with his large dark eyes, silky coat and knobbly, wobbly legs, already quite frisky at a few hours old. His mother would be keeping a very watchful eye, making little contented mooing sounds and giving him a good licking-cum-clean- up all over.

My father never had sheep, although they were kept by our neighbour William Henry and later Stanley Hocking at Tregerthen. They were frequently found hobbling through our fields, with two legs tied together on one side with a piece of rope, supposedly to stop them trespassing. During March our favourite walk was through the fields to Tregerthen and Wicca to watch the baby lambs. They skipped about in groups, for all the world like small children playing tag, then up onto the rocks, pushing each other off, as in 'I'm King of the Castle'. Suddenly, hunger would overcome them, they would race to their mothers, and kneel down on their knees to suck like mad, their little tails wagging at great speed.

Pigs were always very much in evidence on the farm. If one couldn't hear the cacophony of sounds coming from the young ones at feeding times, the old sows might be seen peering through the yard gate with their tiny eyes half covered by large floppy ears, mouths watering, eagerly awaiting some kitchen scraps. Their whole world revolved around things to eat! These sows could be very cunning. One pair discovered that by both pushing the sliding door together with their snouts, they could open it and so gain access to the forbidden garden and vegetable patch, where untold damage was done. We had another couple, a fast and a slow eater. While feeding from the two granite troughs on either side of the yard, the fast eater, having quickly gobbled up her own food, would set up a squealing until the slow eater rushed over to see what was up. The quick sow then dashed to her companion's trough and finished off the lot.

As ungainly and perhaps unattractive as the old sows might seem, this was more than compensated for by the tiny delicacy of their pearly pink babies. We would watch them for hours from the piggery passageway, the old sow lying down grunting contentedly, with ten or twelve piglets lying in a tight row, each one plugged onto a teat, or maybe tripping around the pen on their tiny, pointed, polished trotters, like ballet dancers, tails curled in a tight S. If a sow had a large litter, there was usually a small one or 'piggy-widden' among them. He might be pushed out into the cold by the stronger ones and had to be taken into the kitchen in a cardboard box and placed near the stove or in the oven, if it was not too hot. When he started squeaking and jumping about to let us know he had recovered, he was returned to his mother.

My father never kept a boar. One was kept at Tregerthen and it was brought over when required, an ugly brute with gnashing teeth; we all gave him a wide berth.

The motley crowd of vociferous poultry was everywhere. They were always on the scrounge, cleaning up the pig troughs, pecking at tubmeat crumbs in the cowshouse, searching for grains of corn in the mowhay, scratching for grubs in the manure house and trying to steal the kitchen scraps from the sows, or off into the fields for a bit of fresh grass. The majority of hens were the flighty, 'peckety', cackling white Leghorns. They had nervous dispositions and were always making a fuss. The Light Sussex, of which we kept a few, with their black speckled collars and black-edged wings and tail feathers were much nicer and better behaved.

Most of the hens occupied a large wooden hen-house in the mowhay. The hen-house had come all the way from Invergowrie in Scotland, sent down by Uncle Hope. It was the very last word in hen-houses, down to its grand name of 'Invergowrie'. It comprised four good-sized rooms, one for the grain bins, etc. and three for the poultry. These were well furnished with hay-lined nesting boxes, perches over sanded shelves, long feeding troughs, holes through which heads poked to reach the drinking dishes, floors inches deep in chaff and many other such 'henny' luxuries including window shutters and little ladders up to the doorways. Another smaller hen-house stood in a pen at the top end of the mowhay, where pullets were kept separate from the older hens, who could give them a rough time if allowed to meet.

Feeding the 'Invergowrie' hens was quite a hazardous task. We would go armed with a stick and wellington boots. Firstly the food-house door was given a few taps to ensure that any mice feeding off spilt grain had scuttled away. Then, if some of the pecking hens were still in the nesting boxes, these were removed by placing a wellington-booted foot against their heads, grabbing a wing and throwing them out amidst much fluttering and cackling, in order to collect all the eggs. The greatest hazard came from the two Leghorn cockerels, who ruled the roost. They were always very fierce and mean-tempered. They would dance at you sideways, one wing down, ready to attack with beak and spurs. This is when the stick came into action. Many a time, a child found herself trapped in the pullets' pen with the two cockerels waiting to attack at the gate.

The ducks, geese, turkeys and various other poultry lived in the outer yard and behind the piggery. An ancient two-storied barn stood on the present site of the garage. Poultry lived on the ground floor and such things as sacks of food were kept up aloft, where great care had to be taken not to put a foot through one of the many holes of the rickety old floor. The ducks who lived under the barn steps were usually to be found waddling up and down the stream, bills shovelling in the mud for titbits, or swimming in the duck pond where the stream runs under the hedge into the well field. In the evening the ducks went slugging; they marched down the Well Field towards the cliff in single file, very much like children playing 'follow my leader', the drake with his shiny green head bossing them about.

The gander marched around the yard followed by his two wives, keeping a sharp lookout with his beady eyes for some unsuspecting person, at whom he would rush with neck outstretched, making a great hissing sound. He might even grab at one with his beak. Sometimes, after one of these unwarranted attacks, I have seen the poor gander picked up by the neck and flung over the yard gate by one of the men.

Poultry of different hues and sizes came and went, including the very nice-natured, rather foolish Guinea fowl, known as 'gleaners', who would sit round the yard in a friendly fashion, decked out in neat grey spotted pinafores, making a terrific din with their incessant call. The turkeys, as they grew older, strutted about the yard, the cocks with their tails fanned and wing feathers spread out, getting very red in the face, trying to gobble.

The farm was home to many cats and dogs which, as well as being pets, all had their uses. The cats were expected to keep down the vermin: rats and mice always find a living near animal foodstuffs. Young rabbits also fell victim to the cats.

A number of rather timid pussies lived outdoors, around the farm buildings, and one or two tame ones were allowed into the house. All the feline population congregated in the byre twice a day during milking times, sitting in corners or on bins awaiting their dishful of warm, frothy milk. Blackie, a small, shy female of the outside contingent, must have lived a great many years. On looking back I think of her as a permanent fixture, while the other pussies came and went. Although willing to come for her daily food and milk, she kept herself aloof and was not keen to be petted. Every once or twice a year, a family of kittens would emerge from some hiding place in the hay house with Blackie, the proud mother, in attendance. The hay house was an ideal nursery for kittens; it was comfortable and warm and a safe retreat was easily found in the face of danger. A doorway into the garden had a space of several inches between door and floor. Here the kittens would first peep out, and gradually venture into the garden. We used to stand for ages with a ball of paper tied to the end of a piece of string, dangling it in the space, hoping to see a tiny paw come out and give it a pat. These miniature Blackies, if confronted by one of the dogs, would be up on their toes, backs arched, tail up straight, spitting and hissing like tiny fireworks, before fleeing to safety.

Saul, with his battle-scarred ears, and yellow-eyed, fat, black David were two outdoor tomcats. A succession of friendly indoor cats, by name of Tommy, Moppit or Mittens, entered our bedroom every morning by way of the roof and window. They would jump from bed to bed, purring loudly. My father and I have birthdays on consecutive days in September so we usually held a joint celebration. One birthday morning I came downstairs to find, on the breakfast table, for my father a large green painted wooden wheelbarrow, made by the local carpenter, Mr Stevens from Rose Cottage, and inside it a dear little fluffy grey kitten for me. Sad to say, kitty's life was a short one: she was lain on by a large cow in the cowshouse; and was buried with ceremony in my own little patch of garden. I believe a large granite stone still marks the grave.

The first dogs I remember were Cluny, a brown and white collie who helped drive the cows in at milking time, and Trotter, a brown and white spaniel. Trotter enjoyed hunting and accompanied my father while out rabbiting. He disliked anyone a little out of the ordinary. The postman in his uniform, carrying a sack of mail on his back, or the baker with his large basket of round white loaves, often received a nip on the back of the leg. One year when someone dressed up as Father Christmas and walked through the Shoot Field for the benefit of us children, Trotter nearly went mad and had to be warded off with a stick. For a short time, an Old English sheepdog called Cooly lived outside. She had a litter of puppies away out in the fields in a hole in the wall. Eventually she was given away and we heard later that she came to an untimely end by jumping over some obstacle while tied up and hung herself.

The next batch of dogs were Tweed, Fairy and Nethy: all birthday presents. Tweed for my father, Fairy for me, and Nethy for Flora. Fairy and Tweed, both Shetland collies, arrived by train about the same time: small puppies in large crates. Tweed, who was black and white, travelled the long journey from the Orkneys and Fairy, a chainy eyed blue merle (mottled grey), came from kennels in London. They both grew very fond of the family but kept quite aloof from strangers.

Tweed was a most extraordinary dog, so alert and full of energy. While being taken a walk on the cliffs, he continually raced from headland to headland in pursuit of a gull or some other bird on the wing, his feet hardly seeming to touch the ground. One might almost think he too was airborne, his speed was so great. On reaching the rocks by the sea, off he raced once more, flying like the wind over the uneven rocks, maybe having spotted a seabird by the water's edge. Fairy would try to follow with much yapping and excitement, having no idea what she was chasing, and was soon left miles behind, while Nethy went her own sweet way hunting rabbits in the undergrowth. Tweed was also a marvellous ratter. You only had to mention the word rats to him and he would be up on his toes, ears cocked, waiting for the fray. We would tiptoe very quickly and quietly to the flour house door, open it, and switch on the light. Tweed was in, in a flash, and any rat or mouse present had no hope of escape: one toss in the air and its neck was broken. Fairy would appear on the scene all excited, usually a good few minutes after the fun was over. Despite this vast amount of exercise, Tweed was never interested in food and had to be tempted to eat. His food was placed under the kitchen table and minutes always passed before he deigned to notice it.

Fairy idolised Tweed and followed him around like a little grey shadow. She loved to be made a fuss of. We dressed her up in a doll's bonnet and shawl and pushed her around the garden in the doll's pram. She would lie there looking as though she were in her seventh heaven with a large grin on her face. She also loved sitting on our knees in front of the fire. Every so often she had a litter of six or so pups. They lived in the passageway in front of the cows and when old enough, came waddling out into the garden, little round barrels of fluff, Fairy in attendance with a look of great maternal pride on her face. Occasionally we took Fairy to Talland, Granny Dow's house in St Ives. She hated this journey when undertaken by bus and was extremely nervous, dribbling all the time. Quantities of newspapers were taken to catch the dribbles, and sometimes she was sick, much to the bus conductor's annoyance.

Flora's dog Nethy came from a friend who lived at Nethybridge in Scotland. She was a golden cocker spaniel and very different from the shy, retiring collies. She was very friendly, rather boisterous and needed frequent chastising. One angry word to the collies and they were offended for hours. Not so Nethy. She paid little heed. Drastic action had to be taken sometimes. After she had killed several baby chicks, one was tied to her collar for two or three days and this cured her. Tummel, a black and white hound-like mongrel, had a brief stay at Tremedda, but owing to his great addiction to eggs and poultry, he had to go.

Occasionally foxhound puppies were reared for the Western Hunt; Critical and Crocus one year, Gratitude and Gladness another and Chorister on his own. A silver teaspoon with the hound's name on it was donated for each puppy reared. Gratitude and Gladness were judged the two best puppies of their year and we were given the prize of a silver teapot. These puppies seemed to grow far too quickly for their strength; they raced around the garden falling over every little obstacle or simply going too fast for their unwieldy limbs and turning somersaults as they went. Everyone was sorry to see them go when they returned to the Hunt kennels.

23. Sows at the trough, with hens awaiting their turn, Boswednack Yard. p. 56

24. Annie Christopher ready to pluck a fowl. p. 46, 105

25. The outer yard, Tremedda, with ducks, hens – and the dolls' pram.

There was a much greater affinity between man and beast in those days. There were fewer animals and a larger workforce and all the animal husbandry was done manually. Farming has become much more mechanised and specialised. Certainly this increases production and decreases labour tremendously, but the fate of some of the animals is quite appalling, the intensive rearing of pigs and calves, for instance, where the poor creatures are herded in small pens hardly seeing daylight and never a green field. A quick look to ensure all is well, or being given a jab with a large needle, filling them with one of the many present-day injections is about the sum total of their contact with humans. The feeding and watering is mostly mechanical. This goes also for hens kept in batteries, where three to five hens are cooped up in a tiny cage and very often their only occupation, other than eating, drinking and laying, is pecking out each other's feathers. They must all suffer complete and utter boredom, without even the change from daylight to dark, lights being kept on permanently.

I can hear voices raised saying "We must produce as much food as cheaply as possible for our increasing population, even at the expense of some animals leading a decent life." To me this argument is made void by the fact that so much good food is wasted today. You have only to look at the leavings on people's plates in restaurants, hotels, schools and in the home to see this waste. There is also a tendency to eat too much. The whole population needs to be re-educated in their eating habits. If everyone in affluent countries ate less and wasted little they could afford higher prices, providing extra money to improve the conditions of these poor creatures.

I once bought half a dozen ex-battery hens and was quite horrified when they were taken out of their travelling sack. They were clothed in a dozen or so feathers and were barely able to walk. The expression of surprise on their faces, when set down on green grass was quite comical; each step to them was a major operation, lifting their feet right up under their chins as they went along. Instead of killing them off for the deep freeze as intended, we felt we must allow them the pleasure of roaming a large field in the sunshine. They soon grew glossy black feathers and rewarded us with many bright orange yolked eggs. Cows are much better off as they have the freedom of their pastures, but often the herd is so large that the dairyman has recourse to tags on their tails to identify the animal. No longer does the farmer have the satisfaction of feeding a hungry cow a large armful of sweet-smelling hay and listening to contented munching all around. Instead the cow, when hungry, walks to the self-service silage bar in a vast impersonal shed, similar to an aeroplane hangar, and helps herself. Even the pussies no longer have a small cosy hay house, full of soft loose hay for their bedrooms and nurseries but merely a large barn full of brick-hard, square bales or more recently large plastic- covered round bales. The presence of certain animals such as the fearsome majestic bull and the lordly cockerel with his evocative cock-a-doodle-doo is missing on many farms today owing to artificial insemination and the many hatcheries where day-old chicks can be bought. The free life of a wild fox, who may on very rare occasions be chased by a pack of hounds, is much to be envied by some of our farm animals today.

A Winter's Day

TREMEDDA Farm consisted of 40 acres of arable and 100 acres of cliff, hill and croft land. A typical quota of animals on Tremedda during the 1930s was 16 milking cows, a fierce Guernsey bull, a young bull very playful but not quite so fierce, 10 heifers, 6 yearlings, and 6 or 7 calves. Pigs were kept; 4 to 6 sows and their offspring, which were reared until ready for bacon at about six months old. Sometimes porkers were sold; these were a bit younger. Very important in those days, before tractors took over, were the horses. Lion the carthorse and various riding ponies all had their uses. There was always an abundance of poultry, both for eggs and the table: hens, ducks, geese and often turkeys; and of course the usual assortment of cats and dogs.

The workforce consisted of my father and mother; Cecil Thomas, who was a son of the stonemason and lived in the workman's cottage; Sylvia and Maggie Carlyon from Treen; and Ernie Brookham. Sylvia lived in and helped with the cooking and dairywork. During the evenings she sat in the kitchen, and we admired her patience and skill as she crocheted at great speed, making beautiful heavy lace to edge tablecloths and bed-spreads for her bottom drawer. Maggie came daily to do the housework. Simple Ernie Brookham walked the five or six miles over the downs from Castle-an-Dinas to dig the garden, clean out the hen-houses, turn the butter churn and do many other such unskilled jobs. During bad weather he stayed the night, sleeping in the loggia bedroom. Annie Christopher, a great favourite, came from the little red bungalow at Poniou when extra labour was required. She told wonderful tales and had a grand laugh. Then of course us children; we all had small tasks to do on the farm, I suspect mainly ones we enjoyed.

A typical winter's day on the farm started at half past six, when my father and Cecil, decked out in stout boots and 'tousers' (coarse aprons made from sacking) and carrying lanterns, would go to the byre.

The cows' troughs were cleared of hay and straw, and tubmeat was mixed up by hand in a large metal pan – bran, flaked maize, cow cake and crushed oats. This mixture was carried to each trough and half to two and a half dippers measured out, according to the quantity of milk given by each particular cow. The cows were then brought in. They were usually waiting nearby during the winter months, as they were most eager for their food and shelter; a few calls of "cup cup" and in they would dash, each one to her own stall, where they were tied up with chains or yokes. During the spring and summer months one might have to walk out through several fields to find the cows, as they were then reluctant to leave the lush pastures.

My mother and Sylvia, wearing overalls, tousers and headgear, now appeared on the scene, carrying a milking bucket each and a pail of warm water and a cloth for washing the cows' udders and teats. The lanterns were placed on the bins and together with Cecil they started milking.

Hand-milking on an icy winter's morning was a real 'hot you up'; sitting beside the large radiator of a cow, with one's hands immersed in warmth, was far superior to scalding cups of tea and firesides.

The cows' udders were well washed, the teats greased with stuff similar to vaseline, and then the milker with bucket and stool sat down on the right hand side of the cow, holding the bucket tight between the knees with head pressed into the cow's side. The men wore their caps back to front when milking as the peak would get in the way. It took an average of ten minutes to milk each cow, alternately pulling and 'viceting' as muscles tired. When pulling, one pulled the teat between first finger and thumb from top to bottom; and viceting, one squeezed the teat between finger tips and the palm of the hand starting with the first finger and so on down to the little finger. It was most important to milk fast and get a good froth on the milk, especially so for fastidious milkers. If no froth formed, the milk splashed all over the milker's hands, wrists and knees, whereas a good frothy head prevented this.

During milking, cats appeared from all directions and sat patiently waiting until their dish was filled with warm sweet milk and they were able to feast on this richness.

The milk from each cow was poured through a strainer into a large bucket, which hung from a spring balance with a white dial marked out in pounds. The weight of each cow's milk was noted down in a large blue ledger on the sand bin. When full, the bucket was carried to the dairy and Cecil poured the milk into the big metal bowl on top of the separator. When all the cows were milked the separating began. It was fairly hard work and had to be continued for half to three quarters of an hour, depending on the amount of milk.

Cecil usually operated the separator, which stood on a raised granite platform with two lower granite slabs on either side, one for the cream pan and the other for the large buckets of separated milk. A small tap at the bottom of the metal bowl was turned on and the milk ran down through a series of revolving conical-shaped discs with holes in them. Centrifugal force divided the lighter cream from the skim milk, sending them separately to long spouts on either side of the separator, from which they flowed into the cream pan and the skim milk bucket. The pans of cream were put on slate shelves to await buttermaking day, and the separated milk was fed mainly to the pigs. The milk profit came indirectly from butter, pork and bacon. Two little oval ovenproof dishes were filled with cream for the house. These were slowly heated to just below boiling point on the cool end of the range, and left in the larder overnight, when the cream thickened and a delicious crust formed on top – the real Cornish clotted cream. We all loved bread with 'thunder and lightning' – a layer of syrup topped with a thick layer of cream.

While the milking took place my father carried large pikefuls of hay from the hay house along the walk in front of the cows and gave each one an armful. Then he fed the rest of the cattle.

The bull, heifers, yearlings and calves were all given tubmeat of different mixtures and hay. The horses, Lion and Tony, often in by night, were fed crushed oats and hay.

Calves were taken away from their mothers when ten to fourteen days old. Most of the bull calves unfortunately had to go to market, but the heifer calves were put in a loose box and fed with milk from a pail for several weeks. My mother and us children fed the calves. They were given a mixture of raw milk with warm water or hay tea, a brew with a rich hay-ey aroma, made by pouring a kettle of boiling water onto a pailful of hay. Giving the calves their milk was quite difficult. There were usually four calves in one loose box, and they all had different mixtures of milk and water according to their age. Two of us, carrying two pails each, arrived at the loose box door. As we opened it, the elder and more pushing calves made a mad dash to the nearest pail, so they had to be put in order by giving them really hard cracks on their skulls with a stick, until all the right heads were in the correct pails. Silence, bar sucks and gulps reigned for a few minutes. Next, one had to watch the quick drinkers. Having finished their own, they tried their utmost to finish off that of the slow drinkers. Every so often a new calf had to be taught to drink from a bucket. A finger was held in the calf's mouth for him to suck and his nose pushed down under the milk. Many a cut finger resulted as the calf, instead of sucking, bit with his sharp little teeth.

After separating, Cecil fed the pigs and poultry. He carried large pails full of warm water and separated milk to the flour house, to mix in the meal. He had to be agile and speedy, when feeding the fatteners, in order to nip into the pen and empty the large, heavy pail of food into the iron trough before these lively vociferous creatures had time to engulf him, and send him sprawling on the ground with his pail upset. The sows were fed in the yard in two granite troughs. They stood with their front feet on the trough edge and generally ate 'like a pig', munching and chopping their teeth, with food flying in all directions to be cleaned up by the waiting poultry.

A similar mixture, only much thicker, using water instead of skim milk, was fed to the poultry. It was put in various dishes in the outer yard and the large mowhay, then all the little hen-house doors were opened and out streamed the feathered flock, racing to the nearest dish.

Feeding all these animal souls who were so appreciative of all they were given, eating up every scrap and showing such contentment when replete, gave one a great sense of satisfaction, unlike feeding members of the spoilt human race who all too often push their plate aside saying "I can't eat this" or "I don't like that".

The last outdoor job before breakfast was washing the buckets and separator parts in the large sink in the wash-house, then stacking them neatly away. Around nine o'clock everyone went indoors for breakfast of porridge, bacon and eggs, bread and marmalade, and cups of tea.

After breakfast the cows and heifers were turned out into the fields to graze. Their houses were then cleaned out. The manure was swept into piles, forked into a wheelbarrow and taken down to the manure house. The floors and gutters were sprinkled with sand and fresh bedding given where needed: straw for the cattle and ferns for the pigs. The cowshouse looked really smart after cleaning. As we grew older we often undertook this job when the men were busy. The rest of the day, if dry, the men might be out ploughing, harrowing, dung skudding, ditching; or if wet, indoors making repairs, creosoting or whitewashing the interior of the farm buildings. All woodwork was given a coat of creosote and the cowshouse walls were whitewashed up to a height of about six foot from the floor. Creosote and lime kill many a pest. The hay house needed frequent replenishing. My father, kneeling on the hayrick or the hay in the Dutch barn, cut out square chunks with a large hay knife. These were thrown onto the ground and carried into the hay house by the pikeful. Sheaves of corn and bundles of straw were also carried in.

Flatpol cabbage, turnips and mangolds were all fed in succession to the cattle throughout the winter months. The cabbages and turnips were brought in from the field by the cartload as required. The mangolds were all harvested in late October and stored in a pile in the mowhay. The pile was covered with the 'seal' from the base of the threshed cornrick and a layer of turf, to keep out the frost. Mangolds kept well in a clamp and

27. So alert – Tweed. p. 57

26. Fairy, the proud mother, showing off her pups to Elsie Griggs. p. 59

28. Going to feed the calves, p. 65. Alison, Little Dan and Flora.

29. Maurice Griggs in later life, complete with touser, 'taking a spell' on a winter's day. p. 63

were used at the end of the winter when the cabbages and turnips were finished. During dry weather the cattle were fed these crops in the field. Cecil or my father drove Lion in the cart out to the green crop field, to cut the cabbages or pull up the turnips and trim off the earth with a large knife and throw them into the cart; a very cold job in icy or wet weather. The cart was then driven over to the cows' field, which Lion walked slowly across while the load was thrown onto the ground behind, leaving a delicious trail for the cattle who followed, jostling each other for the best bits. During wet weather cartloads were dumped in the passageway in front of the cowshouse and fed to them indoors. Calves were given chopped turnips and mangolds and the horses and pigs were often fed chopped mangolds.

These root vegetables were chopped in the old mangold chopper. A long handle raised an iron weight, which when brought down pressed the root through two cutting blades, till the chopped pieces fell into a pan underneath.

Simple Ernie spent much of his time digging the garden vegetable-patch and trundling to and fro with wheelbarrow loads of manure, almost as big as himself, to trench-in for vegetables. Or he might be found bent double in one of the small hen-houses, scraping, brooming and throwing the chicken dung into the wheelbarrow; then giving the floor, when clean, a good sprinkling of sand topped with a layer of 'ushan' (chaff) and finally relining the nesting boxes with hay. He was often given the job of churning the cream. He could be heard singing away "Jesu lover of my soul, let me to your bosom fly", then he would look up at the ceiling, see a fly, say "good ol' fly", and laugh uproariously to himself. He always wore a touser, often 'more holey than righteous' round his middle, and more old sacking around his shoulders during wet weather. Ernie was never idle and he sang and laughed while he worked, his little blue eyes twinkling and a clay pipe in his mouth. When my mother gave him instructions he stood attentively nodding his head and touching his cap saying "'Es 'um, 'es 'um".

Around four o'clock in the afternoon the cows were all brought in once again and the morning's performance of milking, separating and feeding was repeated, with slight variations. The cattle were now fed sheaves of corn instead of hay, and sometimes green or root crops. A delicious crunching and munching pervaded the byre as their teeth sliced through large tender cabbages or juicy turnips. The poultry, fed by the women or children in the afternoon, were given grain instead of mash, and the eggs were collected in baskets and taken to the wash-house, where they were counted and the number written down on a chart. All these eggs had to be carefully washed and transferred to strong wooden boxes ready for transporting twice a week to Hoskings the grocers in St Ives.

The mood of the evening milking was very different to that of the morning. Few people felt like chit-chat and song at 6.30 a.m., so the mood in the morning was rather silent and dour, but the evening milking was quite a social occasion. Children sat on little stools playing with the cats, or doing homework with a lantern between their knees to keep warm or maybe trying their hand at milking Old Kervis, while sitting on a low stool with the pail standing on the ground, their small hands struggling with the teats, the milk going everywhere but in the bucket, and Old Kervis standing patiently chewing the cud. As we grew older and more proficient, we were expected to help regularly with the milking. Visitors often came and sat on the bins and chatted, and sometimes we sang our favourite rounds. The cows enjoyed this leisurely milking time, turning their heads to regard the singers with large kindly eyes and ears pricked forward with a listening look. But sometimes the peace was shattered by a flighty heifer giving a vicious kick, her muddy foot perhaps landing in the bucket of milk and often sending the milker flying backwards into the gutter, or a cow, having painful scratches on her teats from brambles in the croft, fidgeting and jumping about.

About 9 or 10 p.m. my father turned the cows out once more to spend the night in the fields. He differed from most of his neighbours in that he turned the cows out by night throughout winter, with the exception of the wettest and stormiest nights, stating that it was much healthier for them. The bull had to be let out to drink at the water trough in the yard and maybe a cow, kept in because she was about to calve or had recently calved, was given two or three buckets of water. Seeing that all the animals were comfortable and secure last thing at night was called 'tending up' and was my father's last job of the day.

A winter's day took on a much more dramatic aspect during the fierce north westerly gales that swept in from the Atlantic. Then the men wrapped themselves in flour sacks, oilers and sou'westers, tying everything well down with binder twine, so that they resembled bundles of sodden old clothes. They bent their heads to the wind, finding it difficult to keep an upright stance, and voices had to be raised in order to be heard. Hands of leather clung to pails, pikes and doors as the icy winds tried to snatch them away. Doors banged and lanterns were blown out. A gust of wind might take a pikeful of hay and blow it a couple of fields hence. The cows would come racing into their stalls, glad to be out of the storm, their coats steaming in the warmth and dripping in little pools around them. On such occasions they were allowed to stay in all night, in comfort. The hens, wet and bedraggled, struggled across the yard to reach their food, gobbled it up and retreated to the nearest shelter. The pigs were a sensible lot and knew where to go, keeping to some warm corner in a shed until things improved. Horse-and-cart work, unless essential, was postponed.

I am sure that there were days when milking was just one more chore that had to be done twice every day seven days a week, but my memories of it are pleasant. Work on Zennor farms during the first half of this century was certainly varied and on the whole healthy, and the country lads seemed larger in stature than their town contemporaries. Work continued seven days a week and fifty-two weeks in the year. A week's holiday was as yet an unheard-of luxury.

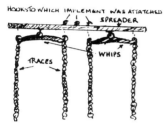
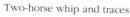

Two-horse whip and traces

Mangold and turnip chopper, p. 24

Baby chick brooder

Cream skimmer

Scotch hands, p. 33

PART THREE: FIELDWORK

Fields and Fieldwork

THE farmland in Zennor Parish was mainly grazing. Granite soil produced pastures most suitable for rich milk production. The nature of the small rocky fields and their exposure to fierce Atlantic gales made much ploughing and crop growing impracticable.

During the early 1900s all the fieldwork was done by horse and manpower; labour was plentiful, tools and implements were simple. The Zennor farmers were poor during the first half of this century and changes were few. Hand tools were gradually replaced by horse-drawn implements. Some of these were fitted with seats, allowing the farmer to sit while driving, instead of walking behind as in previous years. As the availability of labour decreased, the farmer was still able to increase his acreage under the plough with the aid of these improved and more efficient implements.

The Zennor farmer carried out a three-yearly crop rotation system. A certain acreage, 20 to 25 per cent of the total arable land, grew corn for three years. The third year corn fields were seeded out with grass to provide grazing the following year, when another set of fields was ploughed. In this manner most of the fields came under the plough in turn. Most farms in Zennor had the occasional field so full of rocks that it was impossible to plough.

The main crop grown during this period was oats, plus a small amount of barley or dredge corn – barley and oats mixed. The straw and some unthreshed sheaves were fed to the cattle and the grain, when crushed,

30. 'All the fieldwork was done by horse and manpower; labour was plentiful'. p. 72. Old Dicka, seated. On his left: Robert Osborn; right: David, Edie and Jane Berryman.

31. Eglos Meor. The last working mill in Zennor, p. 74, run by the Stevens family.

was fed to the horses and young stock. Each farm also grew one or two fields of green crop such as mangolds, turnips (swedes), and later flatpol cabbage, and a small strip of household vegetables and potatoes. During the Second World War, potatoes and broccoli were added to this list. A different field was chosen each year for the green and root crops. At the beginning of this century a small amount of wheat was still grown to provide 'reed' for thatching. Before this, the farmer grew his own wheat to be ground into flour for breadmaking and other household uses. It was ground by one of the many mills which abounded in the nineteenth century, powered by large water wheels. The last working mill in Zennor, Eglos Meor Mill, was run by the Stevens family and stood in the Zennor valley halfway between the village and the sea. This building was washed away by a great flood in 1894.

Haymaking was carried on throughout this period. At first only a small acreage was grown and used as winter fodder for the all-important working horses. In the 1930s, when buttermaking ceased and the sale of raw milk began, the number of dairy cattle increased and extra hay was grown to feed them. About 20 per cent of the arable land was used for haymaking at this time.

In 1920 Trevail Farm, with 70 acres of arable land, grew 14 acres of corn, 10 acres of hay and 2 or 3 acres of green crop. In 1930, Tremedda Farm, with 40 acres of arable land, grew 9 acres of corn, 8 acres of hay and 2 acres of green crop.

Farming continued on these lines up until the Second World War when high prices were paid to farmers, making them more affluent. After the war things changed drastically. The Zennor farmer could afford tractors and the sophisticated machinery that goes with them and horses disappeared. Aided by electricity and modern transport, mechanical farming had come to Zennor.

Fields

THE field pattern in Zennor varied little during the first half of the century. In fact many of the fields on the hillsides date back as far as the Bronze Age. The fields formed a patchwork of irregular shapes bordered by Cornish hedges, some drystone, others clothed in bracken, brambles, gorse and a myriad of other plants. The average field size in 1900 was one and a half acres; this gradually rose as hedges were taken away, turning two or three fields into one. Very small fields were called quillets.

On closer inspection, these Cornish hedges had great beauty with their multifarious collection of exquisite little plants, each patch forming a little garden of its own. The stones were liberally covered with lichens of different textures and shades of grey, some flat and some bearded. These lichens softened the outlines and the feel of the stones. Tiny patches of starry-eyed stonecrop hugged the hedges, interspersed with brilliant green mosses, while the flat pennies of moneywort gathered in sheltered crannies. Many ferns both large and small and most of the local flora could be found growing on these hedges, and a wealth of blackberries was gathered every year from the brambles rambling along, conveniently at picking height.

All the fields were referred to by their own names, which were often derived from the old Cornish language. The following are the names of the Tremedda fields, as I remember them. On the sea side of the farm leading off the yard was the Meadow, a long field with a stream and a tiny garden full of fuschias and a rose bush at the bottom. To the east of this came first the Dormullion ('dor' means ground and 'mullyon', clover) and below it the Horse Park. Again to seaward were the Crow Field ('crow': sty, cot) and nearest the cliff edge the Boggy Moor, as its name implies, very wet and clumped with rushes.

A lane ran east from the farmyard above the Dormullion into the Rocky Field, beyond which was a patch of moor called the Druzel Moor ('drushyer': thresher) with a small field below it of the same name. Seaward of the Rocky Field were the Higher and Lower Clover Fields and to the east of these lay the Long Castle Skudjack ('scosek': sheltered) and the Higher, Middle and Lower Castle Scudjacks. Going seaward again, were the Gallalas or Rabbit Field (a large rabbit warren occupied one end of this field), the Cocks Field and the Cliff Stitch, running along the cliff edge.

The fields above the farm were the following: adjoining the mowhay, the Near and Far Park Leata ('lyth': damp); above these, the Lower and Higher Cross Close; and next to the croft, the Dalvins ('tal veyn': stony slope). Directly above the garden were the Shoot Field and the two Higher Shoot Fields. The last three fields and the Dalvins, at that time, were farmed by our neighbour, Jackie (Johnnie) Osborn.

As a general rule the cows were sent 'down below' by day, where they could wander far and wide, often onto the cliff if the gaps were left open. By night they were sent 'up above' ensuring one hadn't far to go to fetch them for the early morning's milking, especially during the dark winter mornings.

The field path from Zennor to St Ives, well used in those days, ran through the Shoot Field and the Lower Cross Close. The field-path fields were also known as the 'roadway' fields. This path wound its way from farm to farm with a Cornish stile in the hedge between each field. The stiles were built of three or four large flat granite slabs set about one foot apart on their edge into the ground. The walker could trip easily over them, while the more ungainly four-footed beasts found them inaccessible. No bull was allowed loose in the roadway fields. Most farms with a field-path to the village running through it had a roadway field called the Cross Close and often enclosed a Cornish stone cross. This field was a resting place for funeral processions. A granite platform, to rest the coffin on, was often built at the side of the stile. Every route used by coffin bearers was a right of way.

All the grazing fields were criss-crossed with neat little paths made by the cattle, which they used when passing from one field to another. No doubt their reasoning was to trample as little as possible of their precious pastures.

Each field had its gaps; some were open, some had picturesque old iron gates to open, while many more were stopped up with iron bedsteads, bits of wood or anything to stop the passage of the four-footers.

The plateau of fields between moors and cliff made a grand picture when viewed from above, with its irregular patchwork of greens, browns and yellows, varying according to the season, with here and there the little grey homesteads surrounded by a few stunted and wind-blown trees, nestling into the ground.

Implements

IN the early 1900s the soil was tilled by horse-drawn implements, with the farmer walking behind, and with various hand tools. The most up-to-date was the reaper, the first horse-drawn machine to have a seat on it. Other horse-drawn implements included the simple one-horse, one-furrow plough, the chain-and-tine harrows, the scuffler and the heavy granite roller. Owing to the nature of the small rocky fields, hand tools were used for many jobs. The Cornish shovel and eval, the pike, scythe, hook, rulling hook, 'tommyhawk', digger, hoe, scraper, biddicks, pygal, hayrake and seed drill were but a few. Tools were bought in Penzance: Mitchells and Holmans were two good ironmongers. Sometimes the local blacksmith made them. A two-wheeled wain and cart and later the wagon were used for transport on the farm.

Change was slow, as farmers could not afford new machinery. Gradually much of the manual work was taken over by horse-drawn implements; and the most notable of these was the binder for corn harvesting, first used in the 1920s. A horse- drawn hay rake and an assortment of new ploughs came in at this time, including the two-horse butterfly plough and the one-furrow turn plough.

It was always the custom for the small farmer to borrow the larger implements from relations or neighbours on bigger farms. The farming community was very interdependent as far as labour and machinery were concerned.

Various bulky old machines stood around most of the farmsteads such as the barn thresher, the winnower, the mangold chopper, the chaff cutter; and a few had a corn crusher.

Manures

THE main manures in the early twentieth century were farmyard manure and mixed dressing. Very little artificial fertiliser was used. Farmers at that time had little knowledge of soil chemistry. Small quantities of bone manure and phosphates were used and fields were sometimes dressed with sand or lime. Phosphates cost £3 a ton. Basic slag was first used on Tremedda fields around 1918. The old farmers said "You'll never git good grass down they cliff fields", and were mightily surprised to see the bright green grass growing after a dressing of basic slag and lime had been applied. Nothing was wasted in those frugal days. Liquid manure from the sheds and yard all ran into a catchment area and was spread over pastures from a barrel in a cart with a makeshift sprayer attached to it.

All the farms had a 'dung pile', usually in the open yard. At Tremedda it was in a large open-ended shed. All the manure from the outhouses and the yard was dumped here throughout the year. Mixed dressing was a mixture of waste vegetation and farmyard manure. A pile was made each year in the corner of a suitable field, of weeds, potato haulms, hedge trimmings, etc. which were carted here, and every so often a layer of farmyard manure added. This pile was turned once, using a tommyhawk – a digger with two claws 'turned down and looking towards you a bit' – when the pile was dug down and then thrown up onto the new pile with an eval. Often an old cartwheel or suchlike was placed at the bottom of the pile to ensure that the very bottom was reached when it was turned.

All the fields to be cut for hay and the third-year corn fields were spread with farmyard manure and the fields for grazing with mixed dressing. Manure spreading was carried on throughout late winter and early spring. The farmyard manure and mixed dressing were carted out to the fields where the back of the cart was removed and the cart half tipped while the farmer scraped out some of the manure with a tommyhawk to form a small pile on the ground. He then led the horse on six or seven paces, repeating this process until the field was liberally scattered with dung piles. On average there were six piles to a cartload. The fields were now ready for 'dung scudding' – manure spreading. The mixed dressing was spread with a shovel; the 'long dung' – farmyard manure – with an eval or long-handled, five-pronged fork. On the fields to be cut for hay and the grazing pastures, the manure was chain harrowed but on the third-year corn fields the manure was ploughed in.

Sand and lime were spread in a similar fashion. Rock lime was put out in piles and quenched with rain or dew before spreading.

Small quantities of artificial manures were broadcast by hand from a bucket: phosphates for the first and second year corn fields and turnips, and basic slag for grass. Mangolds, flatpol cabbage and vegetable patches needed farmyard manure. In the 1930s one field might be sown with nitre to provide an early bite for the cattle in March. It was all very different from the rivers of artificial manures that were to flow onto the fields in later years.

Ploughing and Tilling

PLOUGHING took place during the first three months of the year, whenever the weather permitted.

As previously mentioned, the one-horse, single-furrow plough was used at the beginning of this century. In the 1920s and '30s the butterfly plough or banker and one-furrow turn-plough were used. The former had two shares and turned out a right- and left-hand furrow. The turn-plough had one share working and one idle on its upper side. When the end of the row was reached, the plough was up-ended and turned right over, placing the idle share underneath, ready to turn out the next furrow. This facilitated turning at the end of a row.

Flocks of birds, mainly seagulls, followed the ploughman, rising in the air in front of the horse to alight again in his wake like a large billowing wave. They greedily ate all the unsuspecting insects rudely awakened by the plough from their underground homes.

After ploughing, the soil was worked to a fine tilth with the scuffler, tine harrow, chain harrow and granite roller. These were all horse-drawn with the driver walking behind. The scuffler was a frame on four wheels, with two small ones in front and two larger ones behind, to which could be fitted either of two sets of cutting shears, long or short. The short shears were called chislers. The shears could be raised or lowered according to the depth required. The scuffler cut up the sods and a light, many-toothed tine harrow was used for working the soil to a fine tilth. The chain harrow was a mesh of heavy iron links. It was in two parts which could be hooked together, so that either a half or a whole chain harrow could be used. It helped level the ground and rolled up weeds. The spring-tooth harrow, first used in Zennor about 1930, was something between a scuffler and tine harrow: it had almost circular sprung teeth tipped with strong digging points.

As a general rule, ley to be ploughed for the first year corn was chisled (with a small tooth scuffler) to tear up the turf, ploughed, rolled to break up lumps, and scuffled with the long shears to cut up the sods. It was finished with alternate tine harrowing and rolling until the soil was ready for seed sowing and, if required, the broadcasting of phosphates. Finally, about two weeks after sowing, when the corn was two inches high, it was rolled with the heavy granite roller. Tilling the third-year corn field differed in that it was spread with farmyard manure before ploughing and nine or ten days after sowing the corn, grass seed was also sown and worked in with the tine or chain harrow to provide grazing for the following year.

In the autumn, the 'arrishes' – first- and second-year corn fields after harvesting – were chain harrowed to roll up loose straw and weeds which were then hand raked into piles and carried to the mixed dressing pile. Sometimes the arrishes were 'combed' – ploughed very shallow, about one inch deep, leaving the width of a comb between each row. Finally, the hedges were trimmed and the ditches cleaned out, leaving the fields all 'fitty' for ploughing in the following spring.

When tilling the greencrop field it was combed before Christmas. This turned the turf over and helped to kill the grass before ploughing in early spring.

When working a very weedy ploughed field, it was chain harrowed to roll up the weeds which were carted away to the mixed dressing pile. When ploughing ley, it was most important to get the 'tubbans' (sods) out on top as much as possible. Leather-jackets and other pests live under tubbans. When on top of the ground, crows turned them over every day and ate the grubs. If the tubbans were buried, leather-jackets throve. The use of insecticides was still a thing of the future.

At Tremedda, my father usually undertook the horse work while Cecil, the farm labourer, carried out the spade work, digging around rocks and hedges, clearing ditches and hoeing. Lion the carthorse pulled the heavy implements, and when the load was too heavy he was helped by Tony, a half-Arab pony.

When working two horses of equal size, side by side, in whip and traces, the implement was attached to the middle. When the horses were of unequal size the implement was attached towards the side of the larger horse, giving it the heavier load and the smaller horse the advantage of the whip. The saying 'a fair crack of the whip' originated here.

The farmers of yesterday would be amazed if confronted with some of the present day methods of cultivation, such as burning off a field with chemicals and killing every living thing, or mechanically seeding out a field without so much as ploughing it. The modern methods have many obvious advantages, but whether in years to come all these poisons will upset the balance of nature and cause adverse long term effects, time will tell.

Seed Sowing

MOST seed sown on the farm was saved from the previous year's crops. Willie Berryman from Treen Farm saved hay seed in the following manner: he made hay when the grasses were seeding, fairly late in the season. Every day when the horses were fed hay, it was shaken out over an empty stall with a board across it. Every so often the hay seed, which collected here, was taken to the barn and winnowed. The winnowing machine was a large wooden box-like affair with an iron handle. After putting the seed through a coarse sieve to remove bits of hay, it was poured into the winnowing machine and on turning the handle the seed dropped through vibrating graters, while rotating wooden beaters caused a wind that blew away the dust etc. The seed was winnowed five or six times, each time with a finer-meshed grater, resulting eventually in clean grass seed.

Corn seed was also winnowed to get rid of wild oats and dust, and before winnowing or grinding barley, the beards were cut off by chopping the seed with a seed 'piler'.

During the early part of the century all seeds were hand sown. Corn and grass seeds were sown from a 'seed-laps', a pan curved to fit the body with two straps over the shoulders, or a round pan with a rope attached to either side and slung around the sower's neck. Handy farmers could sow seed with two hands, throwing it to right and left, but others could only manage it with one hand. Some farmers used a 'fiddle'. This was slung over one shoulder and consisted of a bag to hold the seed, which ran out through various fittings worked by pushing a long stick

32. Two 'ansome workers' ploughing. p. 78

33. Seed sowing – Leonard Berryman. p. 80

34. Rex Whelan spring-tooth harrowing at Towednack Churchtown. p. 79

back and forth, resembling the action of a fiddle bow, causing the seed
to be flung out in the required amounts. Stripes in the field when the corn
came through meant bad sowing. The poorer farmers simply used a
bucket.

It was the custom for Zennor farmers to finish tealing (sowing) corn by
Zennor Feast, the nearest Sunday to May 12th. Root crop seed, such as
mangold and turnip seed, were drilled in rows. For many years it was
dropped by hand or from an old treacle tin with a hole in the bottom and
a wooden handle fixed to the top. When using the latter method, the
seed was mixed with sand to help thinner and more even sowing. It was
shaken out as you walked down the row. The seed drill was first used
in the 1930s. A container holding the seed was pushed along on two
wheels, dropping the seed from a hole in the bottom; the size of the hole
could be set for different kinds of seed.

Green and Root Crops

IN 1900 turnips and mangolds were grown as fodder for the animals. In
the 1920s and '30s flatpol cabbage was added. These crops were grown
in the ratio of one to two acres per forty acres arable.

On Tremedda, one ley field was ploughed every year for these crops,
including a small patch for vegetables for the household. Mangolds were
sown in the middle of May, turnips in July and flatpol were planted in
June. Soon after the turnip and mangold seedlings appeared in neat rows,
they were 'cut out' with a hoe, leaving small bunches of seedlings. These
in turn were singled out by hand and thereafter kept free of weeds by
frequent hoeing. The ordinary garden hoe was used up until the 1930s
when the introduction of a hand-push hoe on one wheel speeded up
this task. The patch of ground for flatpol cabbage was marked out in
straight rows with a wooden marker (akin to a large rake with four
pointed teeth about two feet apart). When ready for plant dropping, my
father went ahead with a long-handled Cornish shovel, slicing it deep
into the brown earth with his foot and pulling the shovel to one side a
bit; the helper, often one of us children, followed on behind, carrying a
bundle of plants and dropping one in behind the shovel, which was
then removed and the plant well stamped in. Up and down the rows we
went with a rhythmic slice-drop-stamp until the whole patch had a neat
covering of plants. A shower to water them in was most welcome at the
end of the day.

Wartime Crops

DURING the Second World War, farmers were encouraged to grow more food. A certain acreage of potatoes and corn growing was compulsory. On Tremedda Farm, a half to one acre of potatoes had to be grown. At this time crop returns were good and many of the Zennor farmers also grew broccoli.

A good supply of potatoes was always grown for home consumption, both earlies and lates. At the beginning of the century a few farmers grew some for sale, taking them to market in 'mawns' covered with straw. With the advance in transport, potatoes were not really an economical cash crop to grow in Zennor. The north-facing aspect of this area caused them to mature later than in more sheltered districts and the Zennor farmers missed out on the high prices paid for first earlies.

At Tremedda during the war when potato growing was compulsory, all available hands helped with this crop.

The potato field was prepared by ploughing, then spreading with mixed dressing which was ploughed in as the potatoes were planted.

The seed potatoes were bought soon after Christmas and were put to shoot on the floor of the little loft over the bottom loosebox. We climbed the ladder and helped arrange them, placing each one with eyes looking heavenwards and leaning on its neighbour, until the whole floor was carpeted with potatoes gazing at the ceiling.

In March, when planting time came along, each eye had grown into a sturdy shoot half to one inch long. Immediately before planting, we cut the potatoes in half, ensuring each half carried a shoot, placed them carefully in large potato baskets and loaded them into the cart. With planters perched around the edge or sitting on the shafts, Lion took his load out to the fields and the back-breaking and very often freezing job of potato planting started. Lion was unhitched from the cart and attached to the plough, my father ploughed out a 'vor', or furrow, and several of us followed behind, bent double, carrying our potato baskets and placing the potatoes nine inches apart along the vor. As the next furrow was ploughed out, so the preceding row was covered. The job often lasted two or three days, the planters finishing with aching backs and rough, red hands.

When the potato plants were showing well above the ground, the skilful job of driving the large carthorse up and down the rows with hoe and banker was undertaken. Great care was needed to prevent his large hooves from treading on the young plants. Some farmers gave a stream of shouts and commands when working their horses, while the more successful only gave the occasional command in a quiet voice.

Potato picking or lifting was another back-breaking job in which all willing hands joined. It was now June and usually hot, sunny weather. We wore wellington boots and little else, vying with each other for the best suntan. Once more, Lion pulled his load of empty baskets and sacks to the field, where he then took over the ploughing. My father ploughed up the rows and Cecil dug through the combs, shook the potatoes off the stems and threw the haulms (stems) into piles. Then followed the pickers, once more bent double and armed with large baskets which, when full, were tipped into hessian sacks placed at convenient intervals along the rows. At the end of each picking session the sacks were loaded into the cart and taken back to the farm where each sack was weighed on a 'stilliers' – this was a spring balance, although the word suggests a steelyard, or scales with a single weight movable along a graduated beam – to a standard weight of half a hundredweight of potatoes to each bag, before being sewn up with a curved needle and string and stacked to await the buyer's lorry.

A race down the cliff and a dip in the sea in the evening was very refreshing and cleansing after a day in the potato field.

Deciding when to lift the early potatoes was a tricky business. Much discussion on the subject took place and the price of the day was eagerly sought. Either they were lifted when still quite small and the price was high or left maybe until almost doubled in size but the price perhaps halved. The latter was much more satisfactory, having a fine show of potatoes for all one's labours. Usually about two or three tons of potatoes were sold, the price varying from £20 – £30 per ton early, dropping to £12 – £16 per ton later.

Late potatoes were grown for the household. They were lifted in September, put in a pile in the loft and covered with sacks.

As soon as the potatoes were lifted the ground was cleared, worked and made ready for broccoli planting, which was carried out in the same fashion as cabbage planting. These wartime crops meant much extra work but the farmer was compensated by the high prices paid.

Haymaking

HAYMAKING on the Zennor farms was a regular part of the yearly activities. During the early 1900s, a small amount was made: about six or seven acres to forty acres arable. It was fed mainly to the all-important working horses.

Most of the hay was cut with the scythe, but the mechanical reaper was beginning to take over. After cutting, the hay was left to dry for a few days and was then hand turned with pikes – two-pronged forks. The whole family often undertook this job, each taking a swathe and following one another around the field. When dry, three lines or swathes were taken and the two outer ones were turned in, onto the middle one, to make one long, thick 'dram' of turned hay. The hay was now 'pooked', or stacked, in small shower-proof mounds four feet high, as a protection against rain. The hay was later carted into the mowhay on horse-drawn wains and built into a rick. The field was raked clean with a three-foot-wide hand rake and the last remnants carried to the mowhay.

This method of haymaking continued for many years. The horse-drawn tumbler rake replaced the hand one in the 1920s. During the 1930s the acreage of hay increased to around 25 per cent of the arable land, owing to the growing importance of dairying.

My childhood memories of haymaking at Tremedda were of endless delights: everyone joined in, new games and activities presented themselves, and picnics were the order of the day. On the more practical side, it meant long hours of hard work for the grown-ups, whose frame of mind very much depended on the state of the weather. A rainy April and a fine, late May and June produced a good crop of clean hay and gave great satisfaction. During the occasional wet season when rain poured down on the cut hay, the fields looked sad with the hay turning a nasty greyish black and shrinking as much of the goodness washed out of the grasses. The farmer was helpless against the elements as he watched his winter fodder slowly deteriorating in quality. Fortunately a reasonable supply of hay was usually gathered in.

In April all the fields to be cut for hay, previously spread with farmyard manure, were 'stopped in', with all the gaps closed, hopefully barring entrance to all grazers, to allow the grass to grow long and thick.

Preparations for haymaking began in late May or early June. The reaper was pulled out of its winter quarters and well oiled. The reaper knife, with its triangular, saw-like teeth, was sharpened with a file and the scythes were sharpened on the grindstone which stood near the front door. This large, round sandstone wheel was slung on an axle between two round, granite posts. An iron handle was turned and the scythe blade held in position on the rim of the revolving stone. We were often called upon to pour pails of water over the blade to prevent the blade over-heating. Finally, Lion and Tony were hitched into the reaper, one on either side of a long pole, and driven out to the field by my father. Cecil followed behind with the scythes and pikes and cutting began.

One or two cuts were made around the field, then one in the opposite direction around the edge, with Cecil walking beside the knife, forking

35. Gathering in the pooks of hay at Treen Farm. p. 85

36. Sharpening the blade for hay-cutting. Cecil Thomas holding the scythe blade on the grindstone, Ernie Brookham turning the handle.

37. Sweeping in the last remnants. p. 85

up the hay trodden down by the horses on their first circuit. So cutting proceeded. My father sat on the reaper driving the horses round and round the field, while the knife out on his right cut down the grasses, with its quick to-and- fro movement leaving a neat green swathe in its wake. Great care was taken to circumnavigate the rocks. Occasionally a jolt and clattering brought the reaper to a stand still as the knife hit a hidden rock, causing delay and possibly speedy repairs. The horses knew what this meant and the great beasts stopped immediately. The loud shouts of "Whoa, whoa," from their master were more a case of letting off steam than anything else. Cecil meantime cut all awkward corners and around rocks with the scythe. Frequent sharpening of tools took place in the field, with a file for the reaper knife and a whetstone for the scythes. My father used to say with a smile "Always sharpen your tools before they're blunt, always have a drink before you're thirsty and always leave work before you're tired." I can't say he followed the last maxim.

The children, with shorter-handled pikes, often helped turn the hay, the small ones trying to keep up with the more practised elders. One felt in a trance-like state as round and round the field one went: step-turn, step-turn, step-turn, shoving the pike under the swathe and lifting it up and over, like a green wave rising and falling. This turning might be repeated two or three times if rain fell.

When sufficiently dry, the hay was raked into drams with a horse-drawn tumbler rake, then with the help of all hands the hay was pooked. If rain seemed imminent a great race against time ensued, everyone working at full tilt and with little comment. During all this work a great sense of urgency and much weather forecasting prevailed.

Finally the hay was pulled into the mowhay. Lion was harnessed to the wain, a long flat sideless cart with two wheels in the middle and removable wooden 'riggers' at each end. Two long ropes were attached to the rear end for tying down the load. The riggers and neatly coiled ropes lay flat on the wain when empty. Our neighbour Johnnie Osborn and his workman Bert came over to help, bringing his carthorse Doll, also pulling a wain. My father reciprocated when he and Cecil with Lion and the wain in turn helped the Osborns. It was customary in the parish for relations and neighbours to help each other during the busy seasons of haymaking and corn harvesting, providing labour, horses, wains and wagons, etc.

The horses were driven out to the field, the riggers fixed in place and the ropes thrown out behind. They were led from pook to pook as each in turn was loaded onto the wain by the pitchers, and the load was built by one man who rose higher as the wain filled up. When the load was large enough, the ropes were thrown over from back to front, crossing in the middle and securely fastened to the shafts on either side. This large top-heavy load was driven carefully into the mowhay, swaying wildly as it passed through uneven rocky gaps, with the loader perched precariously on top. It was unloaded into the Dutch barn and when this was full the rest was built into a rick. Children were often called upon to trample the hay down tight when filling the Dutch barn, to get as much in as possible. As the hay neared the roof, one had to scramble about on all fours, often bumping one's head on the hard concrete roof above.

After all the pooks had been carried in, the hayfields were raked with the tumbler rake, and the last remnants gathered up. In my early teens, I very much enjoyed being allowed to rake the hayfields. Sitting high up on an iron seat with a sack on it for comfort, I drove the horse, every few yards raising the rake prongs with an iron handle and dropping the gathered hay in neat straight rows across the field. The rakings were gathered and the hay was saved.

Then the farmer could sigh with relief and relax a little until the corn harvest, with the knowledge that once again his labours had provided him with an adequate supply of hay for the coming winter.

Haymaking had a social side to it, and kept children and dogs happy for many a long hour. Mountains of food were consumed and the kitchen was a busy, bustling hive of industry. All the food was home cooked and delicious smells of roasting, baking and boiling, mixed with the more delicate odours of yeast and saffron hit you as you entered the kitchen. My mother, Sylvia, Granny Griggs, and often Katy Osborn, bustled about preparing vegetables in large enamel pans; up to their elbows in flour, making dough and rolling out large slabs of heavy cake and pastry; filling the oven; and stoking the stove. Katy was always full of good humour and had a joyous laugh to go with it. Her daughter Mary came with her to join in the fun with all of us.

One of my mother's favourite dishes for these large gatherings was rhubarb cake. A large round of pastry was rolled out, about fifteen inches across. This was heaped with chopped rhubarb and sprinkled with sugar, covered with another such round of pastry and the two edges crimped together. After baking, the top was cut off, inverted, filled with half the rhubarb from the bottom of the tart, and both halves spread with masses of cream, making two large rhubarb cakes which were cut into slices and often carried out to the field on platters.

If the men were working all day in the field, croust was carried out at mid-morning: heavy cake, saffron buns, sausage rolls, two large blue enamel tea-pots full of steaming tea and an odd assortment of kitchen cups. The men sat in the hedge for a well-earned break while the women and children handed round the food and kept the cups filled. At one o'clock the workers, including Johnnie, Bert and Cecil, after watering and stabling the horses, all trooped in for a large cooked dinner. We all sat around the long, scrubbed wood kitchen table eating, chatting, joking, teasing the young and laughing until the last dregs were drained from the tea cups. The men departed to recommence their labours, leaving the women and children to clear up the kitchen chaos. We helped clear away and wash up under protest, eagerly awaiting our release so that we could race out to the fields with the dogs and continue the fun of the morning.

Tea was the last meal for the haymakers . . . Large potato baskets full of sandwiches, splits spread with cream and jam, heavy cake, saffron buns and rhubarb cake and the much-battered blue tea-pots were carried out to the field. Sometimes a ride was hitched on one of the empty wains. Everyone perched round the edge, legs dangling, trying to protect their precious load as cups clattered and tea-pot lids danced about. These field teas were a delight, with the whole family plus neighbours and often a visitor partaking, the dogs sitting with watchful eyes waiting for titbits to drop on the ground, and the horses standing by, having a well-earned rest and an armful of new-mown hay to munch. Granny Griggs often made herb beer, which she carried out to the field during hot weather. This was greatly appreciated by the men.

For children there were rides out to the field on the bumpy wain as its iron-bound wheels clattered along the rutted ways and, if lucky, a ride back to the mowhay on top of a load of soft new hay. There was hide-and-seek around the pooks and endless fun with the long ropes that dragged along the ground behind the wain as it was being loaded. We swung on them, skipped with them, stood on them as they moved, high jumped and snake jumped over them, with someone holding the rope up or making it ripple along the ground in a snake-like fashion. The dogs often joined in the fun, making a dive at the rope ends, picking them up with a ferocious shake, pretending they were some quarry to be killed. Every so often we raced back to the mowhay for yet another ride out to the field. One day we surpassed ourselves and received one of the very rare scoldings from my father for making houses in the newly-turned hay. He even went so far as to whack us with the 'taws', a sort of leather hand which was a Scottish 'child chastiser' inherited by my mother. However, in the evening when we were all safely tucked up in bed, he came up to us, full of forgiveness, to make sure we were all friends once more. I think it hurt him more than it hurt us.

During these busy times, the evening's milking and animal feeding were often left entirely to the women and children. Although the cows were producing their maximum yield at this time of year, the feeding was down to a minimum. The cows were given a small amount of tubmeat to encourage them into their stalls and the horses were fed a handful of crushed oats only when working.

This method of haymaking was carried on for many years. A few variations occurred as new implements were tried out, but the great labour-saving mechanical hay turner and the baler were still machines of the future in Zennor.

Corn Harvest

THE corn harvest began in late August or early September. Many aspects of it were similar to those of haymaking. A field of ripe corn rippling in the wind like a golden sea looked very beautiful.

During the early part of the century most of the corn was cut with the scythe or hook; the horse-drawn reaper was just coming into use on the bigger farms. Before 1900, when more wheat was grown for thatching and milling, it was the custom for women to do the reaping. The old men could remember four women taking two days to reap one field – about one and a half acres. After cutting, the corn was left on the ground to dry for a few days. The saying was that nine dews must fall on the corn before binding. If it became too dry it would crack and break. When sufficiently dry, the corn was 'taken out' with a 'rulling' hook, which scraped into a pile the required amount of corn for one sheaf. One harvester might rull up corn for the hand binder. Women were thought to be better at taking out the corn as they wore long skirts and aprons which kept it all in place. If the corn was very tangley it had to be taken out by hand. The sheaves were bound by lengths of twisted straw, the two ends being twisted together and turned under the band; or coir twine was wound twice round and tied in a clove hitch.

Queen Victoria's Jubilee year was exceptionally dry and the straw was so short that the harvesters had to carry lengths from the odd taller patches to bind the sheaves. The following spring, owing to the shortage of feed, the cows were so hungry they ate the leaves off the brambles.

As soon as the sheaves were bound, they were built into knee 'mows'. These native-hut-like little stacks were about eight feet in diameter and eight feet tall in the middle. On reaching a certain height the builder had to climb aloft and finish building on his knees. Sidney Berryman, who lived in the Row at Zennor as a lad, could remember his 'granfer', a sprightly octogenarian in a blue 'frock' (smock) nimbly building a mow on his knees. These mows were perfectly weatherproof and were left standing in the fields until the farmer was able to carry them in on the wain to the mowhay, where the corn was built into ricks.

While harvesting in this fashion, Sidney recalled as a lad helping his father cut corn in The Darmarth. The weather was hot and a gallon flagon of beer stood in a shady part of the hedge for the grown-ups. Every time the elders were out of the way, the boys would have a drop of the beer, until Sidney, who had become quite tipsy, was asked to go and fetch the croust. This was packed into a wheelbarrow and Sidney was to push it out to the field along the cart ruts. Unfortunately, as he was slightly unsteady over went the barrow, spilling all the food and drink and breaking half the cups. Poor Sidney!

As time went on, methods changed. On some farms the reaper was replaced by the reaper sheaver, which in turn was replaced by the more efficient binder.

The reaper sheaver had two seats, one near the knife for the driver and one for the man working the sheaver. This had a sheafing rack onto which the cut corn was raked. When enough corn for one sheaf was collected, the man pressed his foot down, dropping the rack, and the corn fell off onto the ground. This did away with rulling, but the sheaves still had to be bound. Johnny Nankervis, a Zennor farmer, had one of his legs nearly severed at the ankle by this machine.

The binder, which first came to Zennor in 1919, was a real step forward in harvesting methods. It was worked by one man and both cut the corn and bound it into sheaves. It was a great labour saver. One man could cut an acre of corn with a scythe in two days. With the binder and two horses he could cut and bind an acre in two hours.

During the 1930s oats were the main crop on Tremedda Farm. Eight or nine acres were grown.

The corn fields were 'opened up' with the scythe around the hedges, thus making room for the horses to pull the binder around without trampling down the standing corn. Then the corn was cut and laid flat on a wide, moving canvas belt with rotating windmill-like flails. A second moving belt carried it up and over to the sheaver, where a pair of rotating prongs did the job of rulling hooks, and the knotter bound it with coir twine from a ball and cut the twine with a knife, before dropping it in neat rows of sheaves up and down the field.

Sometimes parts of the field were beaten down with rain or the frolics of badgers, who liked nothing better than a good roll in the corn. In such cases, a man had to walk along with a pike lifting up the corn in front of the knife. Cornish oats, black in colour, when grown were inclined to run up lank and tall and were 'a villain to go to lie'. This type of corn might be cut loose and on the green side, then pulled in to a rick. It made very good feed.

After cutting with the binder, all available hands went out to the field to 'shock' the corn. These shocks were little wigwam-like structures of eight sheaves, each one standing on its butt with the grain leaning in to a point.

38 Cutting corn with the scythe.
p. 90

39. Building shocks on Boscubban
Farm. p. 91

40. Well-earned croust. p. 88. L-R: Johnnie Thomas, Bert James, Johnnie
Osborn, Cecil Thomas, Bob Osborn (backview), Maurice Griggs.

The corn when shocked was left to dry for some days. If the weather remained fine, the corn was left in shocks until it was pulled in. If, however, rain threatened, all hands rushed out to the field to help mow the corn. A shock was chosen for the centre of each mow, and all helpers carried sheaves to a circle round it and handed them to the builder. He built outwards until the diameter measured about eight feet, then upwards. The beard of each sheaf pointed towards the middle and slightly upwards. As the mow grew taller the builder had to climb up onto it and continue building, circling the mow on his knees. On reaching six feet in height, the mow was gradually brought in to a point, which was firmly bound around with lengths of twisted straw. The corn was now safe from all weathers and birds.

Finally, with the help of our neighbours, the corn was carted into the mowhay on wains and built into one large rick, later to be threshed, and one smaller one for feeding corn in the sheaf.

As with haymaking, all the family and neighbours helped with the corn harvest. The rattling old wains plied to and fro and vast quantities of food were prepared and eaten. The picnickers often swelled in numbers as relations and friends staying on the farm for their summer holidays, joined in. It was not quite such comfortable work as haymaking and by the end of the day arms and legs were covered in red scratches from the sharp ends of the corn stems. A dip into the salty sea was very painful during harvest time. We played our games, rode on the wain, drank drinks through home-made straws and ate the tiny kernel from the middle of the oat grain.

Many unfortunate rabbits and mice, who had made their homes in the field, were speared with a pike or pounced upon by the ever-waiting dogs.

It may seem from this account that the skies were always blue while harvesting. Of course this was not the case. Sometimes rain prevented the start of cutting and the corn grew riper and started losing its seed and the long stems were bent over by the downpour. A short dry spell, and rained-on shocks had to be pulled abroad to dry out the sheaves then re-erected at speed at the first signs of yet more rain. Fortunately, memories of sunny days and blue skies far outnumber those of downpours and spoiled crops.

'Fernyscat'

THE last harvest of the year was the 'fernyscat' or gathering in of ferns (bracken) for bedding. This usually took place in October or late September. A suitable piece of croft was chosen where there were not too many rocks or gorse bushes. The ferns were cut with the scythe, allowed to dry for a few days, then gathered into small pooks and subsequently carried in on the wain. Rather hazardous and bumpy rides were to be had on the wain when gathering ferns, as the cart tracks in the croft were often sloping and most uneven. It has been known for a full load to topple over.

A fern rick was built behind the piggery, and thatched. Most of the ferns were used for pigs' bedding and some for the calves and yearlings.

Rick Building and Thatching

RICK building was a skilled job; if badly done it could result in the end of the rick slipping out. The size of the rick depended on the amount of corn or hay grown. A good-sized cornrick might be 17 yards long by 3⅓ wide and 6 high. Hayricks were usually smaller, and shrank as the hay settled. During the winter months, one often saw little, old, wizened hayricks looking as though they were trying to shrink from the fierce Atlantic winds and rainstorms.

The base was prepared by covering it with the 'seal', a good layer of hedge trimmings, brambles, furze and ferns known locally as 'browse', which kept the base of the rick dry. Later when the rick had been dismantled, the seal would be re-used to cover the mangold pile. Rows of sheaves, grain pointing inwards, were laid around the edge sloping outwards and kept well in as they tended to slip out as the rick grew. The middle was well filled and made slightly higher than the edge. The last ring of sheaves on the stem was laid with a slight overhang to shoot the rain clear of the sides, like the eaves of a roof. This was called the ovice. The rick was then gradually brought in on both sides to form the 'head'. When the head was narrowed to about one yard wide the builder finished it off by 'fixing the blow'. Starting at one end, he worked backwards on his knees the length of the ridge, making a good weathertight finish, often adding a layer of ferns as extra protection. Hayricks were built in much the same fashion, a pikeful of hay taking the place of a sheaf.

Thatching was done as soon as possible after the ricks were built. Many old farmers on finishing a rick would thatch it before going to bed.

Wheat, grown to make what was known as reed for thatching, was carefully prepared, and this might take three weeks. It was either threshed by the barn thresher in handfuls, making sure the straw was kept neat and straight, or had the grain beaten out on a roller or barrel in the barn. With the advent of the mobile thresher, which tended to crush the straw, reed-making died out and wheat straw was bought in.

Before the introduction of coir rope, the reed was kept in place with rope made from straw. The last man to thatch in this fashion in Zennor was Will Berryman who farmed the Glebe, in the late nineteenth century.

My father, with the help of Cecil and a child, thatched with bought-in wheat straw and coir rope. After carefully arranging the reed, five 'broaches' of stout blackthorn were hammered into each end of the rick head. The broaches were joined together with rope forming semi-circles. Starting on top of the rick, long ropes were laid lengthways six inches apart, working down on either side to the ovice. A child carried the long ropes attached to a twelve foot bamboo between the two men mounted on ladders at either end of the rick. Each long rope was firmly secured to the broach ropes at both ends.

Next the frame ropes, of thicker yarn, were woven into place. Holding on to one end, the rope ball was thrown over the top of the rick and down the other side where the correct length was cut. The two men mounted their ladders, one on either side, and wove the frame rope down through the long ropes, giving a half hitch on each one and tying a heavy stone at the bottom. These frame ropes were placed along the rick every three feet. This snug covering worn by the ricks withstood all the winter gales and lashing rain that often swept in from the Atlantic and kept the winter feed perfectly dry.

Threshing

IN early times corn threshing took place throughout the winter months. As it was a lengthy and arduous task, only small amounts were threshed at one time. Around 1900 most Zennor farms had a barn thresher, but a few of the very small farms still threshed corn with a 'threshal', which was a very simple implement made up of two sticks, four foot and two foot six inches long, joined together by an eight-inch leather thong. The longer stick was the handle and the shorter one the beater. The farmer beat the sheaf with the threshal with such skill that two beats caused the grain from the topside of the sheaf to fall out and the sheaf to turn over. Two more beats on the second side and the sheaf of corn was threshed.

The barn thresher was a much more sophisticated bit of machinery. It was powered by a horse whim, which was situated near one end of the barn and had a raised circular granite platform, paved with rab, called a whim round. A heavy iron bar was attached at one end to cog wheels sunk in the centre of the platform and its outer end carried a whip and traces, or shafts, to which a carthorse was harnessed. Sometimes when the workload was heavy, two horses were used. The horse was driven round and round the whim pulling the bar behind him, the driver holding long reins and walking round with the horse on its inner side. The bar turned the central cogwheels, which rotated a long shaft running under the platform through a bolt or tunnel and into the barn at ground level. This shaft drove a large flywheel at one end of the cowshouse. A long belt attached to the flywheel reached through the ceiling to the loft above, where it was attached to a small wheel on the barn thresher in order to turn its various wheels and wooden beaters. The actual threshing consisted of holding the beard of a sheaf of corn in the thresher drum, where the rotating wooden beaters caused the grain to drop out, turning the sheaf over, and pulling it out again. This method of threshing was carried on throughout the winter. Often on a rainy day oat sheaves were carried into the barn and 'ragged a bit', each sheaf held in the thresher drum, turned over and pulled out. A ragged sheaf still contained some of its seed and was good feed for the cattle. A threshed sheaf was known as a liner.

The mobile threshing machine was first used in Zennor about 1909 and came from Mr Jeffrey of Trannack, costing £3 5s.7d. per day. Both thresher and steam engine were horse-drawn; it took from four to six horses to pull the thresher. As time went on the steam engine came under its own power, towing the thresher behind it.

During the early days, a lifter driven by a belt from the thresher was often used. The loose threshed straw was carried up a long platform on moving, spiked chains and was dropped onto the straw rick which was being built. This was replaced by a bundler attached to the back of the machine.

With the change from the barn thresher to the large mobile machines, threshing took on a completely new look. It became one of the big yearly events on the farm. All the corn was threshed at one time and many neighbouring farmers came to provide the extra labour required.

Threshing: a Child's Eye View

THRESHING was one of the most exciting times of the year for us children, and no doubt very hard work for the grown-ups, but certainly a great social occasion. The machine that threshed for us belonged to Phil Rogers from Trevethoe Farm. After the harvest had been safely gathered in, this and one or two other machines started out on their rounds, going from farm to farm, accompanied by the engine driver and his mate. It took one or two days to thresh on each farm. Our turn came in October, with the weather as usual determining the date. Threshing could not proceed during wet weather. Catering for the vast numbers of large, hungry men was a bit tricky, as one was never sure of the day until all the deciding factors were known. Had the machine finished at a neighbouring farm? And would the weather be fine on the following day? Large quantities of saffron cake, splits and bread were bought; also a succulent roast of beef of vast dimensions was obtained from the same Phil Rogers' butcher's shop in St Ives. The barn was thoroughly swept and cleaned in readiness for the new grain and two beds made up for the men who came with the machine.

The thresher resembled a gigantic wooden box with many wheels and gadgets attached to it. It was powered by a large, coal-fired, steam-driven traction engine, to which it was coupled by a long leather belt six inches wide. This traction engine also pulled the thresher from farm to farm. It had a tall smoke chimney and various steam vents. The bundler, a small separate piece of machinery, was horse-drawn in the early days and brought over by Lion. Later on it was attached to the thresher.

We were allowed to take the day off school on threshing days and to stay up late the previous evening, in order to herald the arrival of this exciting machine. As soon as we heard the engine chugging up Jonah's Hill near Zennor village, we raced up to the stile by the Osborn's cart-house to catch our first glimpse of the vast iron and wooden monster. The many iron wheels made a tremendous clattering and clanking on the main road. At last there it was, appearing round Quarry Corner in all its majesty, the noise increasing and great puffs of smoke and steam shooting skywards. Being evening by then and dark, the red glow of the coal fire was dancingly reflected on various well-polished parts of the engine, giving it the quality almost of a living creature. As it turned down our lane the general hubbub increased, as shouting men raced from side to side with iron shoe drags, using them as brakes and to skid the machine to one side or the other and thus guide it around bends. Lanterns were held aloft by us children, to give light to these labours. All our senses were excited by now, with the sights, the noise, the smells of hot oil and smoke, the feeling of heat from the coal fire on our faces and lastly, tasting in our minds the feasts of the following day.

It took a good hour for this machine to manoeuvre its way down the lane, across the yard and into the mowhay. Both the yard and mowhay gates had to be dismantled to widen the gaps.

One beast who did not relish the arrival of the thresher was Lion. I remember seeing him standing in the yard, having brought the bundler over, all of a quiver at the many strange sights and sounds. As soon as he was unharnessed, he galloped off down the meadow, determined to put as great a distance as possible between himself and these unfamiliar activities.

Having settled the machine in the mowhay to their satisfaction, the two machine men had a wash in the wash-house, then came in to take supper with my parents, and after a few yarns retire to bed in the loggia room. Maurice, the engine driver, was a very worthy old fellow who seemed an integral part of his engine, being of the same hue and smell, black from coal dust and oil. He had bushy eyebrows and a large drooping moustache, and fascinated us children.

Everyone rose early on the following morning, their first thoughts about what sort of weather heralded the day. As soon as it was confirmed that threshing could commence, everyone set to, preparing for the mammoth task of the day. The women and children undertook most of the milking and animal feeding, while the men, having breakfasted, repaired to the mowhay to make sure all was in readiness. The thatch was removed from the cornrick, the ropes and reed being carefully stored, ready for re-use on the straw rick. All the pikes were gathered together and hessian sacks were collected for the grain, while 'broccoli crates' were found for carrying the ushan. A broccoli crate was a large wicker basket carried on the back by a rope slung over one shoulder.

While these and many other jobs were being carried out, Maurice fussed over his engine, filling the boiler with water, lighting the fire, making sure it was well greased and that there was plenty of coal to hand. The large leather driving belt was slung securely in place between engine and thresher. Finally, around eight o'clock, sixteen stalwart neighbouring farmers arrived, armed with pikes, having already finished their own morning's work. They came on foot or maybe bicycle, as very few farmers possessed cars in those days; they wore caps, tousers and 'kitty bags' as protection against flying dust and ushan. Kitty bags were pieces of hessian sacking tied round trouser legs. Among the helpers were Dick and David Berryman from Churchtown Farm, Arthur and Bill Nankervis from Wicca, Stanley Hocking from Tregerthen, Charlie Jelbert from Carnellow (who was constantly chewing a straw or piece of grass), Edward Noy from Trewey, James Osborne from Trevail, Claude Eddy from Bosigran, Jack Osborne from Boscubban, and of course our neighbour Johnnie Osborn and his nephew Bert, while Roberts and Pietro came out from Talland. Roberts always found himself a nice easy job but was ready enough to shout and criticise everyone else. The engine came to life with much clanking, steam flying, and smoke belching forth, until it settled down to a steady rhythm, turning all the wheels and cogs with its large unwieldy belt, which flew round at a fair old speed. We were most careful to keep clear of it. Shrill blasts were sounded on the whistle, and threshing commenced. Maurice stayed on his engine, the sweat

41. Threshing at Tremedda in later years. Mow in foreground. p. 90

42. The mobile thresher, p. 96, at Treveglos Farm. L-R: Rex Whelan, Edward Noy, Harold Harfoot, Johnnie Osborn on rick.

43. Croust on the wain in the Dutch barn. p. 88. L-R: Elsie and Maurice Griggs, Little Dan, Dan Quick, Johnnie Osborn, Arthur Oft, Garfield Hosking.

pouring down his blackened face as the fire grew hotter, shovelling on coal, allowing hissing bursts of steam to escape from various jets, and making sure all ran smoothly. These steam jets had their uses; one blew the whistle, while baccy pipes were held over others to be thoroughly cleaned before being refilled.

Two men on the cornrick passed sheaves to the top of the thresher where another man, kneeling, cut the binds and a fourth fed them beard-first into the machine, in whose innards they were separated into grain, straw and ushan. The grain went through a series of different-sized sieves which graded it, then finally ran out of five or six apertures into hessian sacks suspended on hooks at the front end of the thresher. The streams of seed ran out in three grades: two of large, two of seconds and one or two of small seed and dust. This was all stored in separate piles in the barn. A procession of men carried the full sacks across the yard, up a flight of stone steps and into the barn, tipping them onto an appropriate pile on the floor and returning with the empty sacks to replace the full ones. The straw came out of the rear end of the thresher and was fed into the bundler, which tied it neatly in two places with binder twine. The large bundles were ejected onto the ground and in turn built into a new straw rick.

The ushan came out underneath the thresher from a shaking sieve-like contraption; it was raked out, stuffed into broccoli crates and carried away to a pile, to be used later as litter for the hen-house floors. This job was usually delegated to Ernie Brookham or maybe Jimmy 'Limpots'. (Stevens was his surname, Limpots his St Ives nickname).

Indoors, the preparing and serving of food, and the washing up, seemed to continue all day. The kitchen was a hive of industry, bursting at the seams, what with our mother, her two helpers Maggie and Sylvia, Granny Griggs and our cousin Alice, our neighbour Katy Osborn and her daughter Mary, who joined in the fun with us girls. The American stove roared away, stoked up with plenty of good coal and supplemented by one or two oil stoves for all the large saucepans and big black kettles. Good smells of baking, roasting and boiling came wafting out of the windows. All the children helped serve the food and gave a hand with the washing up.

At half past ten the whistle sounded and all the men downed tools for croust. Food was carried out to the mowhay in large potato baskets – hot sausage rolls, buttered splits, heavy cake and saffron buns and, to wash this down, large steaming cups of tea or camp coffee. The dusty men sat on bundles of straw or, if it was windy, settled themselves in the hay house. Those without caps sported a regular halo of ushan on their hair. We helped hand round the food and came in for much teasing. Our greatest dislike was being referred to as boys, which happened frequently, as our mother made us have the short back and sides haircut common to boys of that period; only when we reached the great age of ten were we allowed to grow our hair, my mother hoping that by then we would be able to look after it ourselves.

The next meal, around half past one, was a large cooked dinner. Once again the whistle blew, the traction engine stopped, and the men had a clean-up in the wash-house before coming in to sit round tables in the sitting-room. We all helped carry in large plates piled high with roast beef, Yorkshire pudding, roast and boiled potatoes, cabbage, mashed turnip and gravy, followed by dishes of rice pudding, apple tart and cream, and finishing with cups of tea and much talk and laughter. Finally everyone got up steam again, the engine included, and work started once more. We then had the terrible task of clearing the tables and washing up before we ourselves were allowed to eat, being by this time absolutely starving. When at last it was all done, the women and children sat down at the kitchen table to eat their own large, well- deserved dinner.

The next and last meal was tea at about four o'clock; a similar meal to croust, carried out to the men in the mowhay: sandwiches, splits, cream and jam, and saffron cake, with plenty of tea to drink.

Finally, around dusk, the last sheaf was fed into the thresher, the streams of grain came to a halt and a brand new straw rick stood tall and proud in the mowhay. The traction engine gave one last shrill whistle and slowly ground to a halt, the steam gradually dying down to a murmur. The weary dusty men, now too exhausted for tomfoolery or talk, said their goodbyes, were thanked by my father and set off for home, where still more chores awaited them. The machine was made ready for its departure and finally chugged up the lane and on to the next farm, or maybe only over the stream and into Johnnie Osborn's mowhay. We watched half-heartedly as the machine drew away, too tired to show much enthusiasm and rather sad that the day was over. All were more than ready for 'early to bed'.

My father, and often Cecil the workman, would spend many more days away, helping with the threshing on the farms that had supplied him with labour.

Much of our day had been spent having tremendous fun. Smooth, shiny grains of oats ran through our fingers into the sacks, ladders leaning against ricks were climbed, and up in the barn we rolled, sank and swam in a sea of good- smelling grain, some golden, some black. We had corn fights, corn and prickly ushan were thrust down our necks, we were stuffed into sacks, slung over strong shoulders and carried from barn to mowhay, with much shrieking and laughter, being both frightened and pleased at the same time. The dogs enjoyed the day as much as anyone, dancing around the dwindling cornrick, ears pricked, tails wagging, always on the alert, ready to pounce on the mice as they fled from the homes they had made between the sheaves.

It is doubtful whether everyone looked on threshing in the same light as we children. Maybe there were those who, having been at it for days on end, thought it dusty, scratchy, eye-watering, wearisome and darned hard work. But for us it was a glorious day.

Crushing

THE grain stored in the barn was fed crushed to the horses and cattle, and whole to the poultry. Some of the best seed was saved for sowing in the fields the following year.

If the grain in the barn was damp, it had to be turned with a shovel to prevent it becoming mildewed.

Two or three Zennor farmers had a grinding mill for crushing corn, with a Blackstone engine run on paraffin that was started with a handle, to drive the rollers which crushed the grain.

At Tremedda, every so often throughout the winter months, the cart was loaded with sacks of corn and taken to Willie Pascoe's farm at Treen to be crushed. My father sat on the back end of the nearside shaft and drove Lion with long rope reins. Occasionally, much to our delight, we were allowed to go along for the ride. We sat on top of the sacks, well wrapped up in coats, leggings, hats, scarves and gloves. On the return journey, the cart bulged with well-filled sacks of crushed oats.

Busy Times

SPRING and early summer were exceptionally busy times on the farm. Weather permitting, the men worked out in the fields all the God-given daylight hours, working the ground, sowing seed, planting, lifting potatoes and haymaking. Then would come a slight lull before the corn harvest began in late August.

Everything grew with a rush and weeds had to be kept at bay with much hoeing and cutting. Thistles, docks and nettles in the grass fields were cut with a scythe and later with the reaper, where practicable. Thistles and docks in the corn fields were chopped down with a paddle. Leats and streams needed cleaning to keep the water running in the right direction.

Between haymaking and harvest a brief respite ensued for the farmer. During this period, as time went on, many farmers' wives, including my mother, took on the added burden of summer visitors. At Tremedda during July and August all the sleeping quarters were full to bursting with London relations plus their friends and helpers.

During the autumn as the evenings drew in and the growing season came to a halt, so the work in the fields eased off. This was the time for effecting repairs, cleaning out forgotten corners or removing yet a few more rocks from the fields.

The work of stock feeding and keeping the animals warm and dry was of prime importance during the winter months.

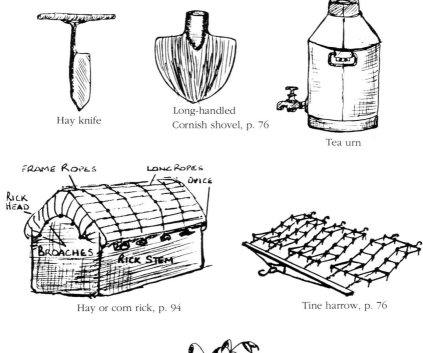

Hay knife

Long-handled
Cornish shovel, p. 76

Tea urn

Hay or corn rick, p. 94

Tine harrow, p. 76

Oats, p. 72

PART FOUR: NECESSITIES AND ETCETERAS

Labour

DURING the early part of the twentieth century labour was plentiful. Families were large, the tin mines were closing down and agricultural wages were low. All the family helped on the farm; the women and girls undertook the milking, calf-rearing, dairywork, and poultry feeding and rearing. They also helped in the fields when required, as at haymaking and harvest time. The men did the horse work, cattle and pig feeding, tilling the fields, 'pig-sticking' and many other jobs. Certain tasks were performed each day, as well as animal husbandry; washing on Monday, ironing on Tuesday, two days for buttermaking, marketing on Thursday, baking on Friday and slight spring cleaning on Saturday. Sunday was kept as the Sabbath, with only essentials being undertaken. Church and chapel were the order of the day, and often Bible reading. Farmers with large families often had to send some of their sons and daughters to work elsewhere. The boys worked in the mines, on the local roads or on farms with insufficient labour, and the girls went into service, mainly. Labour on the farms decreased as the years went by; miners emigrated, people moved into the towns, families were smaller and the machine took over many jobs. In 1900, one man could work ten to twelve acres. In 1940, two men worked forty to fifty acres.

During the First World War many Zennor lads were called up. The government helped to overcome the resulting labour shortage by forming a Women's Land Army. Old Mrs Kennedy, who stayed at Tregerthen

Cottage for a time, took in three land girls for periods of six weeks. They were trained in dairying by my mother and in horse work by Aunt Mary, then moved on to other farms. They did awful things during their first week's training – drove carts into the hedge in gaps and when using the separator forgot to replace the cream and milk pans under the spouts! Canadian soldiers also worked on the farms during this period. Jimmy Thomas the stone mason, John Hocking, a brother of Stanley late of Tregerthen, who was invalided out of the army, and Tom Berryman from the Row, all worked for my mother at Tremedda during the First World War.

During the 1930s most Zennor farmers employed one labourer, who often lived in the farm cottage. Some employed relatives or home boys (from an orphanage), who lived in.

During the Second World War a succession of German and Italian prisoners-of-war came to Zennor to work on the farms. My father, who had fought during the First World War, was not keen on our German help, Gerhart. Although a good worker, he was much too 'uppity' and infuriated my father when he found him using his shaving gear or sitting in the sitting-room listening to the German news on our radio. The Italians were quite a different kettle of fish; they were a merry lot, willing to please and delighted to find themselves in such congenial surroundings; they had no wish to fight anyone.

Many people worked at Tremedda when I was a child. Indoors there were nannies, Swiss girls learning English, Sylvia who lived in and helped with the milking, dairywork and cooking, and Maggie her sister who came daily to clean the house. In the early days my mother undertook horse work and always helped with the milking, dairywork, poultry, gardening, and other jobs. Outside, as well as my father's workman Cecil, simple Ernie dug the garden which was quite large, cleaned out the fowls' houses and turned the butter churn. Annie Christopher helped with the laundry, poultry plucking and many odd jobs, and Jimmy Limpots walked five miles from St Ives to earn a few shillings' beer money by chopping up firewood and polishing floors. All seemed a happy and contented lot.

A rather different form of labour came to Tremedda during the late 1930s. The Nazis had started persecuting the Jews and Mrs Arnold Forster took up their cause, finding households in Britain to take them in. She persuaded my mother to take in one such unfortunate. Harry Murray arrived, a penniless, townee young man from Vienna. His family had been comfortably off, running a hat-shop business. He was expected to help on the farm and provide Robina, Flora and me with our education for one year. He taught us mainly the German language with a smattering of other subjects dear to him such as French history and the prowess of

Marshal Ney! For a short while after his arrival, he used to wonder where everyone went when they disappeared twice daily, early morning and evening, not knowing there was such a chore as milking cows. He wore black city suits and shaved every morning. After learning the art of milking, he never undertook this early morning task unshaven. He soon became very much one of the family and grew to regard my parents with great affection, willingly helping on the farm whenever required. When war broke out, all Germans were interned. Harry was sent to a camp in Huyton. Later, much to his great delight, he was able to serve in the Royal Navy, joining the Pioneer Corp. After the war Harry married a Hungarian and worked as interpreter for the BBC but he always thought of Tremedda as his second home.

Fuel

In 1900, turf and furze were the main sources of fuel in Zennor. The vicarage and Gurnard's Head Hotel were the only two households using coal at that time. Long hours were spent on moor and cliff harvesting the yearly fuel supply. Everyone had a furze and turf rick handy to their back door. All the parish had a right to fuel, and the tenant- or owner-farmers of the fuel-cutting areas allotted plots to the rest of the inhabitants.

The turf was cut in May, just before the hay, on suitable sites on the hills and moors. Large slabs about eighteen inches square and four inches thick were cut out with a biddicks – a tool similar to a digger only with a much longer blade. These slabs were brandised (stood up in pairs in the shape of a roof) black side out, and left to dry for a week or two. Then they were built into 'pooks' starting with a circle of turfs and built up in decreasing circles, with the middle well filled and a final large turf on the top. The pooks were then quite safe from the inclement weather and could be carted in to a rick near the house at any convenient time, usually in September. The turfs were handled with a 'turfy pike', similar to the ordinary pike but with shorter, thicker prongs. A turf rick was about 10 by 5 by 6 feet high. It was built by laying several turfs along one end, standing some up against these and building rows back the length of the rick, thus facilitating the removal of turfs when required for the fire. A turf rick needed no thatching. It was built up to a roof-like point and was quite weatherproof.

Some farmers had to go a fair distance for their turf. There was none near the village of Zennor, but it abounded in such places as the Sperris and other moors just below the hill-tops.

Harvesting the furze was not a pleasant job, as the bush is very prickly. There are two kinds of furze or gorse in these parts, known locally as the French and the Cornish furze. The former is the larger bush and can grow up to eight feet or more. It abounds on the cliffs, lower moors and lower hill slopes and is spring flowering. This type was cut for fuel. The Cornish furze grows on and near the hill-tops and high moorlands and downs; it is only ankle or knee high and flowers in early autumn. I think it is fair to say one can at any time of the year find a gorse bush in flower. 'When gorse is out of blossom, kissing is out of fashion' is an old saying.

It was the custom in Zennor to start furze cutting during Feast week, which fell during the beginning of May. Cricket was played on the Monday and Tuesday and on Wednesday the men went off to the furze grounds, each with their rope, stout stick and hook.

The stick and hook had shields to protect the cutter's hands from the sharp prickles. The hook, a slightly heavier version of the ordinary grass hook, had a leather cuff covering the handle and the cutter's hand, which was often made from the leg of a fisherman's old boot. The shield for the stick was also an old boot. The stick was passed through two holes on either side of the foot and the cutter held the stick inside the boot. He used it to hold the furze to one side while he cut it. When cut, faggots were made by taking several stalks of furze and tying them into bundles, either with a 'furzy stick' – a springy piece of itself – or with light coir yarn. The old people could cut a hundred faggots a day. When dry, in September or October, the faggots were carted in and built into a rick and thatched. They were handled with a turfy pike when building the rick and were pulled out of the rick with an iron 'furze hitch'.

All the cottages and farmhouses had an open chimney, a recess about eight feet wide and six feet deep below a large chimney. The fire of furze and turf was lit on the open chimney floor and served as cooker, water heater and house warmer. Large sooty kettles and iron cooking pots hung from a hinged iron bar above the fire or stood on a three-legged brandis over it. Roasting and baking were done on a flat iron baking plate covered with an iron 'baking kettle'. The plate was placed on the hot embers, and covered with the kettle, a round dish-like lid. Hot embers were piled on top and around the kettle. Food cooked in this fashion was very delicious as none of the flavour could escape during cooking. The cook had to be an expert in timing her roasting and baking as she could not peep inside to see if the meal was ready. According to Dick Berryman, if you put two turfs up against two sides of the brandis around the embers at night, "Come down in the morning, turn the turfs around and you'd have fire enough to roast pilchards."

Sometimes ushan and 'claws' (dried cow's dung) were burnt. These were put under the brandis when much boiling was in progress, and burnt for a long time. When yearlings were grazing the cliffs, they would always lie in certain sheltered places which would be covered with their droppings. When dry and hard these were carried up in sacks to use as fuel.

The furze and turf harvest entailed much labour, and came to an end around 1920 when a good supply of cheap coal became available. The open chimney was gradually replaced by the good old coal-burning Cornish 'slab'. This iron stove was fitted into the open chimney recess and had a little rack over it for airing clothes and rising dough. These Cornish slabs often had ornamental iron and brass work on them. The farmer's wife took great pride in her slab, polishing it every week with black lead and keeping all the brass fitments shining brightly. The Cornish slab was the main cooking stove up until the 1950s to '60s. Sometimes it was complemented with a paraffin stove, when masses of cooking was in progress.

Coal was cheap in the 1920s: it cost ninepence per hundredweight if fetched, and tenpence if delivered. The Zennor farmer drove his horse and cart to St Ives, weighed them on the weighbridge outside the Sloop Inn, drove to Smeaton's Pier where he filled the cart from large piles of coal brought by steamboat, returned to the weighbridge for a second weighing, and drove home. One horse could pull a load of thirteen to fourteen hundredweight; even up Boscubban Hill he needed no 'chainer' (extra horse) as the roads were rough and the horse did not slip.

In those far-off days country people ruled their own destinies to a much greater degree than now. There was no chance of suddenly having their sources of warmth, cooking and water-heating cut off completely by the whims of workers miles away, over whom they had no control. Their own labour was the source of most of their needs.

The Most Important Cow on the Farm

ALL the farmsteads and dwellings in Zennor parish were situated by a water supply. In 1900 this meant a stream for the animals and a spring for the homestead. A stone-lined well was built over the spring, from which the water was dipped out. Some farms had a hand-worked lift-and-force pump over the well. The well was usually near the house, although in some cases it was as much as a field's length away, as at Tremedda. One well sometimes served a group of farms, each one having a right of way to it.

At the turn of the century, the water supplies in Churchtown were a well in front of Treveglos Farmhouse, rainwater tanks for the vicarage, a

44. Smeaton's pier, St Ives, where farmers picked up their coal. p. 108

45. A coal-burning Cornish slab.
p. 108

46. Charlie Roberts and the Barrocino in the Talland stable yard. p. 117

communal pump for the rest of the inhabitants and the river for the animals. During a hot dry spell, a steady stream of water carriers went back and forth to the village pump. The water was carried in large 'clome' pitchers (earthenware jugs) and pails to the smaller households, while a horse-drawn barrel on wheels took water to the larger farms. Some people still wore the ancient wooden yoke, curved out to fit the shoulders with a chain bearing a crook hanging from each end. The carrier bent down, put the chains through the pail handles and hooked the crooks into links at the height most comfortable for himself, and then stood up again, carrying the pails.

The well under the communal pump was a very good water supply, and in the very dry summer of 1921 there were queues of fifty people or more at the pump, with someone on the handle all day long – but it never ran dry.

Dick Berryman's mother carried thousands of gallons from the well in front of her house at Treveglos. She could carry a pail in each hand and one on her head. She was a 'bester' for getting out of bed in the mornings and drinking a cup of cold water from the well. She finally died of enteric fever caused, so the doctor said, by drinking infected well water. So the well was filled in: all the old millstones and other rubbish were pushed into it and it was sealed over. Granny Griggs carried water for her toilet cistern upstairs. She was one of the very few who had one, as she took in visitors.

Animals, when grazing in fields with no access to water, were driven to a stream or river twice a day to drink. It was a familiar sight in Churchtown to see cattle and horses parading down to the river in a leisurely fashion, having a long cool drink, then ambling back to the farmstead. In the 1900s many of the domestic animals were allowed to roam free. Poultry and pigs scavenged around the village and farmsteads, while horses and heifers were sent to graze the hills and moors. All these animals gathered at their nearest stream or river to drink. The motor car and tarred roads, causing so many restrictions, were still a thing of the future.

The first piped water supply in Zennor was installed at Tremedda Farm in 1913. My mother, as yet Miss Pilcher, decided this was her first and most important improvement when she moved to the farm. Two gentlemen came down from Truro to advise her. A small reservoir was built over a good spring in the croft and the water was piped down to the farm where it supplied hot and cold water to a bathroom, kitchen sink and wash-house sink. An American coal-burning stove heated the water. The bathers in the very up-to-date bathroom wore straw hats while in the bath as 'creepy crawlies' had a tendency to fall out of the thatch! My father-in-law, Mr Harry Symons of St Ives, effected the installation, as he did many others in the parish in subsequent years. He always claimed that the water supply was the most valuable cow on the farm – and the most neglected.

Up until the Second World War, most Zennor farmers were too poor to make many improvements and household ones were usually last on the list. The farms with a good landlord came off best in this respect. Domestic piped water supplies consisted mainly of one cold tap over a sink in the back kitchen.

In the 1930s, rams were first used for pumping water. The Blake brothers, triplets from Accrington in Lancashire, invented the hydram. A Blake's Patent Hydram was installed at Trevail Farm in 1933. The river produced the source of energy to pump water from a spring nearby up to the farmhouse. Several more rams were installed in the parish, usually by a benevolent landlord. In 1950 the landlord of Treveglos Farm had water piped into the village from a spring in Foage valley. As well as supplying the farm with water, he provided one tap for the rest of the villagers, thus making the old pump redundant.

Today, most of the parishioners enjoy every amenity water can supply. About 1970 a mains water supply came to half the parish, the other half still relying on their own supplies which are often taxed to the hilt with the vast present-day demands on them.

While on the subject of water, I feel I must extol the virtues of the tiny stream at Tremedda, no more than ankle deep and two foot wide. This little rippling stream had its source up in the croft. The overflow from the reservoir started the little stream on its way, a few smaller streams trickling into it. It meandered down through the croft and one or two fields, providing watercress, drink for grazing animals and many delights for children in the form of frogs, tadpoles, newts, and tiny bridges. The stream emerged from the fields through a shute, falling into a large stone drinking-trough from whence it overflowed and crossed the lane. This tiny ford provided excellent bird baths among the stones in the shallows, where tiny birds came and dipped and fluttered and preened. Water-wagtails were much in evidence here, tripping about and nodding as they went. The stream continued on down one side of the lane until it reached the duck pond. From here it ran under the hedge and away down a little valley to the sea. Where the stream ran through the fields and down the lane it was referred to as the leat as it was partly man-made.

Around 1937, this little stream took on a new and very important role; it was harnessed to a water turbine and provided electricity for the house and farm. My uncle, Hope Pilcher, was very interested in this scheme and generously provided us with the turbine. Work on the installation took many months. As the source of power came from the fall of the water and not the volume, the turbine had to be sited as near sea level as possible.

It was installed in a little house built on the rocks just above high tide, with two round port-holes for windows. Two Profit brothers undertook all the digging with help from my father. A small dam was made just below the fields adjoining the cliff, and a pipeline laid from the dam to the turbine. Poles were erected to carry the electric wires from the turbine to the farm. All the materials had to be carried down the cliff on men's shoulders or pulled on a draw to the very edge of the cliff by Lion.

Great excitement prevailed when the electricity was first turned on. Everyone was present to witness this great event, including the neighbours who were asked to tea. We sat under a blaze of electric light bulbs, drinking tea made with water boiled in an electric kettle and warming our feet by an electric fire. All this may seem very dull and commonplace today, but not so then. The tedious and lengthy jobs of cleaning, filling and lighting oil lamps, stoking the range and open fires and heating flat-irons were replaced by the flick of a switch. A great wonder indeed. All our Christmas presents to each other that year were electric: lamps, lampshades, an electric iron. An electric cooker was installed. The boiling plate worked on the same principle as the Aga: a large metal hot block, permanently switched on, stored up heat when the lid was closed.

The great beauty of this electricity supply, after the initial installation costs, was that it was free. Tremedda could be lit like Buckingham Palace and heated to a frazzle without any thought of the cost. I suppose there were certain repairs and maintenance costs, but these were done as far as possible by my father. The only times we had to be careful of the supply was during very dry spells when a water shortage might occur. Then the turbine was switched off for a few hours to allow the water in the dam to fill up.

There were automatic stop and start buttons in the house, worked by batteries. Faults did occur sometimes, the most persistent one being gravels which somehow got into the pipe line and were washed down into the works, causing havoc to the fast spinning parts and often bringing the turbine to a stand still. Another fault that I well remember as it directly concerned me, was the automatic stop-and-start refusing to work. If this happened during a water shortage I was sent down the cliff twice a day to turn the turbine off and on manually. I became so proficient at this job that I could run across two fields, down the steep cliff incline, turn the valves and run up again in nine minutes. The problem of the power going off occasionally caused minor crises such as a cake half-cooked in the oven, fifty baby chicks in a brooder depending on electricity for heat, or maybe a supper party plunged into darkness.

During the declining years of the turbine, the gravel trouble increased and quite often the lights grew dim and went out. On one occasion when this happened, a small boy (Roger Symons) was heard to say "It's that bloody terabine".

The turbine had been a faithful servant for twenty years when Tremedda was finally joined onto the mains electricity supply.

It seemed quite amazing that one tiny bubbling stream coupled with the ingenuity of man could provide such boundless benefits. A magical stream indeed. Why, in this age, when man can reach the moon and drill for oil on the ocean bed, has he not progressed further in harnessing the boundless energies on our doorsteps: streams, rivers, wind, tide, waves and the sun?

Transport

THE great change in transport, which began during the 1920s with the advent of the motor vehicle, has been a major factor in the alteration of farming and village community life. In 1900, 95 per cent of Zennor inhabitants were local families who had lived in or near the parish for hundreds of years. They all knew each other and met regularly at church or chapel. As the motor car became more widespread, making London almost as accessible as Camborne (twenty miles away), farmhouses and cottages began to be snapped up by strangers as they came on the market. The remote wild setting of Zennor parish, between sea and moors, had a great attraction for the fast-living city dwellers. So the community began to get a large injection of 'foreigners', as the Cornish like to call them.

In 1900, apart from travelling many miles on foot, the villagers rode on horseback and drove in various types of traps. The heavier farm cart, tradesman's cart, and wain or wagon, were constant users of the rab roads, and the large Jersey car or four-in-hand (it took four large horses to pull a Jersey car), might be seen carrying its load of sightseers on an outing. Occasionally grand carriage-and-pairs or landaus came to the village when some well-off personage decided to make a visit, or when they were hired for weddings. Granny Dow lent her landau, with Roberts in his top hat as coachman, for a neighbour's wedding. Accidents often occurred but were rarely fatal.

Some men thought nothing of walking nine or ten miles to a distant mine, putting in a long, hard day's work, and returning on foot to yet more chores awaiting them on their own smallholding. Robert Osborn from Boswednack at one time worked in a mine at Hayle. He walked the ten or so miles to work, walked home, did the chores on his own smallholding and still had the energy to walk another eight miles to catch a hare and return home, well satisfied. One might think there were insufficient daylight hours to perform all these tasks. Children in outlying parts of the parish had a two or three mile walk to school and women often trudged the five or six miles to St Ives or Penzance, carrying a heavy basket loaded with butter and eggs for sale. A few visitors, mainly from the artistic fraternity, went on walking tours along the coast or walked to Zennor to explore the cliff and hill, after which they often made a bee-line for Granny Griggs's house between church and pub, where they could have delicious cream teas, with everything home-made by Granny.

Traps were all two-wheelers, pulled by one horse. Two early traps common in the parish were the box trap and the dog cart. Both were square, and had iron tyres. They had seating for three, facing forward. The seat was movable, back or forth, to balance the weight with the horse. The driver's seat in the dog cart was a bit higher, with a box under it for tools and oil. The jingle, a slightly later model, was rounded at the corners, had rubber tyres, and was entered by a door at the rear. It seated four, two on either side, with the driver's seat at the rear, to the left of the door. The rally trap was much more swanky. It was a two-seater, had rubber tyres and was entered from the front. With a good horse it could travel at speed. Traps had to be licenced at a cost of fifteen shillings per annum. A nearly-new jingle and harness cost twelve pounds.

On coming out of church one Sunday evening, Sidney Berryman was walking up the Gurnick when he saw a jingle carrying four fishermen from St Ives. On reaching the Zennor turning, two wanted to go to the Tinners' Arms and two wanted to go home, resulting in one wheel of the jingle mounting a high bank, so over she went. The driver said to one of the passengers "Silly bugger, I told 'ee to get aft and you got for'ard!"

The donkey shay was a much smaller affair, and used mainly by the poorer people carrying small loads of maybe fish or parcels for the postman. Shays had iron tyres, and a cocoa tin was often tied to the wheel to make a noise to frighten the donkey into action. The shay had an axle to carry the wheels, two shafts that stretched right back the whole length of the cart, across the width a seat for two – this was just a board, and your feet rested on the axle – and a flat piece of wood across the front to carry the parcels. A host of donkey shays worked at Geevor tin mine.

The heavier farm vehicles were the dead cart, spring cart, wain and later the wagon. The dead cart was the ordinary farm cart. It could be tilted up in front and held at the required angle with an iron ladder and ladder pin. The tail board was removable to facilitate loading, unloading and tipping. The spring cart was similar, but as its name implies it was sprung, and

47. 'A spring for the homestead', p. 108. A wayside chat at the well, Trewey.

48. The Talland landau with Charlie Roberts in his top hat. Lent to neighbours for the wedding of Annie Osborn of Tremeadow to James Berryman from Nancledra. p. 113

49. The farm cart in Tremedda outer yard. p. 114. Maurice Griggs, Cecil Thomas and Lion.

open in front. The wain had a long flat base similar to the wagon, on two wheels, with removable riggers at both ends. One pair of wheels and axle often served both wain and cart. The four-wheeled wagon was first used in Zennor around 1912, the front wheels turning on a turntable under the front end of the wagon. These heavier vehicles were usually pulled by one strong carthorse (Shire or part Shire), and occasionally a second horse or chainer was used to help pull an extra heavy load up a hill. The chainer was placed in front of the carthorse and helped pull with a chain fixed on each side. Before motor transport came in, the horse and cart on Treveglos Farm was driven to Penzance at least twice a week to deliver and bring back goods. Dick Berryman's father, Old Dicka, helped Jim Stevens move from Foage Farm in Zennor to Sancreed, fifteen miles or so away. He drove the women, children and chickens over the top of the downs by wain.

The only public transport to use the Zennor roads was the Jersey car, which was hired for outings much as coaches are today. Zennor church choir always hired a Jersey car for their yearly outing. They went as far afield as Gwinear, The Lizard or Land's End – fifteen to twenty miles. Jersey cars were large uncovered wagons with several rows of seats across. They carried twenty-four passengers. The driver sat in front with two people on either side, then there were four rows of five seats and a small seat at the rear for the conductor, who worked the brakes and the shoe drag – an iron shoe put under the wheel to act as a brake or to help turn the wheels around awkward corners. All the seats faced the front and were quite high up; the back seat was the highest and had steps up to it. When climbing a steep hill some of the more nimble passengers would get out and walk. They also alighted for toilet purposes and lined up on either side of the road! John Uren from St Ives had a bigger car which held twenty-eight passengers; it took five horses to pull it up the steep hills. On one occasion, a Jersey car was travelling down the hill from Eagle's Nest towards Zennor, when one of the horses started kicking, causing all four to take off at speed. The driver could do nothing with them, and though they rounded Rab-pit Corner successfully, on the next bend the car toppled over, throwing some of the passengers over the hedge into Tremedda croft. It must have been a work of art to put everything to rights once more.

One-horse open wagonettes were used on short runs around Penzance, and two-horse closed buses, which also carried the mail, had regular routes. Some ran from Penzance to Pendeen, St Just and Land's End. Neither had a regular route to Zennor. There was a stand for wagonettes at the top of Morab Road in Penzance, where they all lined up like a cab rank, each horse with his nose bag, awaiting their turn as passengers came along for runs to Newlyn and Mousehole.

Willie Warren, landlord of the Radjel Inn in Pendeen for sixty years, told me that one of Warren's two-horse buses took a party of men from Pendeen to visit the Tinners' Arms in Zennor. When it was time to return home, the passengers took their seats, and while waiting for the driver the horses turned around and headed for home driverless. They successfully covered the four miles of very twisty roads, with the driver running behind, unable to catch them. He also recalls my mother driving smartly through Pendeen in her baroccino, an Italian trap very similar to the Rally trap.

Other vehicles using the roads were tradesmen's wagons and carts. Two wagons came regularly to Zennor, H.T.P. from Hayle with a three-horse wagon carrying sacks of animal feed for Tom Berryman's shop in the Row and Bazeley bringing out goods for Miss Hosking's shop at the top of the Gurnick. Bakers came in their four-wheeled carts with rounded hoods. One in particular, the penny-cake man, was eagerly awaited by my father as a small boy. He sat on the church steps clutching his penny, which bought a large currant bun with a cherry in the middle. Dick the bread boy came driving his van from St Just. He stopped in the 'court', past Granny Griggs's house, took the bit out of the horse's mouth, slung the nose-bag over his ears and left him contentedly munching while he went round the village with his wares in a large basket. Oats, the night baker, arrived in the village about 9 p.m.; after finishing his business he went into the Tinners' Arms for a drink and then drove very late back to St Just. Yankee Jack came from St Ives with his pony and bread van, always finishing his round in the Tinners' Arms. One evening someone gave his pony a slap on the rump and off he trotted to St Ives driverless. Yankee Jack had to walk the five miles home. Fish 'jousters' came with their carts of fish; they walked round the village shouting "Pilchers, pilchers".

One of the grander carriages that came to the village was owned by John Bramwell, the landlord of Treveglos Farm. He used to come and stay at the Tinners' Arms for his summer holidays. He came in a carriage-and-pair, complete with coachman. The horses, Merrylegs a great dark mare and Penpol a chestnut, were stabled at Treveglos. Bramwell imbibed large quantities of potent liquor and when the time came for his return to Penzance, as soon as he and his coachman were installed in the carriage, off they went at a mad pace, galloping up the Gurnick and away.

My recollections of horse transport, apart from rides in the various farm carts, were driving in my grandmother's baroccino. It had seating for two or three with a padded back rest and a matching long corduroy-cushioned seat, and a large basket under the seat to hold goods. Ariel, a smart bay horse, pulled this little trap along willingly. Roberts, smartly

dressed in khaki breeches, jacket, waistcoat and cap, and highly polished
boots and leggings, drove this little equipage the five miles to Tremedda
and back twice weekly, taking out provisions for my mother and
returning to St Ives with butter and eggs for sale. He was a bad-tempered
fellow, always holding the whip at the ready and prone to bully the
horse. After the roads were tarred, some of the surfaces were like glass,
and Ariel had to wear rubber shoes to prevent her from slipping. During
the mid 1930s there was a period when all four of us girls attended Miss
Baker's small school in St Ives. My father drove us to school on Monday
morning by car, we stayed the week with Granny Dow at Talland, and
returned home for the weekend. School finished on Friday at lunch time.
Pietro, an Italian who worked for my grandmother, brought two hot
pasties well wrapped up, for two of us who would start walking to
Tremedda from school. On reaching the top of Rosewall Hill we sat and
picnicked, awaiting the arrival of Roberts and the baroccino, bringing the
two sisters who had lunched at Talland. Then we exchanged places, the
two walkers now riding and the riders walking. We would sit huddled
together beside Roberts, hardly daring to raise our voices above a
whisper as we were afraid of his loud shouting voice. Ariel frequently
made rude noises and messed on the road, and we had to confine our
giggles under the rug as Roberts was not amused! During cold weather
we were well tucked in with a fur rug; when raining a waterproof canvas
covered all. Ariel and the baroccino was one of the last horse-drawn
vehicles to travel over the Zennor road.

In 1900, all the roads in this district were rab surfaced. During the
summer months men were employed to break up stone for the roads.
These small stones were laid on the roads, then covered with layers of
rab carted from the many rab-pits by the roadsides. A water cart went
over this, wetting the rab. It was then rolled. When dry, this made a firm
roadway. Tarring the roads started after the First World War. A small piece
was done every year. A single track road from St Ives to Zennor was
tarred by 1925. Most of the roads were tarred by 1930 and the bridges
widened by 1935. These roads were widened bit by bit during the
summer months, to make a double track. The tar boilers were very hot
and men worked stripped to the waist, and were often burnt. Some
farmers helped with road work to supplement their incomes, hiring out
their horses and carts, breaking up stone or, as in Dick Berryman's case,
driving the steamroller. Dick's father was paid half a crown for pulling all
the rocks out of the river after the great flood which washed away Foage
Lane at the beginning of the 1890s.

A motor bus service from Penzance to Zennor started in the 1920s.
Many farmers and their wives used this service to go to town on market
day, instead of using the traps. Goods to be sold were taken, or some-

times put on the bus to be collected at their destination. These often included a young calf trussed up in a hessian sack, with only its head showing.

The first lorry came to the district in 1931, owned by Andrew Trudgeon from Nancledra. During the 1920s and '30s motor transport gradually crept into the village. Cars were bought by a few farmers, tradesmen's carts changed to vans, lorries replaced wagons and the bus service increased to include a route from Zennor to St Ives. This bus was used by Zennor school children who attended the St Ives board school after the Zennor school closed in 1933. Farming methods changed, as lorries took cattle to market and live pigs to the killing shops, putting an end to the long arduous tasks of driving cattle on foot to market and the rather gruesome pig-killing on the farm. As I have said earlier, buttermaking also ceased when the milk lorry started collecting the raw milk.

During a period before many farmers could afford a car, motor bikes, often with a side car, were very popular. Annie Paynter from Boswednack carried a pan of cream twice a week to St Ives, riding pillion on a motor bike, and was never known to spill a drop.

Early Cars of Character

CARS in the early 1930s were still carriages of character. They were very well made, from the best metals, wood and canvas. No flashy, trashy nonentities as those of today, which fold up on the least impact, and all look alike to me. The car was still a novelty on the Zennor roads but my father was able to keep one, as he acquired cheap cast-offs from my mother's Scottish relations.

The cars which came to Tremedda were all different. Each one had its virtues and vices. In the main they had comfortable seating and masses of room, so that sometimes eight to ten people were crammed in, the children packed up on the hood-rest at the rear. The hazards were numerous. The hood might blow off in a gale or the water boil, when one would have to walk a mile or two to find water for replenishment, and punctures were frequent, causing the occupants to struggle with wheel changing. Then there were stubborn starters. No car had the indignity of being kept permanently out of doors; they were all housed under cover, but many a car was loth to leave its comfortable garage, or rouse itself from a reverie in the middle of nowhere. Starting the car with a starting handle was often a major operation. The amount of turns depended upon the mood of the engine; sometimes it started fairly quickly and all was well, at others the driver wound and wound the handle until he was red in the face and quite exhausted, feeling not a little annoyed and becoming careless about his stance and his hold on the handle. It was at this point that personal injury might occur. All of a sudden the engine would jump to life, giving the handle a tremendous jerk that might twist the driver's arm, break his thumb, or hit his leg, causing a bruised shin.

These old cars were large, long affairs with folding canvas hoods, long bonnets to house the clumsy engines, rubber-covered running boards under the doors on either side to facilitate entering and alighting, open-spoked wheels, celluloid side windows, wooden floor boards, metal luggage racks at the rear that could be folded up when not in use, and delightful honking horns, the old-fashioned rubber ball type, for which you had to put your hand out of the window to honk. Some of the more expensive models, which had glass windows and a hard top, were fitted with rear window blinds and strap hangers to help keep the passengers stable, the surface of the roads leaving much to be desired. The ventilation was always more than adequate, with winds whistling in through one crack and out through another, and no heating. During the cold winter months, rugs enveloped all of the passengers.

The first car my father had was a small red, sporty Lagonda with a 'dicky' seat. It cost £40. The front seat had a neat little canvas hood. On opening up the dicky there was seating for two or maybe three children, the door or lid acting as a back-rest when open. The dicky seat was completely open to the elements and passengers, usually us children, were encased in large hooded cloaks, and well tucked-in with rugs and a final covering of wind- and waterproof canvas. It was very exciting driving the five miles home from St Ives on a dark and windy night, sitting well wrapped up in the dicky seat, maybe clutching a string tied to a balloon which danced madly in the wind trying to free itself – the last remnant of a Christmas or birthday party. By the time we reached Tremedda the wind would have all but lulled us to sleep. My mother and Uncle George both tried to learn to drive the Lagonda, but my mother kept on changing gear from first to top and Uncle George could never find the hand-brake, so they both gave up.

The steep Cornish hills caused much car trouble. The car, perhaps overloaded, would chug manfully up a steep incline, then die out and stop on a painful hissing note just before reaching the summit. Steam would pour out from under the bonnet as the water bubbled and boiled, and someone was despatched with a receptacle to fetch water from some tiny stream running through the undergrowth at the bottom of the hill. After quenching its thirst and giving the car a good rest to cool off, the journey would be resumed. There was also a downhill hazard. When descending one of these steep roads, a smell of burning might waft up through the floor boards, denoting that the brakes were on fire. All the passengers would have to alight and walk to the bottom of the hill while the driver, after a cooling period, followed on behind. One of my cousins had an old Alvis. One day the horsehair in the back seat caught fire and smouldered away for some time; before discovering the fire my cousin was heard to say "There's an extraordinary smell of baked potatoes in the car!"

My father was driving us into Penzance one gale-whipped winter's day, to take a sick dog to the vet. Rain was lashing down and the wind roaring in from the Atlantic. The car, an old blue Austin, flapped, shook and shuddered in every bit of it, as we sat huddled in the back with poor Fairy shivering and snuffling on our knees. All of a sudden, as we drove over Lady Downs, the car decided to doff its cap, and the hood blew right back, leaving us all exposed to the storm. It was with considerable difficulty, discomfort, and battling with the elements that the hood was finally replaced and well tied down with plenty of binder-twine, enabling us to continue our journey.

One old car that came our way was a Sunbeam, creamy white in colour and vast in size. We thought it very grand and fit for royalty.

During the summer months my aunt and uncle from London came down to Tremedda for the two months' school holidays, complete with five sons, a few friends and helpers, and an enormous car to accommodate this large party. I remember a Buick and a Hudson, but to me they were just enormous cars. Aunt Mary always drove as Uncle George had no inclination for driving. On long journeys she kept a horsewhip handy and when the boys became too obstreperous in the back, she would crack the whip over her shoulder as she drove along. This had instant results. Another punishment for aggravating the driver was to dump the offender by the roadside and drive on, maybe rounding a corner before stopping. The now terrified child would race after the car and, when finally allowed to get in once more, would be very subdued and reduced to his or her best behaviour.

To sum up these delightful old cars, which took life at a leisurely speed – fifty miles per hour was thought to be most daring – here is a story my father told me: two old farmers, Glen Thomas and John Richards drove to the Royal Cornwall Show. On arrival they were asked what sort of drive they had had. The reply was "Brer good; we 'ad a 'eavy shower up Connor Downs so we stopped the car, got out an' sheltered under a hedge for a few minutes, then carried on . . . "

During the Second World War petrol was banned for everything except necessary work. Farmers were allowed a small weekly ration to be used for farming necessities only.

From the post-war period onwards, Zennor became completely mechanised and motorised.

Wrecks and Wrecking

WRECKING was an occupation carried out by most families who farmed the coastal strip, and was well worth the time and energy spent on it. Not the wrecking of earlier times when ships were lured to their doom by fake lights on the cliff, but simply finding and carrying up the cliff anything washed in that could be made use of. This was mainly wood, which was used for innumerable things: repairs, the making of chicken coops, doors, stools, gates, shelves, and of course firewood. After a strong north-westerly gale with the wind sweeping in from the Atlantic, my father would go down to the shore, collect all the worthwhile planks and throw them onto the rocks above the high tide line, whence they could be carried up when time permitted. A great quantity of wreck wood was washed ashore in those days, owing to a greater number of wrecks and the use of timber rather than metal in shipbuilding. The wood was beautifully clean and well pickled with salt water, and there was none of the tarry oily mess that comes ashore today, as the ships were powered mainly by steam produced by coal. Most of the wood used when rebuilding the Tremedda farm buildings was carried up the cliff on powerful shoulders. No one was allowed to walk up the cliff empty-handed, even down to the smallest child who might be given a piece of firewood, a chopping board or a string of corks to carry. Many of the beds in the outer bedrooms were made by my cousins the Kennedys from wreck wood. The first bed my husband and I had when we were married was so made, by a German prisoner-of-war who worked on the farm for a while.

Occasionally, exciting cargoes were washed in. One year a ship called the *Bessemer City* went ashore below Trevega, carrying a cargo of tinned fruit. Hundreds of tins came in along the coast. We all spent hours searching the rocks for them, letting out a whoop of delight every time we came across one. We collected enough to supply the family with tinned fruit for a whole year. The cupboard under the stairs was a veritable store. Every Sunday we opened one of these tins for dinner and as all the labels were washed off, the question always arose as to whether it contained the interminable peaches or if it might possibly be the much prized pears or fruit salad, which were few and far between.

The cargo that caused most excitement came from a ship wrecked off the Channel Islands, which was carrying wines and spirits. Large forty-gallon barrels were washed ashore all around the Cornish coast. A great sense of intrigue pervaded, with comings and goings during the hours of darkness, in order to outwit the Customs officials, while trying to salvage this prize. The Customs men were very much on the alert. If they made a find and were unable to carry it away, the barrel was smashed open and allowed to spill out on rocks or beaches. One might imagine the shrimps, 'mulleys' (blenny) and sand eels having a gay old time in this heady liquid! All the farmers from near and far searched the sea-shore. If a barrel was found in a place where it was deemed impossible to negotiate the steep cliff with the load, ten-gallon milk churns were taken to the spot, the red or fiery liquid transferred from barrel to churn, and this in turn hoisted onto hefty shoulders and carried up the cliff. No doubt numerous sips gave greater strength and purpose to the toil. Often tempers ran high and angry words were bandied back and forth as to who was the rightful owner of a find. When the loot finally reached its destination it had to be well hidden, as searches were made at most of the farms along the coast. Favoured hiding places were in the middle of a corn-rick, under the hay in the hay house, or buried underground. At Tremedda we managed to salvage a forty-gallon barrel of red wine and a ten-gallon milk churn of very strong spirit. These were hidden in the shrubbery until things went quiet.

My mother drank a glass of wine with her evening meal for a whole year.

Many amusing incidents occurred, stemming from the find of this potent liquid. One involved Jimmy Limpots. On this occasion he had been asked to polish all the bedroom floors. The polish used was home-made of beeswax and turpentine mixed up with a stick in a large earthenware jar, and this required very energetic rubbing. Before starting, Jimmy had a large swig of the spirits from a milk churn lid; no dainty wineglass for him! He polished the floors in next to no time, making them gleam, but ended by trying to walk through a large mirror on the landing, thinking it led into yet another room.

There were many stories of horses and carts wandering driverless on Porthmeor Beach at St Ives while their owners lay in a drunken stupor on the sand, to be rudely awoken by the ice-cold waters of the incoming tide. On another occasion, Charlie Jelbert emptied the dregs from a salvaged barrel onto the ground, a sow quickly came and lapped it up and became quite drunk, sleeping for days.

A horrific wreck took place one dark winter's night during a gale. A small coaster called the *Wilson* was driven onto the rocks at Tregerthen Point. The next day nothing could be seen of the ship except at low tide, when the boiler and one or two bits were visible, such a battering and bashing had she had by the fierce waves. The alarm was raised when our neighbour Stanley Hocking found a ship's lifebelt washed in bearing the ship's name on it. Soon, bodies started coming ashore in Wicca Pool. The local farmers climbed down and helped the coast-guards carry them up this very formidable piece of cliff. All hands were lost, about twenty of them, and they were all buried in a communal grave in Zennor church-yard. It was generally thought from the state of the bodies when picked up, that there had been an explosion when the ship struck the rocks. Many years later, the daughter of one of the ship's officers called in on Betty Nankervis in Zennor and told her the following story. The *Wilson* was gun-running to Spain during the Spanish Civil War. Before sailing from Cardiff, her father had walked down the gang plank of The *Wilson* into one of the offices and declared it too rough for sailing. The authorities told him in no uncertain terms the ship must sail and as good as kicked him up the gang plank. She said this was the only time her father ever swore. Apparently the crew had no notion of the ship's cargo when they sailed off to their doom. The daughter went on to tell of her mother who, after a period of five years, married again. However, every time the anniversary of The *Wilson* disaster came round, she sat all day crying, exclaiming she was a sinner, being of the Catholic religion, and her first husband never having been identified as dead. This went on for so many years that in the end it was the cause of the break-up of her second marriage.

During thick fog, a kinder wreck took place off Gurnards Head. A German coaster the *Traute Sarnow*, carrying a cargo of coal, went aground on the rocks. It was a Sunday evening and fortunately the sea was calm. Many locals went down the cliff to help, including the landlord of Gurnards Head Hotel, who was so drunk he had to be sat down on a stile. The ship's crew were able to scramble onto the rocks, the captain carrying a much-prized case of drink. However, while climbing over the rocks he dropped the case and all the bottles were smashed. Hazel Oliver (*née* Jelbert) was given the ship's puppy to hold. In the days to follow, the locals, avoiding Customs men, coast-guards and the company that bought the wreck, salvaged many prizes before rough seas broke up the ship. Charlie Jelbert carried home enormous hatch covers on his power-ful shoulders, and the ship's toilet, even though he and his carthorse had been legally hired by the wreck owners to pull many metal plates and parts of the ship up to the cliff top.

Charlie, a tall, powerful man with a shock of dark curly hair, from Carnelloe Farm, was the most enthusiastic wrecker in the village. It was said he could smell a wreck. Nothing was too heavy for him to tackle nor any cliff face too steep to climb. He spent hours searching the sea-shore, often wading into the water to catch some floating object. From the direction of the wind, he knew exactly which cove to visit. He had many highly polished brass objects in his house including a ship's bell and shell cases, relics of the First World War.

Gurnards Head was the location of another wreck during the First World War. The ship was carrying hay for horses of the British Army in

50. Alison, Flora and Elsie Griggs 'wrecking' on Tremedda rocks. p. 122

51. The *Traute Sarnow* on the rocks at Gurnard's Head. p. 124

France. The hay was tied into bundles with wire and came ashore all along the coast, including St Ives harbour which filled up with bundles. One local St Ives lad, running over the bundles barefoot, had the sole of his foot pierced by wire which eventually caused his death, poor soul. Dick Berryman of Treveglos Farm, who had charge of many a fine cavalry horse during his wartime army days in France, would not have appreciated the fact that all-important fodder, intended for horses on French soil, was floating round the shores of his homestead.

A wreck of a different nature occurred on the rocks off Trevail during the Second World War. Three of us were on the cliff watching two small planes having shooting practice, one of which was towing a target. Suddenly one of the planes glided quickly downwards and disappeared around one of the headlands, and then we heard a thud. We all raced across the cliffs to Trevail, about two miles away. On arrival we discovered the plane miraculously suspended upside down over a pool, the wings resting on rocks on either side. Some farmers were already on the scene helping two airmen out of the cockpit; they were not too badly injured. I was sent up to the farm for rope to help improvise a stretcher for one of these men. I don't think I have ever been so breathless, what with running along the cliffs and then up to the farm and down again carrying rope. What an astonishing escape for those two airmen!

A rather nice story of older times was told me by dear old Willy Warren, landlord of the Radjel at Pendeen.

William Thomas from Boswednack was down at Zennor Bontrove with another old chap, watching a barrel floating out at sea, which gradually came shorewards. The old men assured each other there would only be salt water in it. It finally came ashore and they rolled it up out of the water, still proclaiming the contents to be salt water; however, just in case they were wrong, Willie sent his mate up the cliff for a 'gilmot' (gimlet) and straw. When he returned, they made a hole with the gilmot and stuck the straw in it. Neither wanted to have the first suck, but finally Willie tried it and went on sucking for a few minutes. The other chap said to him "Wat is a Willie?" He replied "I cussent tell 'ee but t'es some good stuff, you." It turned out to be a barrel of rum, so presumably it was carried up the cliff for further drinking delights!

Not all wreckers were so innocent and in earlier times, the inhabitants of Zennor did try to wreck ships with false lights, or sometimes killed unfortunate survivors for their valuables. Halfway down Tremedda Cliff there is a rock called Jack's Lookout. It is said that Jack was a wrecker of earlier times. From Jack's Lookout, with his false lights, he lured the poor unsuspecting sailors onto the murderous rocks below. On one such occasion, the story goes, Jack found a drowned woman with valuable rings on one finger. He could not prise the rings off so he hacked off the finger and in his haste to get to the jeweller in Penzance, took rings, finger and all with him.

The shipping traffic that sailed past our coastline were by and large small coasters, cargo boats, French crabbers and an occasional sailing boat with white sails agleam. Close to the shore were the local fishing boats, some feathering for mackerel and pollack or setting their crab pots; others on their way to the long-lining grounds. A few larger ships, including the white banana boats bound for African shores, crossed along the line of the horizon. The handsome French crabbers were present during most months of the year, coming from Camaret and Audierne in Brittany. They were painted in bright blues, greens and reds and carried large brown sails. After a day's fishing these boats sailed into St Ives Bay in the evening, where they lay at anchor for some hours, the crew maybe resting or making a shore visit, 'skullying' their tiny punts into harbour. They purchased stores, swopped crabs for fresh vegetables and rabbits, and visited the Sloop Inn. They were very picturesque, dressed in much-faded blue cotton trousers, smocks and caps, with wooden sabots on their feet and faces the colour of mahogany, talking and shouting in the Breton dialect. Occasionally one of these large boats edged its way into the harbour and moored alongside the quay to have her freshwater tanks filled up. Sometimes as many as twenty of these beautiful boats, high and pointed at the bow, low and square at the stern, could be seen lying at anchor in the bay. Sad to say, this lovely sight vanished with the introduction of the twelve-mile fishing limit in 1964.

The Harvests of the Deep – On Land and Sea

Fishing

DURING the early part of this century, and previously, a certain amount of fishing was carried on from the tiny Zennor boatcove and Gurnard's Head Boatcove. This must have been hazardous as the coast is very rocky and there is no protection from Atlantic gales. Two brothers from Bosigran were drowned off Gurnard's Head. They went out to pull in their pots in rough weather and it was reckoned the boat sailed under. There must have been quite a thriving little fishing fleet in the Gurnard's Head boatcove at one time, as the ruins of a pilchard curing house is still perched on the cliff edge. Fishing would be a side line for farmers and miners and was mainly a summer occupation. All the boats were small sailing or rowing boats. A small boat was kept in Zennor Boatcove and was worked by two or three farm lads and a mine captain, Dick Eddy, who had started the Rose Mine in Foage valley. Willie Berryman was a keen fisherman as a lad and often accompanied Dick Eddy. One day Willie's brother Dick was asked to take his place in the boat as Willie had gone to a wedding at Lanyon.

The following 'fishy tale' was told me by Dick: "The boat down Boatcove was eighteen foot long and had a little ol' sail on em, brer li'l ol' boat. Dick Eddy was to call for me if 'ee thought a' was fit [the weather]. Course, five o'clock in the morning 'ee was come, 'ee rattling at the window and we got out and went down there. I was sick as a dog. I was all right till I ate something. We come out and we went up Wicca Pool and pulled the trammel, old fish in that, rotten fish and all sorts, enough to turn anybody's stomach up. Got out from there and went out Carracks, Tremedda low water rocks, pulled a tier there. That took us most of the morning, time we done low water rocks and that and the trammel and set them all; 'ee was always takin' so damn long. We come back in the cove and then 'ee was goin' down along; when we got out the tide was going down, so we put up a li'l ol' bit of a sail then. I was starving mind, so I ate something and no sooner gone down, then 'ee had to come up! When we was down Ibbo [Ebbel – a rock off the headland] – you know down Gurnard's Head, – the boat was just in the sway of that, not much sea, going pretty. I was in the bottom of the boat and could 'ear 'im sayin' 'Pull a bit boy, she's going to westard,' and I didn't care where she went. In the end, 'ee's there doing 'is pots and wanting to go back and set them again and I looked up and we's nearly down Pendeen; she was going like a steam-boat, going with the tide see, then we 'ad to pull all that way back rowing, stop at Gurnard's Head and set those pots, then pull back 'ere. As soon as I got my foot out the boat down Boatcove, I was hungry again, but I never 'ad nothin' to eat. Two could skid the boat up over the bowlys [large pebbles]; it was levelled off a bit, made a bit of a pavement there for it. Put the boat in the boathouse in the winter, covered it in; pretty li'l place there. When bringing up fish Fridays, brer li'l crowd down there. 'Ad to carry all the fish up; mostly crabs, lobsters and crayfish, sold them – could knock out seven or eight pound a week each. Crabs weren't worth sending away; we 'ad plenty to eat ourselves. Lobsters and crayfish sent to London in a barrel of wet straw."

I don't think Dick enjoyed his fishing.

There were two full-time coast-guards in Zennor for many years. The first coast-guard houses were at Poniou, the next station was built on Gurnard's Head cliffs and, more recently, they were transferred to two new houses in the hamlet of Treen at Gurnard's Head. The coast-guards manned a small lookout hut on the tip of the headland, which was reached by a cliff path and a climb up a steep ladder at the end of the rocky promontory. There was also a cliff rescue team or auxiliary coast-guard team manned by volunteers from the community.

Mining

I know little about mining, but the following are a few anecdotes gleaned from elderly parishioners:

It has been said that Zennor tin ore is the richest in Cornwall.

Three tin mines were working in Zennor at the beginning of this century, one in Trevail Valley, Trewey or the Gavers Mine and Rose Vale Mine in Foage Valley. Some of the larger farming families might have two or three sons employed in the mines. Some worked in mines further afield.

Harold Semmens, who was brought up at Trevail, led the horse in the 'whipsaderry' at Trevail Mine when he was only four years old, in 1909. The horse in the whipsaderry was 'backened' into the mouth of the shaft then led back out again, pulling up the 'kibble' (mine bucket) full of 'dirt'; back and out, back and out. The kibble was pulled up by a wire rope and the dirt, containing tin, was tipped into a cart and taken across the valley, where it was processed. A small reservoir higher up the valley provided water power to drive the large water-wheel which worked the 'stamps'. These were machines that lifted heavy pieces of iron and let them fall on the stone to break it up. This mine was closed down for a short time in 1909. It reopened when cables were slung across the valley and the kibble was taken across on an endless chain, a sort of pulley. Steam was turned on when the mine was reopened and the pulley was worked by steam power. This mine closed for good in 1913.

The two mines in Foage valley were run by two separate companies. The lower one near Rose was managed by one of the Nankervises and had stamps by the ruins of Old Ennie's House. The other one, the Gavers, was further up, and was reached from the road on Trewey Downs. The 'count house' buildings and the boss's bungalow were situated on this road, opposite the track into the mine.

At Rose Vale Mine, levels were driven into the hillside and a tram on rails brought out the dirt. Dick Osborn spent many, many a night up there watching the stamps. They were worked by a large water-wheel and there were stamps with two, four, six-headed stamps or more. There was a four-headed stamp at Rose Vale. At one time the Zennor river worked the stamps at Rose Vale, a mill by the chapel, a mill at Jownes, Stevens' Mill down the valley and the stamps below Carn Cobba. In November 1912 there were sixteen men on the Rose Vale Mine payroll; in November

1913 the numbers had increased to forty-seven, including my father who would have been sixteen years of age.

My father worked in Rose Vale Mine for a short time, but left when he went to work at Tremedda. Two brothers from Treveglos worked there, one on night shift and one on day shift; they used the same bed and only saw each other when passing to and from work. Dick Berryman's brother Tom worked at Rose Vale Mine with Tom Nankervis and Tom's father. This little team worked what they called three to a pair. They were 'sinking down' (digging down) from the top level. The pair working down the shaft had to have a third man 'up top' to wind up buckets of water and dirt; the water was thrown into a drain and the dirt into a tram. Dick took Tom's place for two nights when Tom was poorly. He had the job of winding the handle of the windlass, bringing up buckets of water and dirt; he was fast (winding) that handle all night long, apart from a break in the middle of the night when they had "a dark old muddy hut to go into". No thank you, – mining was not for Dick.

These two mines closed around the time of the First World War.

Numerous signs of this busy industry can be seen all over the parish. The mine inland from Eagle's Nest, the old tinners used to say 'is as full as she can stick', i.e. plenty of tin is still there. Carnellow Cliff has good examples of mining remains, with the Carnellow Consols Mines to the west of the headland and Wheal Veor to the east.

Shafts were sunk on the very edge of the cliff, one of which was hewn through solid rock only fifteen feet above high tide. Rough steps mark the precarious way down the steep incline to the pithead. Higher up the cliff are two well-preserved buildings, one above the other, which housed water-wheels. A depressed pathway shows the route of a small tramway and various old walls and sunken pits denote the site of the stamps and 'buddles', etc. Higher up are the walls of a small reservoir, whence a good supply of water was carried in wooden launders to turn the water-wheels, wash through the buddles and supply other water requirements. To the east of the headland a horse-powered whim pulled up the kibbles of dirt from Wheal Veor Mine. The whim was worked in a similar fashion to the one which powered the barn thresher. The horse walked round and round on the whim-round, turning a central bar which worked various cog-wheels and pulleys. The central stone, with a hole in the middle, is still visible, as is the small shelter hewn out of solid rock where the young lad, who kept the horse moving, could sit protected from the westerly gales. The ruins of a smelting house stand nearby and a good roadway or donkey track leads inland. On the end of the headland, surveying this busy scene of times past, is the snug one-storied mine Count House, still inhabited today.

Charles Jelbert of Carnellow Farm, a miner of modern times, having

52. The Zennor Auxiliary Coastguard team, p. 129. Back row, L-R: Mr Wenmouth, John Curnow, John Berryman, Ken Berryman, Basil Olds. Front row, L-R: Maurice Griggs, Mr Klisky, Willie Craze.

53. A built-up whim round for raising tinstone on Zennor Head. p. 130

worked in Geevor tin mine for many years and now living in The Count
House, talks of the old mining practices on and under this dangerous
terrain, from which I have gathered the following account.

These mines, already closed in the late nineteenth century, were
worked by water power, horse and donkey power and the sweat of man.
The shafts were between one and two hundred feet deep and ran out
under the sea in places, always following the lode, which could be seen
on the surface as a white line running through the black rocks. The dirt
or tin stones were raised to the surface in kibbles, by water or horse
power. They were then tipped into the tram which stood on the cliff edge
in a small depression, to facilitate loading. The tram carried the stones up
the cliff side to the twelve-headed stamps; the heavy iron heads that
crushed the rock were worked by a tin dresser. Both tram and stamps
were powered by a water-wheel. The crushed rock was transferred to
buddles, small dug out circles, each one surrounded by a stone wall with
a built-up piece in the middle. Water swished through with a circular
movement, washing away the dirt. The clean crushed rock was then
taken by donkey and panniers around the headland to the smelting
works, and from there the resultant tin was taken up the donkey track in
panniers or carts and away to its destination.

There are several mines on Zennor Head including Wheal Grylls, named
after a mine captain, Wheal Sherriffs and Lucky Lace. Before the nine-
headed stamps were put in near Steven's mill garden, tin stone was carried
along the cliff by donkey and pannier to Carnellow stamps to be processed.

Will Berryman from the Row once worked in a mine on Zennor Cliff.
The adits here were so narrow that when pushing wheelbarrows or trams
through them, you had to keep your hands on the inside of the handles.

There was an adit on Zennor Cliff 'down Connows', a piece of cliff
below the Water Field, where you could drink very good water; it was as
cold as clay all the year round. The Berrymans lost two heifers on Zennor
Cliff and searched high, low and level for them. Dick's father said one
day "We haven't looked up the adit, s'pose". Dick and Alfie went down
with a candle apiece; they noticed the water running out of the adit was
a bit muddy, lit their candles and walked in quite some way, and sure
enough found the heifers. There was no room to pass them; they had to
get over or under them, and took one each, backing them back all the
way out. The heifers had gone in to drink the fresh water and when a
'better man' came on, pushing them further in, they hadn't got sense
enough to back out, and kept going forward.

Miners went down the pits with a string of candles around their necks;
candle power was the only form of lighting underground. Candles worn
in the miners' helmets lit the way and were stood in dollops of clay on
convenient rock ledges. The old miners could tell the time underground

according to how far down the candles had burnt. Another timepiece used was an old tin placed under a tiny constant trickle of water. The miner would take his good watch to work for a day and mark off the height of the water in the tin after one hour, two hours or whatever, for the making of a very simple clock. It would be too damp and the work too rough to warrant taking a precious watch underground every day.

Mining must have been very rough and tough in those days. 'What they used to do for te git a shillin'!'

Granite

Granite is not for man's convenience:

> To chip a block into a human form;
> And for its shaping there is but one tool,
> The alchemy of water etching it,
> By constant dripping through the centuries.
> A continuity of handing on,
> In harmony with granite and her mood,
> That finds a worthy setting for her craft
> In the long galleries of cliff and sea,
> Where she has room to show a masterpiece;
> A hundred feet or so from base to top,
> Of square cut pillars like a giant's chair,
> With an extension on the slope above
> Of pinnacles until the ridge is lost
> In the last step that leads onto the moor.
>
> A sculpture that has no advertisement
> Of lofty mountain peaks to catch the eye,
> And needs the last touch of the wizard's hand
> Of sun and shadow to bring out its best.
>> A.W. Andrews, Tregerthen, Zennor

Quarrying was one of the oldest industries in Cornwall. There were two quarries on Tremedda Carn: John White's quarry, not worked as far back as I can remember, and the ancient quarry that was worked by Mr Pascoe and later Jimmy Thomas during the beginning of this century. The latter is described in the following account written by the architect, my uncle G.L. Kennedy, for the Nancledra scrap book:

The Stone Mason of Tremedda Quarry

There are some friends who seem to become an inseparable part of their surroundings, and the granite of West Cornwall is always associated in my mind with James Thomas of Georgia, Nancledra. My first contact with him was in connection with the additions to Tremedda Farm at Zennor in 1912, an illustrated notice of which later appeared in *Country Life*. The material for this undertaking was cleaved from the softer granite of the fields where it interfered with the husbandry. After the first European war Thomas leased the ancient quarry on the slope of Tremedda Carn, and this became his workshop for the rest of his active life, involving a three and a half miles ride or walk over the moors from his farm at Georgia. Here he was to be seen in most weathers, a gentle, sparsely built man to find in single-handed control of such massive stock-in-trade.

In spite of the lonely days spent in these elemental surroundings, he never acquired the airs and uncouthness of a solitary and with the natural modesty of his outlook he was not what is sometimes known as a 'character'. He made no mystery of his craft and was always ready to share his profound knowledge of it with others; artists such as Frank Dobson and Ursula Edgcumbe were able to learn something from him, and Stephen Tomlin, whose untimely death was a sad loss to English sculpture, spent useful time with him.

The war memorial in Zennor churchyard was among his first tasks for me; and since then I came to count on him whenever an opportunity occurred for his craftsmanship and his understanding of his traditional Cornish building material. Interesting local tasks included an incised inscription to commemorate W.H. Hudson on a stone where he was accustomed to rest during his rambles as a naturalist, but much of his work went to other parts of the country. Among examples I can think of are a bird bath at the late Lord Keynes' house in Sussex, and a tomb carried out for the late Sir Ronald Lindsay, sometime ambassador at Washington, to commemorate his first wife. This was probably his most important task and stands in the grounds of Stepleton House near Blandford.

There are two ways of using granite. When employed in cities for public buildings and monuments it can be worked to the same drawing-board details as most other building stones. Treated thus, as at St George's Hall, Liverpool, and in the northern cities of Edinburgh and Aberdeen, it has an impressively dour character in keeping with a dignified purpose. But it has another and more friendly mood as a building stone, when, as in Cornwall, it is the natural material of a countryside. A more 'free-hand' idiom can inspire the design, calling for a closer collaboration between architect and mason, and I think it is in this aspect that the beauty and texture of the stone is seen at its best. It is of this 'country-bred' idiom that James Thomas was such a faithful exponent and it was in this field that he proved himself such a master of his trade.

Wherever you walk on this terrain, the tell-tale marks of the drill can be seen along the edges of innumerable rocks.

The rock formation in Zennor played a large part in dictating farming methods in the parish. Large granite boulders were liberally scattered over most of the fields. These boulders and the small, irregular shapes of the fields were largely the cause of Zennor farms being very backward, in comparison with many other parts of the country, in the acquisition of new field machinery.

The following account of stones in Zennor was written by W.H. Hudson, who sometimes stayed with my grandmother in the village.

There is very little cultivation – hardly more than is required for the use of the farm and in many fields even this little is carried on under difficulties on account of the stones. The stones are taken out and piled onto the walls or hedges at the side and though the process has been going on for centuries, many boulders and huge blocks of granite still remain in the fields. I was amused one day at the sight of a field of only about two acres on which I counted one hundred and thirty five stones appearing like huge mushrooms and toadstools over the ground. Corn has been grown in it, and I asked the farmer how it was managed. He answered that he would laugh to see a man and horses from any other part of the country try to cultivate that field and others like it! Here the men are used to it, and horses know their part so well that if the share touches a stone they stop instantly and wait for the plough-man's word to move on.

By 1900, most rocks of manageable size had been removed from the fields, to be used for hedging and building. The remaining rocks were often several tons in weight and partly buried, and it was very difficult for the farmers of that time to move them. All cultivating and reaping had to be done by hand around the rocks. Rocks just under the surface or hidden in hay or corn, cause untold damage to machinery. A Zennor farmer who made enough money to enable him to move, often left the parish for a kinder landscape elsewhere.

Few granite boulders were removed from the fields during the early part of the century. Occasionally, if a gate-post or a special sized rock was required for building, the farmer might cleave or split a rock in the field and remove it. To cleave a rock, a straight row of holes was made across the rock by laboriously jumping a long steel-nosed iron bar or 'jumper', up and down until holes of sufficient depth were made. Into each hole were put two 'feathers' – curved metal strips, rather similar to a piece of a galvanised bucket handle – and an iron wedge or 'gad' was forced down between them. These gads were all hammered down in turn, until the rock finally split along the line of holes. A more ancient splitting method was to put quicklime and water into the holes and plug them with wooden plugs. The swelling of the material in the holes split the rocks.

During the 1930s and 1940s, when gelignite became more easily available to farmers, rock clearance was one of their yearly tasks, and a few more were removed every winter. A hole was made in the rock with a jumper, a stick of gelignite with a fuse on it was stuffed down the hole with a wooden tamper, the fuse was lit and everyone raced for shelter. The rock was blasted into many pieces, these were loaded onto a draw, a wooden sledge on stout, iron runners, and pulled to the hedges by the carthorse.

I recall one rather hair-raising blasting incident at Tremedda. The hole in the rock had been drilled, the stick of gelignite shoved in and the fuse lit, and the men had retired to a safe distance to await the explosion. Suddenly Panchio, a large black dog, raced out to investigate, stopping on the fated rock itself. No amount of whistling and calling could entice him away before the rock exploded. It shattered into many pieces and lo and behold, instead of a dead dog, something black streaked through the fields as hard as it could go, tail between its legs, heading for home. Being so near the seat of the explosion, the bits of rock had risen into the air and passed over Panchio, luckily for him.

These rocks were a source of many childish pleasures. We were drawn to the larger ones like magnets, always having to climb to the top and jump off. A large rock in the Shoot Field was used for 'I'm the King of the Castle'. A smaller one in the same field, roof-shaped, made an excellent see-saw base. We raced between them singing "I'm on Tom Tiddler's ground picking up gold and silver", with Tom Tiddler after us, trying to catch us before we regained a perch on a rock.

Granite was very much a feature of this piece of Cornish coastline. Every hill-top was crowned with slabs resembling a giant pile of irregular-shaped muffins, stacked one on top of the other. Large boulders of every shape and size tumbled down the hill-sides, were strewn across the flatter farm land and plateau, and continued on down the cliffs to the very water's edge.

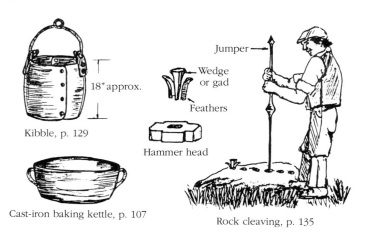

Kibble, p. 129

18" approx.

Jumper

Wedge or gad

Feathers

Hammer head

Cast-iron baking kettle, p. 107

Rock cleaving, p. 135

PART FIVE: SOCIAL AND DOMESTIC

Legendary Lore

ZENNOR folk, during the early twentieth century, seemed very down-to-earth and unconcerned with the supernatural. However, an old book *Hobson and Mathews History of St Ives, Lelant, Towednack and Zennor*, written in the nineteenth century, contains a few snippets of legendary lore about Zennorians.

Trewey, a hamlet near the village, is said to have been the place where all the witches of the west met. A large block of granite here was known as the 'Witches Rock'; anyone touching this rock nine times at midnight was insured against ill-luck. This rock has now been removed, and the last Zennor witch is supposed to have died in the early nineteenth century.

The most celebrated of these sorceresses was an old woman called the Witch of Trewey, who terrorised the neighbourhood with her spells. She assumed the form of a hare when engaged in her supernatural work. After her death, she was borne to the grave by six aged men; halfway between house and church, a hare leaped over the coffin. The terrified bearers let the corpse fall to the ground and fled. Another lot of men took up the coffin and went on their way, when suddenly puss was seen sitting on the coffin, which was once again abandoned. The parson finally persuaded yet another six men to carry the old woman quickly into the churchyard, while he walked before repeating the Lord's Prayer; and all went quietly. On arrival at the church stile they rested the coffin, the parson paused to commence the ordinary burial service, and there

137

stood the hare. As soon as the parson began "I am the resurrection and the life", it uttered a diabolical howl, changed into a black unshapen creature, and disappeared.

It was also told how Sir Rose Price's hounds chased a hare into a cottage at Kerrow. When the huntsman opened the door, there sat an old crone bleeding about the head and face with her hair hanging loose. The sportsmen had hunted a witch.

Hobson and Mathews state that according to the writings of Bottrell, the attribute of a 'mean parsimony' was fixed upon the natives of Zennor. There were many stories illustrating their supposed poverty and meanness. It was said that by their thrifty habits they could live like goats, hence their nickname: Zennor goats.

'Zennor Charmer' was another name commonly given to women and men of the parish. It was traditionally believed that many inhabitants possessed magical powers. Their power of stopping the flow of blood was said to be so great that if a pig was sticked and a charmer was present who simply thought his charm, the pig would not bleed. The charm used was commonly thus worded:

> Christ is born in Bethlehem,
> Baptised in the Jordan;
> The river stood –
> So shall thy blood,
> Mary Jane Polgrain [or whoever]
> In the name of the Father and the Son,
> And of the Holy Ghost. Amen.

Also, according to Bottrell, Zennor people were credited with great musical and vocal talents. No wedding, funeral or merrymaking was considered perfect unless a Zennor man was present to raise his tuneful voice.

Henry Quick was a Zennor poet. He would hawk his rhymes about the streets of Penzance, wearing a tall hat and carrying a bell, as he tells us:

> Oftimes abroad I take my flight,
> Take pity on poor Henny;
> To sell my books 'tis my delight,
> To gain an honest penny.

The legend of the Zennor mermaid is told under the chapter on Church and Chapel.

People

ZENNOR Parish had many colourful characters. They could be divided into two categories; those ancients who were part and parcel of the farming community, and the fraternity of artistic-minded folk who were drawn to Zennor like moths to a candle flame, trying to capture some of the wild grandeur in words, music or paint. Other gentry, of one sort or another, were also dotted around the parish.

One of them might have been thought to be a modern witch. Miss Frost lived part of the year in Veor Cottage, known locally as The Cats' House; this was a little granite bungalow perched on the edge of the cliff above Veor Cove, originally built as a mine count house. She kept sixty cats, and people rarely saw her. She slept by day and went about her business by night. One of the Thomas family from Carnellow worked for her, but only occasionally set eyes on her. Hilda Jelbert carried post to her for years but never saw her. Food for the cats was quite a problem. At one time a very unwilling postman had to carry fourteen pounds' weight of fish out from St Ives every day. On reaching the village he went straight to The Cats' House by the cliff path, to rid himself of his heavy and unsavoury load. For a period a man from St Ives took the fish out twice a week by donkey and shay, relieving the postman. The Thomases augmented the cats' diet with rabbits and offal. Every now and then Miss Frost packed all her cats in wicker baskets and travelled with them to St Blazey, where she spent part of the year in her second home. She had a great wish to keep two lions and had even started having a house built for them, but the uproar in the village was so great that her desire was never fulfilled. The foundation for the lions' house is there to this day. When Miss Frost died, she was buried in a wicker coffin.

Eagle's Nest and the Old Poor House, perched high up on a hill above Tregarthen, were filled with hordes of Westlakes and their servants during the summer months. Mr Westlake was a judge who gave lectures to the children in school. Mrs Westlake, when attending church services, peered at the congregation through her lorgnettes to see who was present. She also presented the children with prizes for good attendance. The Old Poor House was the original poor house for the parish of Zennor. The story goes that a parishioner, while carrying his aged father to the poor house, stopped to rest on a stile. As he sat there, his father said to him "Dam'mee, this is the very same stile where I stopped to rest when carrying my old father to the Poor House". On hearing these words, the son, bearing in mind his own future old age, turned round and carried the old man back home.

The next family to live in Eagle's Nest was the Arnold Fosters, known to me as a child. They were nicknamed 'Big Stick' and 'Little Stick' by my cousins. Mrs Arnold Foster was tall, stately and beautiful and had once been a girl friend of Rupert Brooke, the poet. Mr Arnold Foster was just 'a little stick'. He was a great talker, always discussing politics, and was a champion of the League of Nations, of which he was once Secretary. This organisation was similar to our present day United Nations. He also painted, wrote books and articles and made the most marvellous garden around his windswept perch at Eagle's Nest.

His garden became quite famous throughout the country and further afield, among garden lovers. Will Arnold Foster collected plants from all over the world. He would find just the right spot for them in the garden and they all seemed to thrive. As the garden was on top of a small hill, topped by a rocky outcrop, there were large slabs of granite and big boulders everywhere. The largest boulder, known as the Snuff Box, was an enormous square rock about eighteen feet high, which could be scaled with difficulty by the young and nimble. The garden was divided into small parts, each well-protected from the wind by stone walls and tall, thick escallonia bushes. The driveway was bordered to windward by a row of much-buffeted sycamore trees, which leant away from the wind, forming an archway over the drive. In February, the grassy bank under these trees was covered with a white sheet of snowdrops with, here and there, a delicate pink cyclamen. The real *forte* of this garden were the camellias, rhododendrons and azaleas, of which many different exotic and sweet-smelling species abounded, all very suited to the acid soil. Pink, purple and white heaths of all sizes from ankle height to the large Mediterranean tree-like heath grew round the rocks. One small garden had a plantation of ash trees. A patch for vegetables was backed by a large greenhouse filled with mimosa, jasmine, passion-flower and a grape vine. Brilliant flame trees, *Embothrium*, flowered in the cave garden below a rocky precipice, to which one descended by a long flight of stone steps or climbed precariously down by a wooden ladder. Clumps of hydrangeas spread themselves around in pinks, whites and blues. Little treasures appeared in every nook and cranny; bright blue alpine gentians grew on a low gravel-covered wall and strongly sweet-scented tiny white violets peeped out of a rockery. Amongst all these rocks, hedges, trees, and shrubs, a lawn the size of a tennis court and once used as such, was laid out. There were magnificent views from here on the sea side, of farms, cliffs, headlands and the sea. This garden was Will Arnold Foster's real life's work.

Granny said he was a painter, politician and gardener, and the only thing he was any good at was gardening!

Mrs Arnold Foster was a kind and gracious lady and helped on many committees. Sometimes we were asked up to tea and the big treat was to play with her son Mark's clock-work train, which was set out in one of the small gardens. It fascinated us to watch the little trains winding their way around the paths and through tunnels.

One day Mrs Arnold Foster was asked if she would spend a night in the cottage on top of the carn. The young couple living there had heard strange noises in the night and thought the cottage was haunted. Mrs Foster agreed and went up there to sit with them and listen. Sadly, she died of a heart attack during that same night.

Mr Foster eventually married again. His second wife was the widow of the Mallory who died on an expedition climbing Mount Everest. During hot summer weather Will and his second wife were in the habit of sunbathing in the nude on Tremedda rocks by the sea, often causing us great embarrassment when we went down to bathe.

Mr Arthur Westlake Andrews, a nephew of the judge, came to live in the Old Poor House. He was an enthusiastic climber and started the climbing club at Bosigran on the high cliffs beyond Zennor. He was also a photographer, being the first person to bring colour slides to Britain from America, and a topographer. He wrote poetry, made marmalade, and played tennis well into his eighties, practising with an enormous racket in a small high-walled court built near his house. Towards the end of his life, his sister, Miss Andrews, joined him. She was a sculptor and drew beautifully. After Mr Andrews' death, she collected an entourage of elderly ladies with ear-trumpets and walking sticks and looked after them.

The Lloyds lived in Bridge Cottage by the Wesleyan Chapel. Mr and Mrs Lloyd had three children. Mr Lloyd composed symphonies and concertos and played the flute, and Mrs Lloyd, a great friend of my mother, dressed in brightly coloured scarves and clothes and wore long dangling earrings and played the harp. Their youngest son Walter was always up to pranks as he roamed the village with his donkey and cart. One such prank concerned me and two of my sisters. Walter and two accomplices tied us to the bridge railings. We were rescued by Granny Griggs, who came down the road waving her stick and shouting "You villains!" The following day Walter was brought to Tremedda by his mother to apologise.

Colonel Hirst, an antiquarian, lived at Kerrow. He had a fine collection of museum pieces concerning the local trades, farming and mining. His real name was Shirt, but being so much teased at school, he altered the placing of the 's' and called himself Hirst.

D.H. Lawrence and his German wife Frieda lived for a while, during the First World War in one of the cottages near Tremedda. My mother knew him slightly but did not take to him very well. Hilda Jelbert from Carnellow, when only fourteen, worked for them. Katherine Mansfield and Middleton Murry, known in Zennor as Jack, were living in a cottage next door and the four of them always dined together. Hilda was not very struck on D.H. Lawrence; she thought him moody and sarcastic. She found the German wife who was 'jokey, stout and fair', much nicer than the other three. According to Hilda, Katherine Mansfield was a marvellous-looking woman, but was ill at the time with a terrible cough, and she died of consumption some time after in France. Hilda was asked to make pasties for their dinner one day and to her horror was provided with mutton instead of beef. During their stay in Zennor, a coal boat, the *Emanuel Espana* was wrecked on Tremedda rocks. The foursome went down the cliff to look at the wreck and described it to Hilda on their return. Fortunately no lives were lost. The locals thought D.H. Lawrence and his wife were spies and that they signalled to German submarines at sea. My mother's explanation was that Lawrence was asthmatic and in order to get enough air into his lungs, he opened his sea-facing window and the black-out curtains, thus showing a forbidden light, a strict black-out being in force at that time. After a few months people came snooping around, and a detective interviewed Hilda, asking her many personal questions and embarrassing her greatly. Finally, Lawrence was driven from his Zennor residence by the law.

My father's mother, Granny Griggs, was much admired as a landlady and provider of cream teas in the late nineteenth and early twentieth century. She lived in a coffin-shaped house between the pub and church. Fortunately she kept a visitors' book which is full of artistic gems: witticisms, poems, prose and drawings. Many satisfied visitors wrote in a vein similar to the following, some in the most beautiful copperplate handwriting: 'A Perfect Holiday. Zennor Churchtown – Zennor Pasties, Zennor Cows – Zennor Pigs, Zennor Heather – Zennor Sunshine and Zennor Teas – at Mrs Griggs'.' Among her illustrious lodgers were W.H. Hudson, author of many delightful nature studies, of birds in particular; Sir Alfred Munnings the artist and one time President of the Royal Academy; the writer Edward Sackville-West of Knole, Sevenoaks; the actress Masie Gay; the artist Emily Stones; and the novelist 'Ranger Gull', better known as Guy Thorne.

W.H. Hudson always seemed to be nursing some ailment and was no doubt much cosseted by Granny. He roamed the wild countryside, fed the birds outside Granny's window and gave talks on birds to the schoolchildren. Will Arnold Foster had the inscription 'W.H. Hudson often came here' chiselled out on the face of one of the large slabs of granite near the top of Tremedda Carn.

Sir Alfred Munnings brought his horse to Zennor and my father, as a young lad, often held it up on the hillside for 2d. a time, while Munnings painted it. Granny called him a perfect gentleman.

Guy Thorne wrote under the name of Ranger Gull. He drank a bottle of

54. A page by Sir Alfred Munnings from Granny Griggs's Visitors' Book. p. 142

whisky a day and when quite drunk he returned to Granny's house and wrote until one or two in the morning. The next day he was 'very bad' until he started on the bottle again. He wrote part of the novel *When It Was Dark* at Zennor. This book was quoted by the Bishop of London from the pulpit, causing many copies to be sold and making a good income for Ranger Gull. Despite his successes Mrs Guy Thorne was left a legacy of only £7 and a collection of his works. Ten years after his death the poor widow was broken in health and had a distraint on her furniture in her house in Ealing. Presumably the fortunes had all been drunk away.

Borlase Smart, a St Ives artist, stayed with Granny as a young man. He once put his box of paints and painting gear down on the church steps to speak to someone, when a local from the Row took the paint box and hid it in the churchyard for fun. Borlase Smart got into a terrible state about it, going quite mad. Granny thought he was about to have a stroke.

On being asked her opinion of D.H. Lawrence, Granny replied that many people disliked him but she always found him a gentleman. My father inherited this virtue of Granny's of never speaking ill of anyone.

I suppose Granny was quite a character in her own right. She was very industrious, and found time to mother the schoolchildren who had walked afar to school, warming their dinner-time pasties, making them mugs of hot cocoa during cold weather and drying their coats when wet. She and Dick Berrryman were fined five shillings, quite a sizeable sum of money in those days, for gambling in the Tinners' Arms! One day during hot weather, Granny opened both her front doors to let some air in. The table was beautifully laid in the front parlour for the visitors' evening meal, complete with starched white table cloth. Granny was peeling potatoes in the kitchen when she heard noises in the parlour. She went to see who it was and found a cow in there. David Berryman came in to help get it out as it was one of their cows. They had to go very quietly to prevent the cow getting excited and doing even more damage. As it was, it had already messed all over the white cloth. It took poor Granny two hours to clean up her parlour.

As a girl of ten or twelve, Granny remembers a woman who had lived in a cottage on Jownes Green, down the valley below the village, having a baby out on the grass. This cottage has long since disappeared. Jownes Green was one of the loveliest places to go and pick early mint – it grew right by the stream. Sweet-scented white violets also grew there.

An old Zennor character, often mentioned by the Zennor elders with affection and amusement, was Racco. Whether he was foolish or just different I am not sure, but he was kindly and wouldn't hurt a worm. Racco's real name was David Thomas; he lived with his brother Billie and the two of them worked a farm at Treen. Billie was always known as 'Farmer'. In the winter months Racco hibernated, retiring to bed while

Farmer tended the animals and presumably provided some sustenance for his brother – although he wouldn't need much while hibernating! Once the first cuckoo was heard at the end of April or beginning of May, it wouldn't be long before Racco emerged, full of life. He rose very early and would start out at three or four in the morning to shout under anyone's window "Aren't 'ee gonna git out the bed for the day? Tes four o'clock". My mother once looked out of her bedroom window early one morning and saw Racco standing on his head in the lane. If anyone missed a pike or a scythe or some tool, they would ask if Racco had been seen around, as he would take anybody's tools to give a hand where he fancied. One day while Racco was helping Sidney Berryman's father cut hay up in the Bridges Field, a bottle of beer was hidden in the hedge out of sight, as Racco would be liable to drink the lot if he found it. A bottle of machine oil happened to be dropped in the gap; Racco came upon it, thought it was beer and tipped some down his throat. He was in 'some state' and as the oil ran down his waistcoat, shouted to Will's Will "Oh, oh God, Will! I shall die, I shall die!" Anything happening in the parish, and Racco would be there. He was musical and could play the concertina, the mouth organ and the Jew's harp. He would go to Tregerthen and pick up Mrs Hocking's concertina, take it away and play like a 'dan'(man), (he being a bit simple) then carry it back again. All the money belonging to Racco and his brother was in both their names. Racco couldn't use it unless Billie agreed, and *vice versa*. When Billie died, a considerable sum of money came to Racco. He must have spent it all, buying guns, rabbit traps and nonsense. He had many 'friends' to help him spend it, right down to the last sovereign. He was the first person in Zennor to draw the old-age pension. As he grew old and more 'touched', the authorities tried to put him in Madron workhouse, but they couldn't keep him there. He jumped the wall; quite a high one; and walked home. Finally, sad to say, poor Racco was taken to Bodmin asylum. Dick Berryman heard his mother say "If they had collected money in Zennor and brought him home when he died, he would have had the biggest funeral of the lot".

Will's Will and Anne Berryman, brother and sister, lived in the Row in the village and farmed the Glebe, milking eight or nine cows. They were uncle and aunt to Sidney Berryman from the Post Office. Will's Will was a great character and loved a drop of drink and a good coose, and had a quick wit. The story goes that a rather superior visitor, intending to take a rise from the simple country fellow, asked Will if he had seen a cart load of monkeys pass by. Will's quick reply was, "No; dropped off, did 'ee?" Anne was always 'ballyragging' him about the drink; she never touched a drop and was very miserly. My father, as a boy, heard Will talking to himself as he walked from the pub up to his cottage, saying

"Well, Anne, if thee de say nothin', I wain't neither". During one of Anne's tirades, directed at Will, he turned to someone nearby and said "Hast she finished yet?" He used to go to Penzance with his pony and gig and after finishing the business of selling butter and eggs and buying provisions, he would visit his favourite pubs and return home fast asleep in the bottom of the trap. The pony knew its own way home very well. On reaching Churchtown, the pony would draw up outside the Tinners' Arms, where a helping hand was always ready to unharness the pony. The story of how the pony, returning with its slumbering passenger, capsized the trap as it crossed the bridge, throwing Will into the river, has been told in an earlier chapter.

Mr Dickson, landlord of the Tinners' Arms at that time, bought cream, eggs, butter and milk from Anne and Will. Anne could neither read nor write so she made out her accounts in her own signwriting: one pint of milk was a crook: J; a quart was two 0s joined together: OO; one pound of butter was a big B; half a pound, a small b; a quarter of cream was one o; half a pound, two 'o's: 00 and a pound was three 'o's: 000. Her nephew Sidney could interpret her sign writing and made out her accounts for her.

Anne was said to be a 'terrible one' for hoarding every penny she could. She kept a pillow case under the mattress containing hundreds of gold sovereigns. This was discovered one day when the chimney caught fire in her house. Young Dicka's Dick and some others made a hole in the chimney from the bedroom and put the fire out by pouring buckets of water into the hole. Anne, thinking only of the safety of her sovereigns, carried them in next door to Kate Sowden for safe keeping. The day Anne died, those sovereigns disappeared, so much good they did the poor old soul.

Every so often, when pigs were killed, neighbouring farmers took it in turns to cart the pigs to the butcher in Penzance. One day Dicka's Dick was taking some pigs in for Will. As he was leaving, Will said to Dick "I fancy a kipper; bring one back for me, will 'ee?" On his return, Dick went up to Will's cottage with the kipper to find he had just died in his chair.

Annie Thomas and her old mother lived in a small cottage at Trewey. Annie took in washing and for a time went to Tremedda twice a week in the afternoons, to help my mother. She spent one day washing and the other baking numerous pasties and saffron cake. She took the clothes home to iron, carrying them on her head in a 'flasket' – an oval shaped basket with a handle at either end. Annie and her mother were very poor and spent many hours 'picking sticks'. They were often to be seen trundling home with great 'berns' (bundles) of sticks on their shoulders; this was the only fuel they had for their open chimney. Annie, when young, had a clandestine love affair with Will's Will; although both were single they never married. It was Annie's son who at the age of nine or ten went with Arthur Nankervis searching for gulls' eggs on the Horseback, where he fell to his death. Three days after the accident, Willie Berryman, Dick Eddy and Parson Vaughan rowed around from Boatcove to these dangerous cliffs and found the body on the rocks. A sad tale, to be sure.

Miss Hosking I recall as a short, stout and very erect little person with twinkling beady eyes. She was a great talker and had a ready, jolly laugh. She always wore hats and a fox fur around her neck. She attended church regularly, always sitting in the same pew to one side of the church, rather isolated from the rest of the congregation.

In the early days she kept a little shop in her cottage at the top of the Gurnick. All children visiting her shop were given a 'sweetie', even if the purchase was only 2 ozs of pepper. She sold everything except coal: groceries, sweets, tobacco, snuff, quarter-dozen tea-sets (three cups and three saucers of different patterns, but no plates), cattle food, fowls' food and oil (paraffin). On the right, as you went in through the door, were huge blocks of salt; the required amount was cut off them for customers. It was very good for buttermaking. The left-hand side was piled up with ginger beer bottles, with a marble in the top; the ginger beer was made by Tuckers of St Ives. On a shelf above was jam, and tea was kept down below. At one end of the counter was a large, round bladder of lard, about four or five pounds in weight, and what you wanted was cut off. "Bacca wasn't weighed in they days, you measured en." The 'bacca' was pulled out from a roll of twist in a tin, measured and cut off. A mark on the counter measured a 'pen'orth'. Clay pipes were a halfpenny each. The flour and offal (barley) for the cattle and whole maize for the poultry were kept out in a shed, also a cask of paraffin. There were two scales in the shop; brass ones for the groceries which were kept shining, and the 'gon' as Miss Hosking called it. The gon hung from the ceiling and was used for weighing fowls' food, etc. in a large scoop. The goods for the shop were delivered twice a week from Penzance, by a three-horse wagon.

On retiring from business, Miss Hosking went to live at Poniou. We were sometimes invited over for tea and were fascinated by her parlour which was full of ornaments and 'trinklements', her father having been a sea captain who had brought things home from all over the world.

The only other shop in the village was the post office and shop in the Row, run by Tom and Katie Berryman, Sidney's parents. They sold stamps and postal orders, sent telegrams and paid out the old-age pension, which had just started. They also sold bacon, cheese, salt, vinegar, lard, sweets and currants, pinafores, aprons and socks, all animal feeds and oil. The bottom cottage in the Row was a veritable store of farming requirements.

Katie also baked bread in the open chimney, for selling. They had two scales, one for the post office and one for the groceries.

A very old-fashioned dear from Bosporthennis was Anne Eddy, the sewing lady. She dressed in tight, padded jackets and long, full skirts, which swept the ground. She carried her heavy sewing machine around the parish and sewed for all and sundry, such diverse articles as bonnets for old ladies, shirts for Uncle George and as already mentioned, coats for goats! The bonnets had a brim in front and a piece that hung down the back and had much complicated padding and stitching. There was an awful lot of making in one bonnet. Everything she made was 'for growing' – too large. Uncle George complained he could get two of himself in one shirt.

A grand old soul was Annie Christopher, who lived with her niece Nellie, at Poniou. She carried the post for years and helped on the farm at Tremedda. She wore long black skirts, a touser and hobnailers, and was very hard working and a great story teller. She told us of the time when she was looking after Harold Trewella as a small boy, who years later became vicar of Zennor. The Trewellas lived in a large dingy old house in St Ives. One evening Annie was left in charge of the little boy; they were upstairs and all was quiet when suddenly Annie heard clump, clump coming upstairs, and thought someone had broken into the house. In a great state, Annie shouted "You can kill me, but spare the cheeld". Nobody answered, and on plucking up courage to open the door, Annie discovered rats were making all this noise. One day my father asked Annie to stand in a gapway to stop one of the sows getting through. Annie stood there, legs apart and waving her arms, when all of a sudden the determined sow made a dash through her legs, picking up Annie on the way, and raced off down the field with the astonished Annie facing the sow's tail, astride.

Another ancient was old 'Aunt' from Trevail, who was born around 1840 and lived to the great age of 105. She could remember the 1850s and '60s when, according to her, the Zennor farmer lived on 'rooties' (turnips) and only had one 'shift' (change of clothing). She could also remember the army, or red coats, practising on Trendrine Hill.

Mr Pascoe, from Hillside, was a stone-cutter and worked the quarry on Tremedda Hill before Jimmy Thomas, who learned his trade from him. On retiring from the quarry, he moved to Treen where Mrs Pascoe kept a small shop in the little house facing the road. Mr Pascoe was all bent up from using the jumper when quarrying. He had a 'home boy' (from an orphanage) to work for him and was a stickler for keeping everything neat and tidy.

Jimmy Thomas from Georgia, Nancledra, was a great help to my mother during her single days. As well as quarrying and running his own small farm, he worked for my mother at Tremedda during the First World War, quietly imparting his considerable local knowledge to her. When my mother and father were married, Jimmy was best man. In later years Jimmy's son Cecil and his son-in-law Walter Palfrey both worked at Tremedda at different times.

Mr Nankervis, granfer of the Wicca Nankervises, kept the Tinners' Arms at one time. On being questioned by the law about opening after time, he answered "What time? My time's up there," pointing to the sundial on the church. He wasn't particular, and he fed the beer drippings to a sow which came down from Trewey every day for its pint.

A Zennor stalwart Charlie Jelbert, apart from his prowess as a wrecker, had a powerful bass voice and could be heard above all the other singers in church or at Christmas time singing carols in the pub. He danced with great gusto and was usually first on the floor at the village dances and socials, adding his own intricate steps to the waltzes, foxtrots, valetas, barn dances and military two-steps. I can see him now with his shock of dark curly hair, chewing a stalk of grass, always with a flower in his button-hole. His wife Hilda was also musical, had a good singing voice and was the church organist for a time, having taught herself to play.

There were many people who made frequent visits to Zennor. Dr Nichols came out from St Ives to tend the sick. He wore brown leggings and was "the nicest man you could drive home with," according to Dick Berryman, who drove him home "times and times", as a young lad. Dick recalled that "the doctor 'ed bring 'isself down to our level and chat with we as if we was 'ansom, all the way down." Dr Nichols had an unfortunate wife who drank too much. On one occasion he came to Zennor with a motor bike and side car; his wife was with him, carrying a parrot on her shoulder. He always went into the Tinners' for a bottle of stout, which he drank from the bottle. When it was time to return home, the bike broke down and "Missus was as drunk as a fool", so Dick was asked to fetch Queenie and drive them back. Meanwhile, Missus and the parrot had started walking to St Ives. Dick took his time harnessing up Queenie, thinking "Let the bugger walk!" When Dick and the doctor overtook her, they were near St Ives, and she was so 'mad' (with fury) she wouldn't get into the trap. The men went on a 'bit a way' until the doctor said "We had better try once more". So they stopped the pony and waited for Missus, and then managed to get her into the trap. When driving up the steep nip on Skidden Hill in St Ives, Dick had to ride sitting on the shaft to keep the trap down. The two passengers sitting back on the seat nearly lifted the pony off its feet. "She was a cough-drop, wasn't she?" said Dick, referring to the doctor's wife.

Dr Nichols often rode a horse or drove one on his rounds. He was very good to the poor and rarely charged them for his services. Any parishioner going to St Ives always called in at the surgery to see if there was any medicine for 'up his way'.

The following account of Johnny Nankervis's accident with the reaper sheaver portrays something of the horrific tasks those doctors took in their stride. Johnny was cutting corn at Carnellow when his leg became entangled in the reaper knife, all but severing it above the ankle and leaving his foot dangling by a tendon. His brother Sam found a piece of old twine with which he put a tourniquet on Johnny's leg and then, leaving him in the corn field, went for help. Someone galloped to St Ives and found Dr Nichols who hastened to Carnellow by pony and trap where he stitched the foot back on. Johnny remained in bed with his foot and leg encased in sandbags until it healed. He was left with a fairly useless foot, but was able to walk with the aid of a special boot. What marvellous work those doctors did under very difficult conditions!

The district nurse was a familiar figure, riding her bicycle along the roads and lanes, and later driving her small, clumpy, black car. She attended to most of the medical needs of the poorer folk in Zennor and Towednack and was paid by voluntary subscription. She attended births, laid out the dead, etc., and was generally a 'godsend', as her services were free. A fete was held yearly in one of the fields near the school-room, the proceeds of which were given to the district nurse. We walked miles with my mother, to all the outlying farms, collecting money for this much-needed service. The fund-raising for the nurse finished when the state stepped in to pay her.

Jimmy Limpots from St Ives might often be seen early in the morning picking mushrooms for sale, if he was not begging odd jobs from my mother. He was a tall, strong man, with a shock of red curly hair and a red kerchief around his neck. Threshing was a popular time for Jimmy to visit Zennor as he could join in the gargantuan feasts as well as earn some pocket money.

Ernie Brookham's father Elisha, a stone cleaver from Castle-an-Dinas, who kept goats, sometimes visited Tremedda. He came by donkey and shay and sat on the wooden form in the kitchen, eating bread spread with treacle and cream which trickled down his long grey beard as he ate.

Tramps often visited Tremedda. They sat on the little wooden chair in the hall, eating a good meal provided by my mother. We children peered at these old fellows through the banisters, half afraid of them, and wondering how they lived and where they came from. After eating, the tramp was escorted by my father to the hay house for a good night's rest. My father was most careful to confiscate all matches, in case of fire.

Postmen played a significant role in village life. During the early part of this century, post was an important item, especially so to Zennor folk, who had many relations living in far-distant lands. With the closure of the tin mines, hundreds of Cornishmen emigrated to America, Canada, South Africa and Australia, taking their mining skills with them, to try their luck in the mines for gold, silver, copper, diamonds, or whatever could be dug from the ground to make a living. Their only means of contact with those left behind was by letter writing. Telephones, for them, were still instruments of the future.

A postman walked out from St Ives, delivering and picking up mail at all the farms on his way. On reaching the village, he retired to a little green hut with a stove in it, near the vicarage back garden gate, where he could sit down and dry his clothes if it was raining, or have a bite to eat. He also had to walk all the way up to Foage and on to the outlying districts of Noonveors, Mill Downs and Lady Downs. Old postman Joe could wring water out of his vest when he returned from Lady Downs in hot weather. At 2.05 p.m. the postman picked up the outgoing mail and walked back to St Ives. The post was carried westward from the village by two locals. Women or men, often youngsters on leaving school, undertook this job, as far as possible on bicycle. One took it as far as Chykembro and the other from Chykembro to Gurnard's Head and various cottages on the cliff. Post was delivered on Christmas morning. It was quite a social occasion, as the post carrier knew everyone on his or her round and was plied with tipples of home brew and pieces of Christmas cake by many households. By the last port of call, bicycle riding had often become rather wobbly and hazardous, so that the rider had to foot it home, pushing the bike.

The postmen varied: some were easy-going and jolly, like Postman Bryant, who would have a cup of tea and a chat in various houses and might even visit the pub; others were more strict. Postman Renowden was a crochety old thing and was nicknamed Mr Grumps by the vicarage servants. He sometimes preached in the Zennor Wesleyan Chapel. He was 'strict like a policeman' and would hold his watch in his hand; on the dot of 2.05 p.m. he would be off through the door. If you ran after him with a letter you would have to catch him up; he wouldn't stop and wait. Will's Will once galloped from Zennor to Tremedda with a cart-horse and wain, sparks flying, to catch him.

At one time the parcels were brought out by donkey and shay, driven by Mr Bryant: "You could 'ear 'ee with a stick batin' into 'un from roun' the corner", as the donkey would get into the ditch. Willie Spry, a very small chap with a peaked cap and turned-out feet, often helped carry parcels from St Ives. Postman Renowden led him on a lead so he shouldn't lag behind. Willie also carried telegrams and fish for sale to Zennor. Postman Cothy, a most obliging and friendly man, often sat on the little wooden chair inside the front door at Tremedda, refreshing

56. Mrs Whelan carrying the post to cottages on the cliff at Gurnard's Head. p. 151

55. Miss Hosking at Poniou. p. 147

57. Willie Spry and Postman Bryant. p. 151. Background: Bob and Johnnie Osborn with the jingle.

himself with tea and chatting. I was told the following tale: while walking down Foage Lane once, Postman Cothay happened to look up and see a cuckoo flying overhead; it laid an egg in mid air and Cothy caught the egg in his cap and took it to the village to show to the schoolchildren.

Postmen had to work hard for very little wages in those days. Kate Sowden from County Mayo in Ireland, and her husband, took over the post office in the Row from Katie and Tom Berryman. Kate ran it on her own after her husband died, and was earning only 7s. a week right up until 1930.

There was never a job or repair left undone in Zennor through the lack of someone to do it. A carpenter at Rose Cottage would make a chicken coop or wheelbarrow, mend anything, and charge wireless batteries. He had fixed up a little water-wheel in the river, to provide power for these batteries. In early times the parish had a blacksmith in the village, a shoemaker at Higher Kerrow, a dressmaker, washerwoman and baker; the school teacher lived in the parish, locals carried the post, others mended the roads, and there was always someone willing to act as midwife or vet. A little farther afield, in St Ives or Penzance, buckets, cream pans, coal scuttles, kettles and harness were all made and sold locally. A hand-made Sunday suit, pair of shoes and a hat could all be purchased without difficulty. Very little came from afar. Things were made to last for years and were often repaired many times.

The busy, hard-working inhabitants of this little parish were very self-sufficient, depending far more on one another than on outsiders. They suffered many hardships and discomforts and had small rewards financially, but the work was varied and healthy. They had their dramas, heartaches and happiness, but I would guess they were never lonely or bored. The farmer was his own master and free to work as he pleased, with very little outside intervention. The weather and the animals were his boss and the unwritten rules of the close-knit community he belonged to were his guide lines. The weather had a much greater effect on his toils than the Ministry of Agriculture.

Domestic

WOMEN worked very hard in the old days. They had to be up early to do the milking. They depended greatly on daylight, as candles were the only lighting they had at the beginning of the century, and horn lanterns: four sides of the lantern were filled with thin horn rather than glass, and one side consisted of a little door which opened to get at the candle in the middle. In the 1920s and '30s oil lamps and lanterns were used. If there were miners in the household, the women had to work according to them; they would come home at odd hours and want their meal and a rest.

The downstairs floors in the farmhouses and cottages were made of lime lias, a mixture of lime and rab or clay, which set very hard. The houses in and around the village probably used clay from the pit at the bottom of Jonas' Hill, opposite the turning into the village. The outhouses might have earth or rab floors. The parlour at Treveglos had a lumpy floor and bits would break off. You couldn't put down carpets or rugs, it was so rough. Once a year a load of sand was brought from Hayle, and this was used for sanding all the downstairs floors. Hobnailed boots 'stank' it and cleaned the floors; the sand was brushed up and the floors resanded and all was clean again. This sand was put to a pile on its own; it was not suitable for spreading on the fields as it would not grow good corn owing to an excess of lime in it. All the walls and ceilings in the house were whitewashed with lime once or twice a year. Every Saturday a bit of a spring clean was carried out. The floors were swept and resanded, being too rough to scrub; the granite doorstep was scrubbed, and pieces of wall inside the open chimney on either side were whitewashed and the nook beside the open chimney was filled with enough furze and turf for Sunday. The Paynters, when they lived at Tremedda, swept and sanded the kitchen floor every day, keeping it spotless.

In the early 1900s Dick Berryman's mother from Treveglos baked saffron cake every day, and she made all her own bread. They were a large family; thirteen sat around the table for years. Most farmhouse kitchens had a long scrubbed wood table with a wood form on either side and a wooden stick-back armchair at one end for the 'cap'en' (captain). All the cooking was done in the open chimney, as I have described in the chapter on Fuel. Dinner 'down under' often consisted of a large round of pastry placed on the flat iron. It was marked with thirteen snicks for thirteen people, a piece of beef was put on each snick and it was covered with the kettle, then plenty of fire was thrown on top. It was called 'toad in the hole' and the cooking was judged to a nicety. As well as mountains of cooking, Dick's mother carried thousands of pans of milk from the dairy down to the open chimney to be scalded and then carried them back again. All the daughters were expected to lend a hand from an early age, as were sons out on the farm.

After pig-killing, the fat was run down, leaving delicious crispy scrolly bits which were made into scrolly cake. Pudding skins made from the intestines were stuffed with dough and raisins and boiled, then put in the oven to brown.

During the 1920s and '30s, most farm houses and cottages had the coal-burning Cornish slab installed, and cooking in the open chimney became a thing of the past, as did the use of furze and turf for fuel. Our neighbours the Osborns, only having three in the family, had just one large baking on Fridays. They made saffron cake, heavy cake and sponge cake. Johnnie was partial to cake for breakfast, I believe. As time went on, most people gave up baking their own bread as various bakers came to the village. The weekly wash took place indoors in winter and outside in summer. Many farms had a furnace house with a built-in copper boiler, in which large quantities of water could be heated by lighting a fire underneath it. Wooden 'troys' or wash-tubs and hard cakes of soap were used and the more soiled garments were rubbed on a washboard. All the water was heated in large sooty kettles or, for the luckier ones, in the copper. Garments were also boiled in the copper. As time went on, the weekly wash was transferred to a sink in the back kitchen.

The household wash at Tremedda was done in the wash-house. Much soaking, bleaching and blueing took place. All the whites, especially bed linen, towels and tablecloths, were soaked, and spread on the grass on the washing green to bleach overnight, then brought in next day and rinsed with a bag of blueing in the water and hung out to dry, or, as was the case with our neighbours, spread on convenient gorse bushes. My mother was a great bleacher; the washing green was always dotted with snowy white patches, large and small, sheets and hankies. Woe betide the dog or cat who dared set foot on these. This dazzling sweet-smelling array of linen, when brought in from the line, was carefully folded and carried to the mangle where it rolled through the wooden rollers, appearing on the other side as though beautifully ironed.

Some of the heavier articles such as blankets and bedspreads were washed in a cumbersome old hand-driven machine. This was a large wooden box with ridges inside. It was half filled with buckets of hot soapy water, the washing put in, the lid closed, then turned so many turns in a forward direction and so many turns backwards. This was repeated with the rinsing waters.

The last job was to arrange the linen on the hot-cupboard shelves for airing. For those who still had no hot-cupboard, everything was aired on a rack over the slab.

The ironing was done on the kitchen table on a piece of blanket covered with some old sheet. Two flat-irons were used, which were heated on the cooking range. One would be heating up while the other was in use, and frequent swopping took place. The iron was held with a piece of cloth such as flannel and an old horse-shoe acted as an iron stand. On taking it off the stove one spat on it; if it sizzled it was sufficiently hot to use. There were several fancy models of flat-irons. One consisted of one or two heavy iron pieces which, when heated, slotted into a shiny metal frame for ironing. Another model had a wooden handle which fitted onto the iron when removing it from the stove. When using the flat-irons, one always seemed to be waiting for them to heat up or cool down. The ironing sheet was covered in scorch marks where the iron had been tested for heat and black smuts from the stove appeared on best Sunday shirts and blouses.

There was little waste in those days; the old people were very frugal. Some household foods and animal feed came in cotton and hessian bags. The cotton 3lb flour bags were used as dish-cloths, handkerchiefs, cow-cloths and blueing bags. The larger ones, after a good wash and bleach, made excellent tea-towels and aprons, and the hessian sacks were made into door mats, tousers, general covering for the outdoor worker in bad weather, and held calves, chickens and what-have-you when being transported.

Every bit of newspaper was used: cut into neat squares for the toilet, laid on newly-scrubbed floors, and covering for shelves and many other surfaces, to protect them from dirt.

There was no rubbish collection: all burnable rubbish went onto a bonfire behind the piggery. Every so often bits of metal, glass and china were thrown into some suitable pit or down a mine shaft and all vegetable matter was thrown to the sows or onto the garden rubbish pile.

A few ancients still wore smocks, commonly known as frocks, in Zennor. They were pale washed-out blue in colour and were made from heavy, canvassy material, coming down just below the knee. They kept the wearer clean and warm; no coat was worn over a frock except maybe in very cold weather.

My memories of farm workers' attire are of baggy, dark brown corduroy trousers, often tied under the knee with a piece of binder twine, or riding-breeches-type trousers flared on the hips and tightly laced down the calf (I suppose this prevented dirt and dust and the odd mouse going up the trouser leg), collarless flannel shirts and black waistcoats that were maybe a remnant of a Sunday suit. Tattered jackets, barely recognisable as such, and kept together with binder twine around the middle, were worn in cold weather. All this was topped and tailed with cap and hobnail boots. When heavy rain prevailed, the more affluent donned large black 'oilers' and sou'-westers, while others shrouded themselves in hessian sacks. Women wore high-necked blouses and long dark skirts covered with long aprons, and black wool stockings. Children wore pinnies. As skirts became shorter, cotton floral aprons crossing over in front and tied at the back, were worn, covering everything except the arms. Sleeves were always rolled up, as arms were often immersed in suds or in baking flour, or thrust under cows when milking or in buckets of milk when teaching a baby calf to drink. All these garments for both men and women were usually covered with a touser when working outside.

My mother wore her own special fashions. As I remember them, the emphasis was on comfort. Her clothes were rather loose-fitting, with nothing to restrict her movements as she raced about, carrying on her many activities. Her summer clothes were two cotton outfits, one in green and one in blue. They consisted of a skirt hung on a bodice and a long blouse-type top with short sleeves, collar and belt. These outfits were beautifully smocked and embroidered in white and were made by Katherine Cockerell, a marvellous sewer, who, as a young girl, spent a year at Tremedda helping with the dairywork and the care of us children. In winter my mother wore Harris tweed and Irish homespun skirts hung on bodices, silk and cotton blouses with a brooch at the throat, blue and grey cardigans and lisle stockings. She went bare legged in summer. Her footwear was flat brown sandals and black shoes with strap and buckle. She always wore aprons; checked and striped cottons and beautifully embroidered Swiss ones. Three Burberrys, all in differing states of respectability, were her most useful items of outdoor clothing. A very worn one was donned for jobs when it was winday or wet or as protection against brambles and gorse. A Burberry of medium condition was worn for local jaunts and visiting. Her very best one she took with her on her annual travel to Scotland or abroad. She always wore coloured headscarves in windy weather. She travelled light, cutting down her luggage to the barest necessities. When off to Italy or Switzerland for a fortnight, she carried a red leather bag containing her night attire and clean underwear, and her money and passport were held in a large pocket sewn onto the inside of her skirt waistband. With these few things and her Burberry, she was ready to travel anywhere.

The farmers of 1900 had few regulations to comply with. Money matters were simple and there was very little paper work. A few bigger farms paid income tax and had to send in a bit of a return, showing the number of animals they kept and their acreage. A few early prices, some mentioned in other chapters, were as follows:

	1900		1920
Pigs	– 5d. per lb.	Pigs of ten score	– £2 per score
Bull	– £12.10s.0d.	Bull	– 15 gns.
Cow and calf	– £5	Cow and calf	– £9
Calves	– 15s. each	Sucking colt	– 10 gns.
Geese	– 8⅔d. per lb.	Dog licence	– 7s.6d.
Turkeys	– 11⅓d. per lb.	Trap licence	– 5s.

Butter   – 6d. and 7d. per lb.
Eggs   – 4d. and 5d. per dozen
Trap licence – 15s.

1929

Salt (for buttermaking, curing ham, herrings etc.) ⅓ cwt.		7s.0d.
Coir yarn (for thatching, the binder and bundler, etc.) 4 lbs.		2s.0d.
Rivets ⅓ lb.		1s.0d.
Files (for sharpening reaper knife, etc.)		2s.0d.
Grease, 7 lbs.		2s.6d.
Footwear		4s.9d.
Chain harrow		£3.0s.0d.
Sand		1s.0d.
Lime		1s.0d.
Straw,	25 bundles	£3.0s.0d.
Bran (cattle and pig feed)	1 cwt.	8s.6d.
Crushed Oats (cattle and horse feed)	1 cwt.	12s.3d.
Maize meal (cattle and pigs)	1 cwt.	10s.9d.
Barley meal (pigs)	1 cwt.	13s.0d.
Sharps (pigs)	1 cwt.	11s.6d.
Maize (poultry)	1 cwt.	10s.0d.
Wheat (poultry)	1 cwt.	16s.0d.
Flour (domestic)	half sack	12s.0d.
Potatoes (domestic)	half cwt	12s.0d.
Clover seed	18 lbs	£1.7s.0d.
Mangol seed	4 lbs	3s.4d.

The hessian sacks, in which these goods were supplied, were charged out at 1s. each; this was deducted from the bill when they were returned.

All the 1929 items could be purchased from Edward Mitchell & Sons, Auctioneers, Penzance.

The more prosperous farmers banked money, which was of gold for guineas, sovereigns and half sovereigns, and silver. In the 1920s paper money came in.

Tremedda as I first remember it was lit by oil lamps and candles. Two Aladdin lamps, with mantles which disintegrated frequently, provided good lighting for reading and sewing. Oil lanterns were used to light the outhouses and for outdoor jobs; these had well-protected glass chimneys and seemed to stand up to any amount of buffeting from the high winds: there was always an assortment of large and small oil lamps. It was quite a job filling, cleaning and trimming the wicks of all this lighting equipment. A large red metal container holding several gallons of paraffin stood in the back kitchen. It had a tap at the top and as one pumped a little brass handle up and down, the paraffin came gushing out.

The cooking was done on a coal-burning American range, which also heated the hot water; various oil stoves helped out when much cooking was in progress, and the house was heated by open fires.

A hot and cold water supply served a bath and basin in the bathroom, a sink in the kitchen and a sink in the wash-house, and a cold tap provided water for the cider trough, the cows' drinking-trough in the yard and the dairy – a very modern provision of water for the 1920s and '30s. Most Zennor folk depended on a private or communal pump or well for their water supplies, which had to be carried to the house in pitchers and buckets.

The upstairs toilet was in a little cubby-hole under the sloping roof, with a skylight. It was equipped with an Elsan and an enamel bucket with a little seat over it. These Cecil discreetly emptied, carrying them by way of the night-nursery, down the balcony steps and out through the back garden gate. The downstairs toilet had the usual wooden seat with lid, over a bucket. A similar, small toilet tucked away behind the piggery for the workmen completed the Tremedda lavatory arrangements.

Modern amenities, such as we take for granted today, gradually came to Tremedda: a wireless with a heavy glass accumulator which had to be carried down to Rose Cottage to be recharged every so often by Mr Stevens the carpenter, a telephone, a flush toilet upstairs, and finally the installation of the turbine in 1937, to provide electricity.

Domestic chores were performed in a much more orderly fashion than today. There were certain jobs allocated to each day of the week, including washing on Monday, ironing and airing on Tuesday, market day and shopping on Thursday, baking on Friday, and extra cleaning on Saturday, which was also bath night. Baths were taken in a tin bath in front of the fire in most households, so all should be serene and spotless with little to do on the Sabbath. In the evening, hands were rarely idle, performing numerous mending jobs. Everything was made to last and clothes were resurrected with countless patches and darns – a dying art today. The women crocheted, knitted and made clothes out of this and that for the children. Granny Griggs knitted socks like a machine, with the end of one long knitting needle held fast in a 'corn dolly' stuck in her waist band. The men had harness to mend and the family boots to repair. For many of these tasks, the more prosperous inhabitants resident in the parish, employed outside labour, such as the washerwoman and seamstress, and took footwear to the shoemaker. Older folk sat on the settle by the fire, maybe smoking a clay pipe, and holding forth on their favourite subjects with a neighbour. In the years before radio and television the art of conversation flourished.

Zennor School

THERE were no 'dame-schools' in Zennor by 1900. I believe before this there had been one at Boswednack, where a penny or so was paid weekly for tuition. In early times there was a school at Porthmeor. The Zennor Church School, already an old building in 1900, stood in the centre of the village. It consisted of one long room, had windows down one side and two chimneys. Inside it was divided in two by a curtain, making two classrooms, one for the older children and one for the infants. Each classroom had a round, coke-burning, iron stove in it. The coke was kept in a pile in the boys' yard. Except during lessons, boys and girls were segregated. At the top end of the schoolroom a door led into the girls' cloakroom, earth closet and small yard where they played. At the bottom end was the porch and the boys' yard and earth closets. Later the curtain was replaced by a wooden screen and the round stoves by two open, coal-burning fires. The coal was kept in a small coal-house in the boys' yard. School hours were from 9 a.m.–12 noon and 1.30 p.m. –4 p.m.

There were seventy-odd pupils in 1900, but then the numbers diminished very fast and in 1914 there were only about twenty. There were two teachers: Mr Bevan the head teacher from Pit Pry, a nice sort of chap; and old Betsy Berryman from Porthmeor, who taught the little ones. She was a cross old thing and hit the children on their knuckles with a piece of one of the slates that had come apart. Poor old soul, she didn't have much patience, according to one of her pupils but she was very good at sewing and could bring any of the girls on at that. Twice a week she took sewing classes for all the girls; they made pinafores. Miss Berryman ate her dinner at school and Mr Bevan went home for his. The children all had little wooden framed slates to write on and slate pencils, and the teachers had a blackboard and chalks; not much paper was used in those days. Miss Marshall was head teacher from 1913 to 1918, during the war years. She lodged in Rose Cottage with the Nankervis family. Every Christmas, she provided the school children with a Christmas tree. She left Zennor on March 4th 1918 and went to Scotland to make aeroplane engines. As a leaving present, the choir presented her with a travelling clock as an expression of their good wishes. In later years a teacher drove out from St Ives in a little black car to teach at Zennor school.

Betsy Berryman must have taught at Zennor for many years. As well as teaching Dick Berryman's generation – he started school in 1900 – she also taught his mother. According to Dick, his mother must have been a very apt scholar; she kept two books on the bookshelf Dick and his

58. The Row, Zennor Churchtown, with Mr and Mrs Sowdon, who kept the Post Office, 1920. p. 153

59. School transport. John Berryman and his smart little outfit. Jean in the shafts, late 1920s. p. 163. Background: the Vicarage and, L-R, Rex Whelan, Harold Harfoot, Matthew Hollow.

60. A Zennor school party, in earlier times. p. 160

61. A Zennor school group, 1933. p. 164. Back row, L-R: Joan Berryman (Boswednack), Claud Eddy (Bosigran), Harold Harfoot (Tinners' Arms), John Berryman (Treen), Edward Noy (Trewey), Basil Hosking (Pit Pry). Middle row, L-R: Jack Tracey (Coastguards', Gurnard's Head), Joyce Berryman (Boswednack), Joyce Trundel (Trendrine), Mary Osborn (Tremeadow), Gonard Trundel (Trendrine), Willie Craze (Trevega), Jim Dunstan (Chy Barnett). Front row, L-R: Henry Hocking (Tregerthen), Jimmy Thomas (Tremedda), Hazel Jelbert (Carnellow), Ken Berryman (Treen).

contemporaries could not fathom out, but when he took up the Parish council work, he could refer to them and learn from them. Her hand-writing was perfect, much better than that of her children's generation. All this although she left school when she was eleven years old to go to work. When Dick started school, he went there with an older sister Winnie and was put to sit beside her. "I suppose I was sent up there out of the way," says Dick.

All the children walked to school, come rain or shine. Some had to come three or so miles along the footpath, through the fields and down the rab roads. Occasionally a boy might ride a pony to school; John Berryman from Treen sometimes rode his Shetland pony Jean of Littleness or drove her in a little cart. The pony was put to graze in the field behind the chapel during school hours. When it came time to go home, Jean was the very devil to catch and had half the school children running around the field after her. The children came from Bosigran, Lady Downs, Trevail, and when Towednack school was moved near Nancledra, Trevega children went to Zennor. If they arrived at school wet they had to put up with it. Coats were hung around the stoves to dry. They all carried their dinners and tea to make at school: the water was boiled on one of the stoves. Granny Griggs, who lived nearby, was a haven of refuge to the school children. She dried them off in her kitchen and warmed up all their dinners, usually pasties sometimes for nigh on seventy! During very cold weather she made them mugs of hot cocoa. When she died, a Berryman from Porthmeor said "I am going to Granny Griggs funeral 'cos she always warmed up my pasty for me when I was going to school".

The girls ate their dinners and played in their cloakroom or outside in their little yard; the boys had the front porch and a small yard, and also played on the Town Plat, a rab-paved piece of ground outside the school entrance bound on one side by railings, where they could run about, play cricket and swing on the railings. Sometimes, during fine weather when the school door was left open, a Tremedda dog was wont to come in and sit down and scratch and have to be ousted by one of the pupils.

My father ended his school days in the following manner: Will's Wioll from the Row came into the school, pointed to my father and said "I want you", my father jumped up, followed him out and started 'leasing' stones. So began his first job.

Willie Osborne from Bosporthennis started out on the three mile walk to the village for his last day at school. On reaching Trewey, he was told Great Aunt Anne had just died and would he retrace his steps to ask his father Mathy, one of the grave diggers, to make the necessary arrange-ments. On returning home, he found his father was unable to carry out this request as he had a bad attack of asthma, so Willie was sent to Mill

Downs, another long trek over the moors, to ask his uncle to make the arrangements. In this fashion Willie missed his last day at school. With barely a break, he went to work for Robert Osborn (Tremeadow Johnny's brother) at Embla Farm in Towednack Parish.

Most of the children started their schooling at the age of four or five and left when they were fourteen. Sidney Berryman from the Row started his schooling in Zennor and at the age of eleven went to Hayle Grammar school where he boarded for a year or two and finally, as he grew older, rode a bicycle the nine or so miles there and back every day. The rab roads were very rough and he always tried to ride up Boscubban Hill, but only managed it once – "Last li'l bit was a villain!" At one time there was a night school in Zennor attended by those who wished to further their education. Sam Nankervis went to night school.

The little Zennor school closed in 1933 and the Zennor children went by bus to the St Ives board school in the Stennack. It reopened for a short period during the Second World War for evacuees, when Zennor inhabitants took in children from Plymouth which was being devastated by bombs. Two little girls, Rona and June, came to Tremedda. June was one of a large family of about nine brothers and sisters and one day my mother had to break the tragic news to her that all her family except one older sister had been killed by a bomb.

The children were well versed in the three R's and much was learnt by heart; discipline was good, helped greatly by the fact that most children were well disciplined at home.

Church and Chapel

ZENNOR church was built in the twelfth century, an aisle was added in the fifteenth century, and it was restored in 1890.

St Senara, the patron saint of the church, is depicted in one of the windows. A legend connects her with Princess Asenora of Brittany, who married King Goello. Her stepmother, jealous of her beauty and virtue, accused her of infidelity and she was condemned to be burnt. However, when it was discovered she was with child her jailers nailed her into a barrel and threw it into the sea to avoid being guilty of murdering her unborn child. She was miraculously fed by an angel, bore her child in the barrel and was eventually washed up on the coast of Ireland. Her son became the Abbot of St Budoc (Budoc means 'the drowned one'). He despaired of the Irish, so he and his mother returned to Brittany at the request of the now penitent King Goello, who had discovered that his wife had never been unfaithful to him. On their way to Brittany they landed in Cornwall, where they founded the parishes of Zennor and St Budoc.

Inside the church is the famous Mermaid Chair which stands in the side chapel. Two bench ends preserved from the Restoration form the sides of the chair. A mermaid holding a looking glass in her right hand and a comb in her left is carved on one of these bench ends. Legend has it that a beautiful woman in a long dress used to sit at the back of the church listening to the singing of one of the choristers, Mathew Trewhella. One evening she lured him down to the lilttle stream and into the sea at Pendower Cove. It is said if you listen carefully on a warm summer's night you can hear the pair of lovers singing together.

The church and Wesleyan chapel were well supported at the beginning of the century. It was here the parishioners gathered to worship and socialise. On the Sabbath they attended the services, visited and entertained relations and read the Bible. No one was allowed to sew or do any unnecessary menial jobs although the livestock always had to be attended to. Much of the village entertainment was centred around church and chapel. There were the Christmas and Easter festivities, Feast, Chapel Anniversary, Harvest Festivals and the annual choir and Sunday school outings. Most of the village activities were held in the church schoolroom. As a general rule, conservatives went to church and liberals went to chapel.

Dick Berryman's mother could remember six chapels in the parish in the late nineteenth century, and all of them full every Sunday. There was the large one in the village, near which stands a big rock from which John Wesley preached, one each at Tregerthen, Trendrine and Porthmeor, and two in the vicinity of Mill Downs and Lady Downs. Many people lived at Mill Downs and Lady Downs in those days and the villagers called them 'mountainy people'. Sometimes revival meetings were held in the large chapel in the village; it would be full to bursting with people. This chapel was built in 1799.

Dick's mother also remembered a round reading room in the vicinity of Treveglos Yard, where those who could read came to glean news from newspapers. The young lads used the old papers for paper chases.

The church owned the Glebe Farm but had no say in the running of it. At the beginning of the century the Glebe was farmed by Will and Anne Berryman from the Row. The Glebe and Treveglos shared the cliff grazing. Later, the two farms were farmed as one unit by Dick Berryman. The Glebe was sold to Mr Brookes in 1940. The vicar, or parson as he was called in those days, kept only a pony and jingle and had a paddock and stables behind the vicarage. The parson usually kept a staff of three; parlourmaid, housemaid, and housekeeper. Our neighbour Katie Osborn (*née* Johns) was housekeeper at the vicarage for a while.

Parson Roe (Farwell Roe) and his wife left Zennor in 1900. The parishioners collected £30 for a present for them. They were followed by Parson Vaughan and his daughter. According to Dick, who grew up in the village during Parson Vaughan's term of office, "He was a nice little chap but poor as death." When Dick left school, he helped with the church accounts. Parson had to give him the statement of his accounts for the auditors. Dick said "he was taxed to death," and when the accounts were finished he couldn't see that Parson had more than £50 to live on for the year. Although small of stature, Parson Vaughan had great authority in the village and was well liked. He was present at all the entertainments in the school, such as dances, socials and concerts. The men used to go to the pub, but if they were the worse for drink they couldn't put their nose in the schoolroom; Parson would put them out and tell them to go home. He wouldn't let anyone in drunk, "No fear!" He relented a little with some of the old folk at Christmas time. Dick's Uncle Will was a great drinker and Parson Vaughan would allow him into the Christmas concert for about five minutes. Will would come into the school in a blue frock and give a little step dance on the stage and then Parson would say "Now you go home, now". Uncle Will had drunk a drop of beer but he wouldn't be drunk.

Miss Vaughan was a good organiser; she played the piano and helped with all the village activities. The organ was installed in the church during the Vaughans' stay at Zennor. They left the parish in 1919 and were followed by Mr and Mrs Harvey. Mrs Harvey was very old-fashioned and, as I have mentioned, grew a vine in the greenhouse adjoining their stables, which she tended with great care, feeding it on pig's blood whenever pig-killing took place.

Twenty pounds a year was taken out of the stipend: every five years, when £100 had accumulated, this money had to be spent on the church in some way. The local carpenter had a good packet from this money. One year it was spent on pulling down the greenhouse where Mrs Harvey grew her precious vine. It had a slate floor and brick wall around it "Done 'ansome. That was that £100 gone and the vine gone with 'un".

Mrs Nankervis from Rose Cottage and later Carnellow Farm, was the church cleaner for some time. She swept the floors, polished the brasses and saw to the oil lamps and the coke stove. She lit the stove every Saturday. It was a large iron one with a tortoise in relief on it and rough bricks inside, and stood at the back end of the church. It held ten buckets full of coke and an extra one was filled in readiness to top up the fire at ten o'clock on Saturday evening. This cumbersome stove was later replaced by a flotilla of small black oil stoves. Mrs Nankervis also filled and lit all the lamps which hung on long chains from the roof, and put them out again, before and after the evening service. She had to lug the heavy buckets of coke and the paraffin up from the cellar beneath the belfry. She also scrubbed the church right through once a year. Matilda Berryman lit the farm furnace and provided her with hot water for this task. All this Mrs Nankervis did for five pounds a year.

At the beginning of the century all parishioners who owned or rented land paid tithes – some to the church and some to the representatives of Miss Johns. It seems no records can be traced of the reason for Miss Johns' tithe. It is thought she probably lent the parish money, either to build the school or help with the restoration of the church. Foage and Treveglos were the only farms to pay all their tithes to the church; the rest paid half to church and half to Miss Johns' representatives. The church tithe was paid in the vicarage study and Miss Johns' tithe in the pub. A clerk from Penzance hired a room in the Tinners' Arms. Everyone paying his tithe was given a ticket worth four shillings or so, a percentage of the tithe due, and this had to be spent in the pub and was for the hire of the room. Even the Wesleyans and teetotallers, rather than waste their tickets, bought beer and spirits. Usually ructions broke out, the pub being full of tithe-payers and most of them tight. Some wore top hats which, when given a bang on the top of the head, fell down over their eyes, at which the wearer was heard to exclaim "You've scat me blind". Jan Thomas always shut his eyes when drinking gin and, when asked the reason, replied "I can't abide to see un goin' away". Dick recalls as a boy playing a trick on the tithe-paying revellers. Old Toby Friggins had been trimming the churchyard and had thrown all the branches over into the church field. Dick and his pals went to pick out the biggest branch they could find, stood it up against the pub door, and cleared off. Mr Dixon the landlord, who was smoking a long clay sailor's pipe, thought he heard something and opened the door. In came the tree, knocking the pipe out of his mouth, and "My gor, there's some swearin' in there, and we's gone," says Dick.

Racco's father, old David Thomas, used to walk from Treen to Zennor to pay his tithes wearing a white frock down to his knees. He could be heard a mile away as he clomped down the road in his 'hobstankers' (hob-nailed boots).

Way back in the 1700s when tithes were often paid to the parson in farm produce, certain Zennor farmers wished to pay their tithes in butter and cheese. The parson would not accept this as he wanted the usual cows and calves. These farmers dumped their butter and cheese in the church, where it remained until it went rancid and stank the place out, but the parson finally won the argument and the farmers had to pay up as required.

Funerals were attended mainly by the men; the women stayed at home to see to the milking and animal feeding. There were always two sets of bearers dressed in their best, with black coats and top hats, to carry the coffin across the fields to the church. All blinds en route were drawn. When the funeral procession arrived at the bridge near the church, the choir took their places and sang a special hymn all the way into the church. There was always a bit of a wake after a funeral; all but the teetotallers trooped into the pub and would stay there till next morning, sometimes finishing up with fighting and blood flowing.

The Feast of St Senara falls on the nearest Sunday to May 12th. In those days it was Zennor's most important church and social occasion of the year. Folk who had lived in the parish and still had relations there all came flocking back for Feast. If they lived far away they travelled to Penzance by train, where they were collected by trap and driven to Zennor. They arrived on the Thursday and stayed the week; it was their yearly bit of holiday. Relations from neighbouring parishes came over for the day.

The week before Feast, the churchyard was tidied up and the grass cut, and parishioners attended to the graves of their beloved ones, sometimes scrubbing the headstones and usually leaving a bunch of fresh flowers in a jam pot on the grave for the spirits to admire. On Saturday, many came to help decorate the church with spring flowers. On Sunday big midday dinner parties were held throughout the parish, Large roasts of beef and 'feasty' pudding known as 'guldise' were eaten. Guldise was a baked, cake-like pudding, full of fruit and spices, and delicious with clotted cream. As a general rule a vicar from another parish was invited over to preach at the evening service. The church would be packed, with everyone dressed in their best, all the women and girls wearing hats and many showing off new outfits. It was the only time during the year when the young 'maids' were allowed, or could afford, to buy a new costume (coat and skirt), hat and maybe shoes. Many of the older ladies threw caution to the wind and also decked themselves out in new clothes.

Feast Monday was a holiday for all, including school children, but of course the milking and animal feeding still had to be fitted in. A cricket match against Towednack was played in a field at Trewey. There might be four hundred people or more watching the cricket. Hamlyns, a baker from St Ives, brought out stalls and set them up at the end of Pump Road near the church steps in the late afternoon or evening. The young lads 'would put a girl down' to the stalls and buy a bag of fairings for her; ginger nuts, sugared almonds and 'clyjjy': bits of hard toffee. There were one or two other small stalls but Hamlyns had the main ones. Johnnie Phillips drove a wagon out with the stalls and stabled the horse at Treveglos. Afterwards, he could be heard driving away home at two in the morning.

On Monday evening a concert, organised and performed by locals, was held in the schoolroom. The cricket team went to play St Buryan on Tuesday as it was also the Feast of St Buryan. On the Wednesday, furze

62. Zennor church in 1874 (restored in 1890). The round reading room is on the right. p. 165

63. Ready for church, Zennor Feast Sunday, 1935. p. 168. The Osborn family and relations at Tremeadow. L-R: Bert James, Jim Berriman, Herbert James, Annie Berriman, Kathleen James, Alma Osborn, Jimmy Berriman, Kit (?), Katie and John Osborn. Front: Mary Osborn.

cutting started and on Thursday the remaining relations departed and Feast was over for another year.

We always went to Towednack Feast as Aunt Amy and Uncle Thomas farmed at Amelveor in Towednack Parish and we had entertained them at our Feast. Granny Griggs and Alice were of the party and much yarning took place, liberally sprinkled with 'ays you's and 'you knaw like's. We ate large quantities of food in Aunt Amy's small kitchen and helped her feed numerous baby chicks. Then we attended Evening Service at Towednack Church before returning home.

One year Dick Berryman rode a colt over the downs to Towednack, on Towednack Feast Monday. It was the first time the colt had crossed these downs. He went to Embla to visit Robert Osborn and stabled the colt there. He and Robert walked across the fields to watch the races. Robert asked Dick to come back in the evening as there was something on in the village. Dick said "I got to go home milky". He rode back to Zennor, finished his work and went off again on the colt to Embla. He and Robert went down Cledry (Nancledra) to the concert and then returned to Embla for supper. When Dick set out to ride home it was as black as ink outside; you couldn't see your hand in front of your face. He mounted the colt and decided to let him please himself which way he went home, so he dropped the reins on his neck and left him alone. The colt turned up Rocky Lane and struck out across the downs; Dick had no idea where he was until he came out by the rab-pit below Eagle's Nest. The colt had returned in the very footsteps he had taken on the way over.

The Chapel Anniversary was another big occasion in the village. As well as the services in the chapel, a chapel-band tea was held on the green in front of the chapel, where long trestle tables were erected and loaded with food, and wooden forms were carried out for seating. When the Osborn family lived in Bridge Cottage near the chapel, Alma Osborn provided large black kettles of boiling water for tea-making, and these were heated on the brandis in her open chimney. All the children were given a large saffron bun each, about nine inches across with a cherry in the middle. Towednack Town Band of about fourteen players used to come over for this occasion. Starting from the chapel and playing all the while, the band marched up the Gurnick to Trewey, followed by two old stalwarts carrying a banner, all the chapel-goers bringing up the rear. The procession continued on through the fields to Boswednack, returning to Zennor by the road, and then went on to Tremedda to give Bob Osborn a tune. Dick and his brothers had to stay at home while the band played: "We should have to stop home to watch our cows see, they'd go out of this world!" (with fright.)

Church and chapel held Harvest Festivals on different days at the end of September or beginning of October. Church-goers and chapelites attended both festivals, when there were various well-attended services, harvest teas and a bit of a dance or social in the evening.

I well remember as a child helping to decorate the church with flowers and farm produce, butter, eggs, vegetables, fruit and sheaves of corn. We dipped water out of an old rain water butt in the churchyard and filled jam pots and potted meat and bovril jars. These were then filled with flowers and arranged around the church, carefully concealing the makeshift vases with moss and greenery.

When we arrived for the different services in the crowded church or chapel the bells rang out from the belfry to welcome the worshippers. Favourite harvest hymns were sung, accompanied by Mrs Harfoot, the pub landlord's wife, vigorously playing the organ while behind the scenes Reggie pumped away at the organ blower to keep up a good supply of air for Mrs Harfoot's loud pedal. 'Come Ye Thankful People Come' and 'We Plough the Fields and Scatter' were sung with gusto, nearly raising the roof, with the voices of Charlie and Hilda Jelbert much in evidence. On dark evenings the church looked mysterious to me, with its rows of suspended lamps and the candles on the altar, yellow pools of light around each flame gradually receding into darkness in the far-off corners and crannies of the old building.

At the close of the service the congregation poured out of the church, and there began a very sociable gathering at the foot of the church steps around 'Monkey's Corner'. The church-goers were mostly related to one another or well acquainted and much chatting and yarning ensued, while the young lads turned their attention to the maids, hoping for a partner to walk home. Certain married women drifted up the Gurnick towards Gurnard's Head, even though home was in the opposite direction, in order to prolong the delight of companionship and a good gossip.

The church harvest tea was held in the schoolroom. Everyone sat down on wooden forms at long tables laden with bread and butter, splits, cream and jam or demerara sugar, heavy cake, saffron cake and carroway seed cake, and were served steaming hot cups of tea from two copper tea urns. Water for making the tea was boiled in a large urn standing on a brandis over an open fire out in the boys' yard. Young lads had collected a pile of furze stogs to keep the fire burning. The Berryman family from Treveglos were a great help on these occasions, often heating extra water in the copper in their furnace house.

Chapel harvest tea was held inside the chapel, as the weather could not be depended on at that time of year. A small American harmonium provided music in the chapel. For many years Mr Noye from Morvah walked six or so miles to Zennor and back, once if not twice every Sunday, to play the harmonium and accompany the chapel singers.

I have a daily reminder of this chapel music, as the little harmonium now stands in my living room.

There was never a shortage of organists in those days of home-made music. Hilda Jelbert, Charity Nichols and Janey from Porthmeor could all play the organ, and most parishioners had good singing voices. Some of the more prosperous farmers sent their children to St Ives for piano lessons. The children rode there on ponies or later travelled by bus. Many taught themselves to play. The church bells rang out for all these services. There was never a dearth of bell-ringers; we all learnt this art when young. Zennor church tower has six bells. I usually rang number six, the heavy bass bell. On one occasion during bell ringing practice with Mr Byfield the vicar, his arm became entangled in the bell rope and he was pulled up aloft and down again, fortunately suffering no more than a fright and breaking his glasses. It was quite a delicate operation keeping the large heavy bell balanced upside down with only a wooden stay to prevent it toppling right over before its next plunge downwards. Many a stay was broken by the heavy handed. In earlier times, hand bells were rung. Johnnie Nankervis from Carnellow, when on his death bed, said he would dearly like to hear these bells rung once more. The ringers came and gave him a tune and he died soon after.

There was much festivity in Zennor over the Christmas period. As well as the church and chapel services, there was some sort of entertainment in the schoolroom for about twelve nights following: dances, a social, the children's party, cricket and choir parties, a concert and sometimes a fancy dress ball and much carol singing in church and chapel, in the pubs and anywhere where a tune might be forthcoming.

Some of the dances were quite grand affairs, the girls wearing long satin dresses and diamante slippers and the men their pin-stripe navy blue suits with well-oiled hair. During those early days, beautifully printed dance cards were used on special occasions, sometimes printed in silver and embossed with ivy leaves. Dances listed on these cards included the cotillion, the gallop, the lancers and the polka. There were always musicians available to make up a small band of drums, saxophone, accordion and maybe a fiddle.

In preparation, the schoolroom was cleared, the desks piled up at one end and forms placed around the room for seating. The floor was swept clean and sprinkled with powdered chalk, to enable feet to glide smoothly over uneven boards, and during the winter months two bright fires burned in the grates. Turns were taken to stand at the door with a bowl and take an entrance fee. This was to pay the band, for the use of the hall, for coal, and oil for lighting.

The maids and older women who liked dancing arrived first, and grouped themselves at the top end of the schoolroom, chatting and dancing with each other. They eagerly awaited the arrival of the men and lads, most of whom visited the Tinners' Arms before rolling in at ten o'clock, to group themselves at the bottom end of the schoolroom. The fun now really began. Occasionally a scuffle broke out at this end of the room but the trouble-makers were quickly ousted from the hall.

We started attending these dances at the age of fourteen or so. Each occasion was awaited with great excitement, and also some trepidation in case our mother should say no to our request to go. Sometimes our workman Walter Palfrey, a keen dancer, came over and put in a plea for us, saying that he and his wife Lena would keep an eye on us and make sure we went home early. Among the dances stepped out were the slow and quick foxtrots, the waltz, military two step, valeta, barn dance and Paul Jones. During my Zennor dancing days, Jimmy Rickard and his band came out from St Ives to provide the music. My father attended all the social occasions in Zennor; he was a good dancer and loved to sing a good tune and was sidesman in church and sat in the choir for many years. His mother often said of him "There's no show without Punch." My mother was not a great socialiser and usually stayed at home.

All the children in the parish were invited to the children's Christmas party. They sat down to a large tea, were given crackers and balloons, and then played games; Nuts in May, Oranges and Lemons, The Farmer Wants a Wife, Blind Man's Buff, Musical Chairs, Musical Bumps, and Musical Mats, to the accompaniment of Mrs Eddy from Bosigran, who played the old out-of-tune piano with zest. The crowning moment of the party was the arrival of Father Christmas, who entered carrying a large sack full of presents, one for each child. The children sat, eagerly awaiting their name called out. When they walked wide-eyed up to Father Christmas to receive their present, he might ask one to sing or another to give him a kiss, and many of the tinies cowered behind their mothers' skirts with fright.

The Zennor concerts and socials had varied programmes of singing, small plays, comic dialogues, tap dancing, reciting, and tunes on the concertina or mouth-organ. The acts were performed on a small stage erected at one end of the schoolroom. My father could tap dance and Johnnie and Katie Osborn could always be relied on to give the audience a good laugh.

At one time concerts were rehearsed in the vicarage kitchen with Miss Vaughan playing the piano and a crowd practising their pieces with Parson Vaughan "killing hisself laughing". Johnnie Osborn was a comic fellow and would often have Parson rolling on the floor with mirth.

Parlours were often used for music making. Most of them contained a piano or harmonium and singers gathered here to enjoy a musical evening, or practise a tune. Most of them could play some sort of instrument: the accordion, fiddle, or mouth-organ.

When the Christmas concert was on, "that school wouldn't hold half the audience", it was so popular. The Zennor people also performed their concert in the neighbouring parish of Towednack.

In the 1930s I was dragged in to perform in some of these acts. Five or six of us in a row dressed up and sang songs such as 'Little Old Lady Passing By' and 'Daisy, Daisy, Give Me Your Answer Do', with an accompanist thumping out the tune on the old piano.

The choir and Sunday school took their yearly outings by Jersey car and later by charabanc, and might drive as far as the Lizard, Fowey, Gwinnear or Land's End. A very popular Sunday school outing was for all the children to pile onto a couple of wagons provided by the Berrymans of Treveglos. These were carefully prepared with forms from the schoolroom for seating, well tied down, and the end riggers and sides fixed securely in place. Then, with willing helpers, drivers and horses, off to Carbis Bay beach and Paynes picnic grounds; what fun!

The annual fête to raise money for the district nurse, held in a field, drew a good crowd to wander round the stalls, take part in games, sheaf-pitching, tug-of-wars and eat a good tea. Once again the large urn was kept on the boil over a hot fire of furze stogs (sticks). Miss Hosking was a very enthusiastic helper at the fête; she and my mother ran a stall, and God help any stall that made more money than theirs – which was seldom!

During the First World War, all sorts of activities were organised to raise money for different war funds including a War Savings Association and the Zennor Knitting Fund. Celebrations were organised when peace was declared.

Many other pursuits were followed. Menfolk rode or drove traps to nearby horse races, fairs and shows. Zennor always had a cricket team; the game was very popular and the women even made up a team at one time. The schoolchildren played cricket on the rab-covered plat outside the school and on the green by the river. The Osborn family from Bridge Cottage were great cricketers; there was no chance of bowling them out and having a turn with the bat when they were playing.

Whist drives were popular, especially the Christmas one when the money taken at the door went towards the cost of the children's Christmas presents.

Hunting was another popular pursuit. Many a Saturday afternoon was spent out rabbiting with shotgun, ferrets and dog. Hedges and banks were riddled with rabbit warrens. Nets about two feet across and bounded by a drawstring were placed over the holes and each one pegged down with a wooden peg, then the ferret, with a little bell hung around its neck and maybe 'coped' (muzzled) to prevent it killing the rabbits, was put down one of the holes. The rabbits raced out of the holes to escape from the ferretand into the nets, the drawstrings tightened and

Zennor.

Vicar—Rev. D. R. Vaughan, Surrogate.

Six of our Zennor boys have suffered in the war. Two were wounded in France, and one got trench feet, and another was gassed there. One was wounded in Palestine, and another has malarial fever in Serbia. Four of these are in hospital in England and are doing well.

MARRIAGE.

Nov. 6. 2ud Lieut. Henry William Dodds and Louisa Hocking.

Zennor.

Vicar—Rev. D. R. Vaughan, Surrogate.

Of course we had our Thanksgiving for Peace on July 6th—thanksgiving for the great peace after the greatest war the world has known.

On the following Saturday, July 12th, we had our Sunday School treat. We were favoured with fine weather, and the children seemed to thoroughly enjoy their tea, games and prizes, the last being presented by Miss Vaughan.

We had very fine weather for the Peace celebrations on July 19th. The village was very gay with many flags. The programme for the day included sports, tea and medals (presented by Miss Vaughan) for the children, and for the parisioners generally tea, sports, hat trimming for men, and dancing. All took place in a field kindly lent by Mr. R. Berryman, of Treveglos. All went brightly and smoothly, and we had a most enjoyable and successful Peace celebration. At a Parish Meeting in the School Room on July 22nd to receive a statement of the celebration accounts, and to decide to what object the balance left should be given, it was decided to give the balance, £8 14s. 3d., to S. Dunstan's Home for Blinded Soldiers and Sailors.

BURIAL.—July 7th, Thomas Millie Dow, aged 70 years.

64. Items of local news: Zennor boys in the War, and Thanksgiving for Peace.

65. An outing to Land's End, 1914. Standing, L-R: Parson Vaughan, Mr Edwards, Mr White, Stanley Hocking, Arthur Berryman, Annie Quick Thomas (feather in hat), Miss Marshall (school teacher), Miss Vaughan. Middle row includes, L-R, Mabel Hocking, Alfred John Curnow, Elizabeth Edwards. Group on rock includes, front, Elizabeth and Janey Berryman; behind, L-R, Mabel Johns, Maurice Griggs, Johnnie Osborn. Right back, Berryman brother and sisters. Front row includes, left, Amy Griggs (later Mrs Paynter) and Katie Johns.

66. A Zennor choir outing to Fowey, 1928. p. 176. Seated, clockwise, from near end of table: Gordon Nankervis, Frank Edwards, Audrey Nankervis, Alice Paynter, Dick Stevens, Annie Quick Thomas, Mrs Harfoot, Reggie Woods. From near end of table, anti-clockwise: Katie Osborn, Mary Osborn, Katie Quick Thomas, Amy Paynter.

the poor rabbits were trapped inside. The hunter had to extricate the rabbits and give them a blow on the back of the head to kill them. The ferret was located by the sound of his tinkling bell and put back in his little bag to await further hunting forays.

Woodcock, snipe, wild duck and pigeons were also shot. They were taken home, plucked, trussed and put in the pot. Nothing was killed that couldn't be eaten, except foxes which were a menace to poultry and young lambs.

Many farmers rode after the Western Hunt. My father rode Mars to hounds; as soon as he reached the top of Kerrow Hill there was no holding him and he was off at a gallop. Others went hare coursing with greyhounds and lurchers.

On special occasions such as a Jubilee or the Coronation, a sports day was organised. We sisters and our friends bought our first pair of shorts for one such occasion, which was very daring! There were races for all ages: running, three-legged, wheelbarrow and sack races, sheaf pitching and all the usual paraphernalia of sports events.

There were various committees in the parish, and the entertainment committee organised most of the activities in the schoolroom.

Shrove Tuesday was known as Rogue's Day, when all sorts of mischief was done, such as altering ploughs, unhitching gates and hiding horses. My father recalled one Rogue's Day when a crowd of boys, including Sam Nankervis and William Henry Hocking, whitewashed every window in the village.

There were pubs in abundance in the late nineteenth century. As well as the Tinners' Arms and Gurnard's Head Hotel in the parish, there was one in Towednack Churchtown, one 'down' Newmill, two in Morvah, one of which was called the Star Inn, and two pubs in Nancledra. One of the houses in the little row going down from Nancledra chapel and on the same side, was a pub. Two old Zennor crones, very partial to a drop of gin, regularly crept into the Tinners' Arms kitchen with a teapot, had it filled with gin and returned home with their well-camouflaged beverage, to enjoy it in secret. To be seen drinking in a pub was unthinkable to them.

In the early days of this century, men went out far more often than the women, and many mothers of small children rarely left their homes.

Summers

DURING the summer months many farmers' wives took in paying guests, some of whom might stay several weeks, becoming very much part of the household. The journey by train and pony and trap, or later taxi, to this far-off corner of Britain was a lengthy one. In general the visitors used the bedrooms and parlour; the farmer and his family if necessary slept in the barn. The visitors occupied themselves by rambling over cliff and moor, and bathing in the coves, while many considered it a great treat to help with chores on the farm. The farmer's wife provided them with all meals; good home-produced and home-made fare: scones, cakes – saffron and heavy cake in particular, tarts filled with apples or blackberries fresh from the hedgerow, all eaten with lashings of butter and Cornish clotted cream from the Guernsey cows, and rich, yellow, creamy milk by the jugful. Roast chicken and boiled fowl, which had to be killed, plucked and trussed before putting into the pot, were served with swedes, cabbage, carrots, onions and potatoes, all grown in a nearby field, followed by creamy rice pudding and stewed fruit or custard and tart washed down with cups of tea. Large Cornish pasties, eaten with great relish, were made from chopped beef, preferably skirt, and finely chipped potatoes, swedes and onions, not forgetting the salt. The mixture was enclosed in pastry cases, crimped down one side, with a hole on the top through which three teaspoons of water were added, then baked in a hot oven for a good hour. Sugary tea was always drunk when eating pasties. High teas of poached, boiled or fried eggs, rich, dark-yolked and freshly gathered from the nest, were eaten with platefuls of thin slices of white bread and butter. A cupful of cocoa at bedtime often ended these gastronomic delights.

Many families and their guests became lifelong friends.

Summers at Tremedda meant hordes of visitors. During the school holidays these were mainly Kennedys, Aunt Mary, Uncle George and the boys: John, Horas, Sandy, Gilbert and Charlie, plus a bevy of helpers and eccentric friends. Many varied and diverse things came with the Kennedy family; kitchen equipment essential to Aunt Mary such as a coffee percolator, the intricacies of which only she could fathom, a Swiss vegetable shredder to help prepare all the healthy raw vegetables fed to the boys and a porridge and fish steamer; also a Dunlopillo mattress to ease my aunt's rheumaticky joints, musical instruments, and mumps, chickenpox and whooping cough. When one of the last three raged, Uncle George could be heard muttering "Tremedda is the most unhealthy place this side of the Gold Coast".

Granny Dow often came out from Talland for a month or so, bringing Susan her Irish cook and Pietro her Italian butler. Beds of all descriptions were found, many made from wreck wood by the boys who were enthusiastic carpenters. All rooms bulged with beds; six in the far loft for boys, one in a curtained-off corner of the loft for Pietro, four in the loggia for girls and more in the loggia bedroom. The house was reserved for the more important grown-ups. Occasionally a tent had to be erected on the washing lawn when numbers were too great.

We girls eagerly awaited the day when it was finally decided we could move into our summer sleeping quarters in the loggia. During stormy weather wooden-framed hessian-covered shutters were fixed in the windows to prevent the rain pelting onto the beds and a similar half-gate placed in the doorway to stop muddy dogs jumping onto beds. This did not deter the pussies, however. Many excitements went with this bedroom open to the elements, where we could lie and gaze at the stars. The boys often squeezed through to reach their bedroom beyond, too lazy to use the yard steps, maybe tipping us out of bed or dropping a spider on our pillow. At dusk a succession of bats flew continually in at the window, out of the door, in at the door and out of the window. Occasionally a dog fight occurred at the end of the beds and worst of all, in the dead of night, cats sometimes brought their newly caught prey under our beds, the poor creature, rabbit or whatever, still kicking and squealing in its death throes.

We felt very snug in our beds when gales blew and rain came lashing down.

We all had various jobs to do; feeding calves and hens and making our own beds. Every now and then Granny Dow took pity on us and went round making all our beds properly. Each day two of us were allotted for vegetable duty. This meant going out into the field where we dug potatoes, pulled up carrots or picked large quantities of peas or beans. These were carried to the garden where, sitting on the stone steps leading up to the loggia we proceeded to peel, scrape or shell, with the aid of large white enamel pans of cold water.

Meals at Tremedda were usually eaten in the kitchen or little sitting-room, or both. There were various other eating places according to the season. If large numbers were to be fed the nursery was used, where two tables were put together. During the summer we often ate in the glasshouse or outside in the top orchard. When our mother felt hot and bothered from the *mêlée* of cooking, children, etc., she took her dinner out into the back orchard, sat on the steps opposite the glasshouse door and ate it in peace and solitude. We had various suppertime haunts, for a fairly portable meal of a large basin of soup with chunks of brown bread in it or a mugful of meal drink and some fruit. My mother's soups were something to remember; there was always a potful standing on the stove. They were made with vegetables fresh from the garden or field, stock from boiled fowl or bones and plenty of barley and lentils. All left-overs, sweet and savoury, went into the pot and all vegetable water was saved for soup. Sometimes it was thick, creamy potato soup with onions, leeks and rich Guernsey milk. These were real soups; nothing ever came out of tins. Meal drink – Scottish fare – was made by pouring boiling milk onto a spoonful of oatmeal and a pinch of salt and stirring well. Oatmeal was bought by the sackful from the Lothians in Scotland.

A favourite supper spot, for children only, was reached by climbing out of the kitchen window to sit on the garage roof, where we were joined by the cats. Sometimes we sat on top of the barn steps, with Fairy and Tweed in attendance, to watch the sun setting below the Atlantic. This it often did in great splendour, emitting brilliant rays of orange and red. A pathway of shining ripples over the sea reflected these colours as the sun turned from yellow to orange and then red, growing in size by the minute, until it finally disappeared below the horizon. When clouds were about they floated in the sky like wisps of pink cotton wool or, if stormier, their fantastic shapes looked large and black, edged with a bright scarlet rim; indeed a grand panorama to watch while supping.

On looking back it seems the weather in those summers was pretty good, although I think one's memory retains more easily the good parts rather than the irksome ones. All jobs possible were performed in the garden and we had a table set out in the top orchard for meals. We girls were usually attired in a pair of pants only while the boys wore minute red bathing trunks made from two triangular pieces of material joined at the points and kept up with elastic. We often went about barefoot, and one summer I remember the soles of my feet became so tough I could walk on thistles without feeling them. We were frequently dispatched down the cliff where we bathed in the rock pools with a grown-up in attendance. Picnics were numerous; down the cliffs, up the hill, on long treks to Trevail and Boatcove, or when hordes stuffed into a couple of old cars, with the canvas hoods folded back to make more room, and were then driven to Porthcurno or Treen beach. An abundance of lettuce and tomatoes, with home-made salad dressing, and potatoes either baked in the oven or boiled in sea water in a billycan over a driftwood fire were eaten with cold chicken and sausages, with dried bananas and raisins to finish off the meal; these were all Aunt Mary's picnic standbys. Not content with merely food to eat, we were also fed music when Uncle George was present, part of the picnic equipment being musical scores and Aunt Mary's clarinet, with which she accompanied us. We all had to join in, and were given various soprano, alto, tenor and bass parts to learn. A variety of songs were chosen, negro spirituals, church anthems, 'Where the Bee sucks, there suck I' from Shakespeare, 'Cherry Ripe' and various rounds like 'Frère Jacques' and 'London's Burning'. Uncle George was quite a hard taskmaster and bits of each song were sung over and over again until quite correct. I know not what local cliff-top inhabitants such as rabbits, foxes and mice, thought had descended upon their homes.

Uncle George was rather a remote background figure to us children, chuckling at the antics of all and sundry but keeping well out of the way

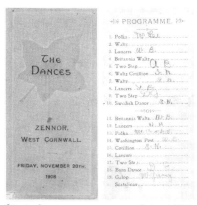

68. A dance programme of the 1930s.
p. 181

67. A Zennor soldier of the First
World War: Maurice Griggs. p. 174

69. 'Picnics were numerous'. p. 180. L-R: The Kennedy and Griggs families on
top of Tremedda Hill. Front, L-R: Maurice Griggs, Robina Griggs, Granny Dow,
Mary Kennedy, Miss Mullen, John and Charlie Kennedy. Middle, L-R: Cluny
(dog), Alison and Ellen Griggs, Horace and Gilbert Kennedy. Back, L-R: Elsie
Griggs, Sandy Kennedy, Flora Griggs.

of commotion and activity unless dragged in by Aunt Mary to take part. The strains of Bach wafted out of the nursery windows where he played the piano for hours on end, his feet working imaginary organ pedals on the floor. He played the organ in many Cornish churches, his favourites being St Ives Catholic Church and Truro Cathedral. While not occupied with his musical interests, he might be found on the lawn coaching his sons in Latin, tucked away in his bedroom writing, or having long and earnest conversations with his many learned and often, to our minds, rather odd friends. Being of a rather tubby build, every so often he was forced by Aunt Mary to undergo a period of strict dieting; one of these diets consisted only of oranges and milk, when the fat would roll off him. He took great pride in the large splash he made when diving into the gully, but the edge was taken off this after one of his dieting bouts. Uncle George was oblivious to such mundane things as clothes and often wore odd socks, a pair of old sand-shoes tied up with string and a pair of tobacco-stained baggy corduroy trousers.

Every so often the grown-ups would have a dressing-up supper party when they all dressed up either as someone in the household or someone well known to them all. We would creep down in our nighties to spy on the proceedings. One very funny example was Aunt Mary dressed up as Pietro. She donned one of his dark blue cotton suits, gave herself a neat moustache and then proceeded to act the part, handing around the vegetables, taking away the empty plates, etc. and addressing each diner in Pietro's very Italian English amidst much laughter. Pietro himself hovered smiling in the background, quite nonplussed as to what his part should be.

Guests of the Kennedys often came to Tremedda. Two of these were Eve Myers, a tall willowy girl, and her friend Diana Matthias. They slept in the loggia room where one night they had such a quarrel that Eve went to spend the rest of the night on the hay in the Dutch barn. In the middle of the night she came racing into the house, screaming, because creepy crawlies had crept into her ears. Madame Vandervelt, known as Lala, the English widow of a Belgian Prime Minister, was extremely odd. She liked to put on a slightly foreign accent and had extraordinary eyes; each one seemed to be looking in a different direction, which was most disconcerting when she talked to you. She had dyed bright red hair, wore much make-up and dressed in bright red trousers, not at all the thing for an elderly lady in those days. All in all, I think she had been quite a scarlet woman in her day. Kaftal, a Russian, came for a short stay; purportedly an excellent cook, he took a whole week to cook a dish of jugged hare with much preparation and wine. Monsieur Sarasie came the summer of the whooping cough epidemic and spent much of his time shouting to the children, "Go away whoopee cough, go away whoopee cough".

Various helpers joined the throng. Nellie McGee from Donegal, a bright young Irish girl who, given the chance, would sing and dance half the night. Zoe and Annemarie came from Switzerland, eager to learn the English language. Lizzie Fitchet, my mother's old nurse from Aberdeen, was a great favourite with the young. She was an endearing old soul, very gentle, always laughing and with an endless repertoire of stories for small folk. 'Jack and his big boots' was a favourite. Lizzie dressed in a long brown cotton dress with a tight-fitting bodice, long sleeves and a high neckline, very neat and trim. Her hair was fashioned in a bun on top of her head and she wore gold-rimmed spectacles, all in all very Edwardian looking. As she advanced in years, when she was staying, one would find in the house oddities such as lamps filled with hot water or hot water bottles filled with paraffin. She thought my mother's friend Mrs Lloyd was a tinker, because she wore large gold earrings and a red scarf on her head.

Katherine Cockerell, sister of Sir Christopher Cockerell the inventor of the hovercraft, often came to help on the farm and in the house. At the age of sixteen Katherine spent some time nursing her paralysed mother and then needed a complete change. Mrs Arnold Forster brought her to Tremedda, where she spent a year learning to cook, make gravy, milk cows, make butter, plant cabbages, look after children, and in fact all the practical jobs of house and farm. She adored every minute of it. She smocked and embroidered beautiful garments for the family and taught us to sew. She kept a chart for us girls colouring in one square for each child daily; blue denoted good behaviour, yellow fair and green bad. This ploy helped Katherine when putting us to bed as we had a sneaking desire to attain blue squares which earned us the added bonus of being read a story from *Milly Molly Mandy*.

As well as the Kennedy tribe and various friends and relations, when rooms were vacant my mother took in paying guests.

One of our favourite p.gs. was Mrs Ashford Hodges, later known to us as Aunt Nitza. She was a short, stoutish Austrian lady with a ten-year-old son Antony. Very shortly after their first arrival at the farm, Antony was lost. He was found, much to everyone's consternation, running across the roof tops. Mrs Hodges was a great talker and entertained us with many amusing tales. She always used superlatives; things were either exquisite, magnificent, formidable or terrible, atrocious or horrific. She painted cupboards, just polished with lovely beeswax and turpentine, with paraffin in case her fur coats got moths in them. She was a marvellous pianist and spent hours playing the piano, often giving us a concert of Mozart, Beethoven, Bach or whatever we fancied, and she also gave us piano lessons. When living in Egypt she gave piano lessons to one of the Egyptian royal family. Owing to the nature of her husband's work in that country, she spent many hours travelling by train so she had a model keyboard made with no sound which she placed on her knee to practise on while sitting in the train. Her husband died while abroad. We all liked Antony. He could never be found at bedtime, and his mother would search the farm buildings shouting "Antonee, Antonee," asking everyone within earshot "Where is that terrible boy?" Antony was very adept with his hands. In later years this flair helped him become a skilful bone surgeon. One of his hobbies was collecting butterflies, of which he had a large collection from all over Europe. An occupation he loved at Tremedda when darkness fell was to dash into the piggery or flour house with a light; any poor rat or mouse which might be visible on the beams or elsewhere would be lashed to the ground with a horse whip or caught in his butterfly net. He would then take the unfortunate creatures to the cows' drinking trough and drown them.

The Hodges became very good friends and came to stay regularly for many years.

Mr and Mrs Marshall Smith, a very correct elderly couple, came every spring. Mr Smith was head of Trinity House. He was tall, with a large hooked nose and rather pompous; we were very much in awe of him. Mrs Smith was very nice; a charming lady. They brought cases of Alicante wine with them which were stored in the cupboard under the stairs. My mother was often invited into the sitting-room after their evening meal for a glass of wine and a talk. The Smiths were great mountaineers and had undertaken several big climbs in the Alps. They dressed the part while trekking on cliff and moorland, wearing climbing boots, thick socks, waterproof trousers and jackets, and carrying walking sticks. We had to try to be on our best behaviour during the Smiths' stay, at the end of which my mother would be presented with the remaining bottles of Alicante.

Honour Davy and Elizabeth Raverat were two musical guests. Honour played the 'cello and Elizabeth was a singer. The sound of scales, both vocal and instrumental, used to come wafting out of the loft where they spent hours practising. Honour's sister Ursula also came as a p.g., accompanied by her large family of small children, the grandchildren of Sir Stafford Cripps, the Labour cabinet minister.

Anne Sinclair, daughter of Sir Archibald Sinclair, once a Liberal Minister for Aviation, came to learn something of the practical side of farming in order to help on her father's estate at Thurso Castle in Caithness. Anne fascinated us by smoking a foot-long pipe.

Although my mother never appeared to get flustered, when the last visitor had departed and we were all back in our winter quarters, she must have heaved a sigh of relief.

Playgrounds

APART from organised entertainment, the pleasures to be had from this marvellous countryside were boundless, especially for nature lovers and children. I daresay some of the old men looked on it only as a rough and stormy terrain which they had to try and tame with horse and plough, but the sight of marvellous sunsets over the ocean, a glimpse of fox cubs playing in the sun or old Brock wandering along a hidden path, and the gardens of wild flowers in spring, were all theirs to enjoy.

Playgrounds for us children were numerous. We roamed the fields, hill, cliff and sea-shore and when raining, the farm buildings provided shelter for divers pursuits.

Around the farmstead we performed gymastics in the heifers' house, played shops in the flour house, rough and tumble in the hay house, and innumerable games in the loft, including indoor cricket when the Kennedy cousins – five boys – were staying with us. The main aim for me and my sisters, when roped in to play cricket, was to avoid a hit on the shins or knuckles by the hard cricket ball; if the ball came in contact with the bat, this was more good fortune than good judgement. Panes of glass in the round loft windows were frequently broken during these games. During fine weather, cricket playing was transferred to a field.

Kick the Can was a favourite garden game, when an old tin can was placed on the path near the front door, someone was chosen as 'he' and the rest went off to hide. The child who was 'he' had to search for the hidden children, and if he saw one, the hider's name was called out and he had to go and stand by the can as prisoner. The aim of the hiders was to sneak up unseen and kick the can. If any one of them managed to do this, any prisoner could escape and rush off to hide anew. When all the hiders had become prisoners, a new 'he' was chosen.

The cider trough, when filled with water, became a pool to bathe in or a sea for toy boats. The Kennedys produced little white oblongs of what was known to us as meter which, when clipped onto the back of a little boat, propelled it along as if by magic, but actually by a chemical reaction between meter (sodium carbide) and water.

The Osborns' little thatched pigs' crow at the bottom of their yard became for us a minute theatre where we made up and acted plays. The long iron bar of the Osborn's horse whim for the barn thresher, on its circular platform, could still be pushed round and round in circles, the pusher giving rides to all who sat on it. Our neighbour's daughter Mary often took part in these games with us.

The hill, or Tremedda Carn, rising eight hundred feet above sea level behind the farm, was one of our winter playgrounds. Every inch of the

71. Paring vegetables on the loggia steps. p. 179. Front, L-R: Ellen and Flora. Back, L-R: Little Dan and Alison.

70. Sylvia and Maggie Carlyon sitting on the old cider press. p. 185

72. Elsie Griggs and her mother Mrs Dow sewing at Tremedda.

path up the hill was known to us. On the lower slopes bracken, brambles and gorse had to be pushed aside as they tried to claim the path. As one ascended, the vegetation gradually became more sparse and shorter and more rocks appeared. If, when halfway up, the right hand fork was chosen one came to a rocky outcrop and Hudson's Rock. The climb up and over these rocks was quite a feat for small arms and legs, but gave one a sense of achievement, so this path was usually chosen. On reaching the summit, magnificent views held the eye. We pranced around the rocks like goats, then ran the downward journey that gave one the feeling of flying through the air, never stumbling or stopping until the road was reached. Dogs always accompanied us on these jaunts, scenting out rabbits or with ears cocked and tails flying in the wind, chasing birds.

Halfway up the hillside is a large granite rock, the top of which is shaped like a saucer. Here we often built a fire, starting it off with dead bracken and furze prickles, then adding furze stogs. When a nice red hot glow formed in the centre of the fire, potatoes, ready scrubbed, were poked into the embers. When cooked, the potatoes were speared with pointed sticks and eaten, blackening our faces with charcoal. We were always most careful to extinguish our bonfires before returning home. It was a great crime to set the hill or cliff on fire through carelessness. My father sometimes burnt patches to allow more grass to grow. This was undertaken in February or March, great care being taken to keep the fire under control.

Hide-and-seek was a favourite game to play on the hill during the autumn, when patches of ferns nearly as high as oneself afforded good hiding cover. It was always a thrill to come across the little stone house built into the hillside, with its wooden door securely padlocked. Sticks of dynamite for blasting were stored here when the quarries were worked. We always wondered if this little house still contained these dangerous sticks or whether perhaps pixies and elves had taken over.

There were two old quarries on the hillside; John White's Quarry and Jimmy Thomas's Quarry. The latter was often used as a site for supper picnics, as the quarry provided large stony areas suitable for a bonfire, and slabs of cut granite made admirable tables and chairs. The evening would be carefully chosen, dry weather and moonlight being the ideal. We walked to the quarry warmly clad, helping to carry the food and cooking pots. The boys collected sticks for the fire while we helped prepare the food. Sausages and onions were fried in a large, black, iron frying pan, which was balanced on stones over the fire, and these were eaten with thick slices of bread-and-butter. Water, boiled in a billycan, made steaming hot mugs of cocoa to wash down slabs of saffron cake, and an apple or banana rounded off the meal. The evening usually ended with word games and singing, especially if our cousins were present. Rounds such as 'London's Burning' and 'Frère Jacques' were great favourites. The quarry had the added bonus of echoes that bounced off the sheer granite cliffs, and pools containing frogs' eggs and tadpoles when in season. Finally, everything was stowed away in baskets, including every scrap of rubbish, the fire was extinguished and we all made our way, weary but very contented, home to bed.

Springtime was the best flower season on the cliffs, and no garden could excel in beauty the patches of sunny primroses, the tiny hidden violets, golden celandine, pin-cushion clumps of sea pinks of rosy hues, sea campions, gowans (large white daisy flowers), and blue seas of pale scillas. All these and hundreds more were followed by bluebells, campions, stitchwort and foxgloves. These flowery profusions grew between patches of bright golden gorse and the bell and ling heathers.

We used to picnic by a large rock adjoining the Cliff Stitch, eating large pasties fresh from the oven, at Jack's Lookout, on Tregarthen Point, or on the rocks by the sea where good driftwood fires could be easily kindled and potatoes boiled in sea water. Then we filled our baskets with bunches of whatever we fancied, tying each bunch with long strands of old grass. Foxglove flowers decorated our hands, a flower on each finger tip, honey was sucked from honeysuckle and the primrose flower, and little houses were fashioned from bracken stalks thatched with heather.

Sometimes we walked across the cliffs to Wicca Pool. A sheltered little valley with a stream rushing seawards, where yellow iris and beautiful ferns grew, afforded us a sheltered spot to sit and watch the fulmar petrels nesting on little ledges on the sheer cliffs. The sea in Wicca Pool is very deep, and sometimes a school of porpoises came rolling by, chasing a shoal of mackerel, or on rare occasions several gigantic, basking sharks, with head, fins and tail showing above the water, might be seen lazing in the sunshine.

During the summer months, the sea-shore was our playground. We spent many happy days on the rocks and could run barefoot over them like goats. There were fascinating pools, each with its own special use and name. The small pools were for small children to bathe in, and grown-ups if the tide was in and the sea rough. We usually sat and ate our picnic here, as conveniently placed shelves of rock made good seating. These pools contained any number of treasures. A variety of seaweeds in greens, browns, yellows, pinks and reds grew here; the soft green seaweed we used as a sponge. There were sea anemones, limpets, barnacles, various little shells in crevices and of course shrimps and mulleys (Blennys) which we used to try to catch – the shrimps in nets and cups and the mulleys on baited, bent pins, attached to a piece of cotton. The Horseshoe Pool was where we all learned to swim. Aunt Mary threw mussels at us until we were forced to jump into the deep end, where we swam a few desperate strokes until our feet touched the bottom. Our cousins had much more terrifying swimming lessons. Aunt Mary took them out in a boat in St Ives Bay and threw them overboard. It was sink or swim for them. However, they got their own back when older by diving into rough seas and in turn terrifying their mother.

The gully was for competent, brave swimmers. It was part of the open sea, a deep inlet between rocks with a sandy bottom where we could dig when the tide was very low. When the tide came in the waves grew bigger as they were forced into this narrow channel. At times someone had to stand holding a rope with a blown up motor tyre attached to one end; this was thrown into the sea to help swimmers get out onto the rocks after diving in.

There were various other named pools of less importance: the Rough Sunday Pool, where our infrequent dips were very exciting as waves came crashing onto the rocks on the seaward side; Zoe's Pool, a tiny bay open to the sea where you could float about on small wavelets during calm weather; and Mr Nightingale's Pool, which was never used for bathing as it was full of seaweed and nooks and crannies where crabs and other unseen creatures might be lurking.

We always visited the little channel where the wreck wood and flotsam and jetsam were washed in. No end of surprises were found: a French fisherman's wooden sabot, strings of corks, green glass floats and maybe an oar. Here we collected material for toy boats. Often we found a small piece of cork with a hole in the middle, pushed a stick through the hole as a mast and stuck one or two seagull's feathers into the cork, to make a beautiful little boat, or so we thought.

A little further along the rocks, towards Tregerthen Point, was the pebble beach. The games played in this area were quite different. One could either search for fascinating pebbles, when sometimes an agate was found, or build a little pebble tower on a rock and take turns throwing stones at it to try to knock it over. A tin can floating in the sea also made a good target for stone throwers. A gigantic boulder, twenty feet high or so at one end of the pebble beach, had to be scaled. It had an iron ring cemented into its topmost surface, once used in connection with a pulley for hoisting wreckage onto the cliff above. This was used when a coal boat was wrecked here.

A secret underwater garden could be found at low tide between the Horseshoe Pool and the pebble beach. A little pool in the flatter rocks had two steps down into it, a path across the middle and two steps up the other side.

Around the half-tide mark, the rocks were blue with mussels, and one walked among these with care, owing to their sharp-edged shells. Occasionally some were collected to add flavour to a risotto.

After these occupations, we collected our bathing gear and a piece of wreck wood each and climbed the cliff back to the farm, having a rest on the way at Jack's Lookout. Sometimes we went along the cliff to Trevail, where a large natural swimming pool, lying between rocks, was uncovered at low tide. This was Cap'n Billy's Pool, where cowries and many other pretty shells were found in the coarse sand, and seals abounded. The Carracks, a large rocky island offshore, afforded them a safe haven. They could be seen swimming about, eyeing us with curiosity, their dog-like heads bobbing about like floats, or sunning themselves on some remote sea-washed rock.

Once a year, during the summer holidays, an expeditionary force, armed with picnics and stout shoes, set out for Carn Galva, a large very rocky hill with two summits overlooking the coast road to Land's End. This expedition was organised mainly by the Kennedys and the Arnold Fosters from Eagle's Nest. Friends and relations were all invited. Having driven to the bottom of the hill and climbed the first peak, a game of Friends and Enemies became the order of the day. The children were divided into two groups, each one encamped on a summit. These groups were subdivided into attackers and defenders. The aim of the game was that the attackers should traverse the hill-top between summits and reach the opposing camp without being caught by a defender from the opposite side. This was carried out with much cunning, and entailed darting from boulder to boulder; crawling silently through brambles, gorse, ferns, and heather; and arriving with scratched and bloody legs. If caught, loud shouts and whoops were heard and the attacker was taken prisoner. Finally, when all the attackers had either reached their goal or been taken prisoner, tally was taken and the camp with the most successful attackers was declared the winner. At this point a mad rush to the picnic baskets ensued, where the grown-ups sat idly chatting, applying plasters to injuries, or presiding as judges over disputes that had arisen. When quite replete, we raced down the boulder strewn hill-side to be driven back to our homes.

Flora and Fauna

THE countryside in Zennor has a rich and varied flora. The first spring flowers to appear are the tiny blue violets in sheltered nooks on the cliff, closely followed by the primrose, a great favourite, and gathered by the bunch for little vases in the house. Small thickets of blackthorn, leaning away from the icy winds, flaunted their lacey covering of tiny white flowers. As spring and summer progressed, a riot of sea pinks, sky-blue scillas, sea campion, stitchwort, celandine, purple scabious and the large gowans or marguerites all appeared on the cliffs in great profusion, sheltered by the French gorse which formed patches of pure gold.

Around Easter-time parts of the cliff and crofts were covered in a blue haze of bluebells; flowering amongst these were pink campions, cranesbill, the rusty red sorrel and the cow parsley family. Flowers giving great delight were the white sheets of wild anemone, delicately tinged with pale pink or blue. These grew in the crofts and on lower slopes of the hills. The tiny white wood sorrel, its petals veined with green, could be found in hidden corners in the undergrowth. Pale blue forget-me-nots and pink cuckoo flowers grew amongst the rushes on boggy ground. Fields were often white with daisies or yellow with buttercups and dandelions; the clovers were of more subtle colours that blended into the background. The tiny scarlet pimpernel, blue speedwell and yellow crowsfoot grew among the short grasses. Foxgloves marched up and down the hillsides and along the hedgerows. As summer progressed, much of this colourful panorama was overtaken by the bracken, clothing everything in a rather dull green.

It was the turn of the higher moors to excel in beauty in late summer and autumn, when the heathers and short Cornish gorse flowered together. Heathers were found from the cliff edge to the hill-tops: the dark purple bell heather, the pink to lilac ling heather and also on the moors, the Lizard or cross-leaved heath in many shades. Among this riot of gorse and heather could be found the tiny milkwort, varying in shade from the brightest gentian blue to almost white, the little golden faces of tormentilla, the crawling ladies' bedstraw, the blue pompoms of sheepsbit and if you knew where to look, the occasional patch of pink orchids. On the higher moors large patches of pale dried grasses rippled in the wind, like water. The colour of the bracken improved immensely during autumn and winter, turning a rich rusty brown with here and there a bright yellow fern. The granite rocks were well clothed in lichens, mainly greeny greys and sometimes bright yellow. Some were flat with frilly edges clinging to the rock, others soft and fuzzy. A pretty little stonecrop, with a mass of pale pink stars, grew wherever it could get a foothold in a rock crevice. Among many of the flora that crowded the hedgerows were the greeny-yellow spikes of the pennywort with its round fleshy leaves. Entanglements of brambles, honeysuckle, vetches and the wild rose cropped up frequently and fronds of many varieties of ferns including the Royal fern, polypody and hart's-tongue, enhanced the background of these floral displays.

The variety of wild flowers is so great in these parts, I am sure I have omitted more than I have mentioned.

The animal inhabitants of the area are mainly the slinky red fox, the stuggy badger with his distinctive black and white striped face and the rabbit, providing food for man and beast alike. Fox and badger setts were found on cliff and hill. There has been an inhabited badger sett in Tremedda Lane ever since I can remember and doubtless long before that. In spring the tell-tale trails of newly-dug rab and bits of dried grass and bracken surrounding their holes denoted the badgers nursery preparations. Hares were fairly numerous during the first half of the century. Both stoat and weasel, with their long furry bodies, slithered through the undergrowth searching for food, sometimes hypnotising their prey. They were fierce fighters, the scream of a rabbit often denoting their route through the ferns. The usual *mélange* of furry creatures: the field mouse, harvest mouse, long-nosed shrew, vole and mole and the prickly hedgehog, all had homes in holes and tunnels, and the sleek adder, with its venomous bite, often lay sunbathing on a warm rock or coiled in some rocky hole. Around and in the ponds and streams were newts, frogs and toads; trout could be caught by delicately tickling their tummies with a finger or dropping a baited hook on the end of a long white horse hair into the water. Slithery eels also come up the larger streams.

Although few trees grew here, the bird population was large and varied. I am no ornithologist so will only mention the ones I knew and liked. The usual sparrows, blackbirds, thrushes, robins and tits haunted the garden and bushy spots. Further afield were the crows, rooks, gulls and magpies. The glossy, metallic-hued, garrulous starlings congregated in noisy throngs during autumn and winter. Up on the moors, during spring and summer, the delightful song of the lark could be heard trilling on high as the tiny speck of a bird hovered in the heavens. Wee brown bouncing birds, whinchats I believe, danced up and down over the gorse bushes as though on springs and the kestrel wheeling overhead or hanging motionless in the sky scanning the ground for prey caught one's attention. It was always a treat to catch a glimpse of the tiny shy wren, a row of pretty yellow-suited yellowhammers sitting on the telegraph wires or the neat little water-wagtail, dressed in black, white and grey, wading in the stream, dipping and flipping his tail up and down as he walked. Goldfinch and chaffinch searched busily around garden and hedges for seeds and a woodpecker often tap-tapped on the trunk of the old ash tree. At dusk bats, having spent the day in some dark corner, came whirring round the buildings. We were always slightly frightened of these creatures, having been told the old wives' tale that if bats became entangled in your hair you would never get them out. During the night the hooting of owls added to the eerie call of the fox. Gulls wheeled in the air and wailed and followed the plough, coming inland by the hundred when a storm threatened.

The arrival of the first migrant birds was a great thrill. One always wanted to be the first to hear the cuckoo; as long as he arrived before Towednack Feast, the feast could take place. Swallows arrived in hordes, their twittering heard everywhere. They built their mud nests up on the beams and ledges in the farm buildings. While milking the cows, one could watch them sitting demurely on their nests or flying endlessly to and fro, carrying insects to their young. The swallows always seemed tremendously busy, I suppose because they had only a short while in which to carry out their social rounds and raise a family before returning south. When the time came, crowds of them sat in rows on the telegraph wires in preparation for taking off on their long flight to Africa.

The winter migrants came as soon as cold weather set in. Woodcock and snipe settled in wet boggy patches; the long-legged, long-billed curlew, with its haunting cry, and the black and white lapwing, with its jaunty head feathers, settled in flocks in the fields. If the country further north was caught in an icy grip, birds including plover and redwing, known locally as greybirds or janshewals, flocked by the thousand to the kinder climate of the south west. The greybirds fluffed out their feathers to keep warm, and the folk here used to say to someone freezing with the cold, "You're humped up like a janshewal".

Down by the seashore gulls swooped over wave and rock or enjoyed themselves floating on wavelets, black cormorants stood like statues on rocky islets, with wings outstretched to dry after diving underwater for a tasty bit of fish, and flocks of kittiwakes or oystercatchers flew by, skimming the tops of the waves. Large gannets were a fine sight when feeding, as they plummeted from on high straight into the sea with a splash. Terns, guillemots, razorbills, shags, puffins; all might be seen skimming past, resting on the rocks or fishing, some on their way to nesting sites on the Scilly Isles.

We sometimes went in search of rarer birds: the large buzzards that always nested on the same rocky ledges on the cliff edge, the fulmar petrels who came to Wicca Pool every spring from their life on the ocean, to raise their families on small rocky ledges on the sheer cliff face, a raven on a rock dining off some unfortunate rabbit, or a heron standing statue-like by the river in Foage valley.

There was always a wealth of bird life to watch around the farm and while walking the countryside.

Walks

MY mother was a great walker and most Sundays, if not picnicking by the sea-shore, we were taken on long rambles on cliff, hill or moors.

We clambered up the hill, to admire from the top the magnificent views of moorland, carn and cliff, and the flat coastal strip of neat, patchwork farmland and the ever changing sea and sky. Sometimes when the extraordinary bright light unique to these parts prevailed, the detail picked out and the brilliance of the colours seemed almost unreal, or should I say over-real. The sky was ever changing, with its hues of brilliant blues and magnificent cloud formations: forboding, mountainous and black; billowing, frothy and white; or delicate and lacy; sometimes hanging motionless, at others dashing across the heavens in a mad whirl. All these different skies were reflected in the sea, which wore a large range of colours, varying from dark navy to the brightest blues and most delicate pale, opalescent blues and greens, and all these shades might be flecked with snowy white as the wind whipped up the sea-horses. On overcast days the sea ranged from dark, steely greys to pale, pearly ones that often merged into the sky on an invisible horizon. At other times large, dark navy shadows raced across the sea as clouds scudded overhead. A small armchair fashioned in a rock with a heather cushion could always be found from which to sit and watch all this magnificence.

On days when mist enshrouded everything, it was a different world. On calm misty days, droplets of moisture hung in the air and on every plant; it all seemed very eerie, and rocks and bushes took on sinister shapes. When windy, the mists swirled about in all directions, completely disorientating the walker. It was easy to lose one's way on the downs when walking in thick mist. The sea mists came rolling up the valleys in great white billows, while the hill fogs descended, capping all the highlands, but often leaving the lowlands and cliffs below clear and sunny.

On windy days when gale force winds roared in from the Atlantic, howling and hissing, and snapping the very words out of one's mouth almost before one had time to utter them, making speech all but impossible when facing this onslaught, even breathing was difficult as the air rushed past one's nose in a mad whirl. We stood up unsteadily, unbuttoned our coats and held them out as sails, and were blown along like ships at sea.

From this rocky perch on a still day, the everyday noises from our farm below could be heard; dogs barking, voices calling to one another, the "cup, cup" of someone fetching in the cows to be milked, the rattle of buckets, the clink of an iron gate or the commands of a farmer to his horse while ploughing. From the village, the sound of church bells, the clatter of the pump or horses walking down the road to drink in the river might be heard. As well as these domestic sounds there were bird songs to listen to, differing according to the season: the joyous lark, the wail of a seagull, the honk, honk of a raven, the cuckoo, and many others; while in the background, to a greater or lesser degree according to the state of the sea, was the grand sound of Atlantic rollers crashing onto rocks.

From the top of the hill we continued inland until we reached the Zennor Cromlech, a large slab of granite weighing many tons, once supported on four granite uprights as a table but now lying aslant, as some of the supports had been moved; the burial ground of an ancient King or Chieftain. Dotted over these hills and moors are many reminders of very ancient and not-so-ancient man in the form of stone-hut circles indicative of stone-age man and the remains, left by the tin miners of the eighteenth and nineteenth centuries or maybe earlier, of their shafts, adits, engine houses and smoke stacks. We walked on from the cromlech to Eagle's Nest, passing on our way the squat ruins of an old mine engine-house, once the centre of a hive of industry on these gaunt now empty, windswept moorlands. Then back home we went, by way of Tregerthen.

Sometimes we walked along the field path to the ruined chapel in the valley between Tregerthen and Wicca. This roofless old building, with its large windows open to the elements and its ivy-clad walls, was an eerie spot. We crept stealthily in through the old porch, which was well protected by stout blackthorn bushes, in order to get a glimpse of the white owl which dwelt therein, sleeping by day in the thick ivy. On hearing us mortals, out he flew through a window. We read the names and initials scratched on the bare parts of plastered walls, trying to equate them with the families of Berryman, Hocking, Thomas, Quick, Nankervis, Osborn, Eddy and Hollow, all still familiar names in the parish. It was hard to visualise this ruin as a neat whitewashed room, with wooden benches full of devout worshippers saying their prayers, singing hymns and listening to their preacher, all walking to and from chapel, there being no roadway or lane leading to it; simply a footpath through the fields.

After a thorough inspection of the chapel, it was our wont to explore the tiny copse of sycamore, elder and blackthorn nearby, a favourite nesting place for birds. A small stream winding its way through the undergrowth was a great attraction. We sat on overhanging boughs watching the water gurgle on, or bared our feet and paddled, be it winter or summer.

Another Sunday walk was to Zennor Head. On the way we passed and climbed onto the Logan rock, which is in Churchtown fields. This gigantic rock was so exquisitely balanced, it could be rocked quite easily. We walked out along the headland as far as the Window Rock, a square hole framed in granite through which one gazed at the sea. Below and to the west was the long narrow spit of land jutting out into the sea known as the Horseback. To the east where the coastline ran inwards and then

73. The ruined chapel at Tregerthen.

74. Maurice Griggs in old age at W.H. Hudson's rock. p. 142

turned again, the little cove known as Boatcove sheltered in the curve. Even in rough weather large rollers always seemed to by-pass Boatcove, making it possible for people to keep one or two small fishing boats there, as they did many years ago.

During the month of September, we walked miles around the hedgerows, especially those of Tregerthen, gathering baskets full of blackberries and sloes. The blackberries were made into jam, jellies, tarts and fools and eaten raw, mashed with sugar and cream, and the sloes were used in the making of sloe gin. We sometimes went as far as Trevail or Foage valley on these blackberrying outings returning home tired, with purple dyed hands and tongue, and scratched legs, but nonetheless feeling very satisfied with our weighty baskets of fruit, weighing them on the scales to see who had picked the most.

I think we should consider ourselves really privileged to have spent our youth in such surroundings as these.

Flat iron – a cast-iron baking plate, p. 154

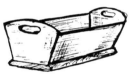

Wooden wash trov, p. 155

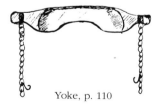

Yoke, p. 110

Washboard, p. 155

APPENDIX 1

Some Zennor Folk – and Where They Lived

DURING the first part of the twentieth century old Zennor families still farmed and worked the land. Most of them found husbands or wives in or near their own parish, resulting in the majority being related in one way or another and all knowing each other, rather like one large family. The following list is a rather complicated ramification of who lived where in the parish and was related to whom.

The coastal farms running from east to west:
The hamlet of Trendrine
1. *Trendrine Farm* – Early – The Eddy family. Later – son Cyril; wife and children Margaret, Rosalind and Phillip.
2. *The Chapel* – Workman Mr Trundel; wife and children Gonard and Joyce.
3. *The Cottage* – Let to visitors. Cecily Courtneidge and Jack Hulbert often stayed here.

Trevail Farm
Early – The Semmens family including son Harold. Old Mr Semmens was a sea captain. Later – Mathew James and Irene Osborne and children Jim, Alma and Clarice. Elsie Griggs (my mother) bought Trevail Farm in about 1930 for £1,500. She first offered the tenancy to John Osborn of Tremeadow but his wife Katie, being of a very sociable disposition, said she would have to put her best clothes in mothballs as it would be too far to walk to church and social occasions in the village, so the offer was declined. Later – John Loosemore (see below), wife Marjory and children.

Trevail Mill – smallholding.

Mr Loosemore, wife Bella (*née* Hollow from Trevega) and son John. Mr Loosemore grew daffodils in a quillet and exotic orchids in his greenhouse. The family took in visitors and cared for an old aunt (Hollow) who lived to 105.

Boscubban Farm

Early – Daniel and Naomi Hocking and sons Daniel and Lewis. Later – Jack Osborne (from Boswednack) and wife Dorothy (*née* Jelbert from Carnellow) and son. Later – brother Bernard, wife Betty (*née* Craze) and son Robert. Elsie Griggs's brother Hope Pilcher, from Scotland, bought Boscubban Farm in 1932.

Wicca Farm

Early – Care family. Later – Mr and Mrs Arthur Hollow and children Mary, Mathew, Arthur and Alfred. Later (1931) Sam and Sarah (*née* Hollow from Trevega) Nankervis (from Trewey) and children Arthur, Irene, Audrey (who taught in Zennor school), Bill (a great boxer), Gordon (Zennor church organist for over fifty years), Uny, who became a GI bride and went to live in America, and Jenny. Sam was often called upon to cure sick animals. Later – sons Arthur and Gordon took over the farm.

Tregerthen Farm

Early – Robert Mitchell and family. Later – old Mrs Hocking, her son William Henry, wife Mary Quick (*née* Eddy from Trendrine) and children Rita, Kitty, Jenny, Henry and John, also William Henry's two sisters Mary and Mabel who were very hard workers. Later – brother Stanley, wife Doris and children Olga, Desmond and Caroline and workman Arther Ost, a home boy. Sadly, Doris died when Caroline was born, and Mary and Mabel brought up the children. Stanley was musical and could play the accordion and fiddle. He was often invited to Tremedda to join a makeshift band for dances in the loft organised by the Kennedys. He was a great talker and knew well his one time neighbour D.H. Lawrence. Every Christmas Stanley visited the Osborns at Tremeadow to listen to the King's speech, having no wireless of his own. No doubt the Christmas cake, drinks and chat were an added enticement.

The hamlet of Tremedda

1. *Tremedda Farm* – Early – Paynter family. Later – the author's family Maurice and Elsie (*née* Pilcher) Griggs and daughters Ellen, Robina, Alison (the author) and Flora. Later, daughter Flora, her husband John Berryman (from Treen) and their daughters Lorna, Bridget and Tamsin.

2. *Tremeadow Farm* – Robert (Cap'n Bob) Osborn went there with his family in 1894 with his wife Mary (*née* Berryman from Treveglos Farm, sister to old Dicka) and children Robert, Tom, Johnnie and Annie.

Later – son Johnnie (often called Jackie) and wife Katie (*née* Johns from Treen) and daughter Mary. The Osborns' workmen were home boys and later Katie's nephew Bert James worked for them for seven years.

3. *Cottage* – Early – used as a dairy by the Osborns. Mary was not allowed to go upstairs here as the flooring was unsafe. Later – Elsie Griggs turned this building into a workman's cottage for Tremedda. Early – Cecil Thomas (son of the stonemason), wife Mary (*née* Craze) and son Jimmy etc. Later – Walter Palfrey and wife Lena (sister to Cecil). Later – Dan and Alice (*née* Paynter) Quick and children Little Dan and Rosalind.

Zennor Churchtown
Treveglos Farm
Early – old Dicka Berryman (lived all his life on the farm), wife Mary Elizabeth (niece of Ben Thomas of Treen) and children Dick, Willie, Alfie, Tom, David, Tilla (Matilda), Winnie, Jane, Aggie, Edie and Charity. They were thirteen around the table for years. Later – son Dick and wife Kate (previously Sowden, widow from the Post Office). Horses were the Berrymans' speciality.
The Glebe (or Churchland) and *the Row* (a neat row of six little cottages)
1. Early – Will's Will Berryman and sister Anne. They lived in the Row and farmed the Glebe land. Later – the Glebe land was combined with Treveglos.
2. *The Post Office* and Store in *the Row* – Early – Tom Berryman (brother to Will's Will), wife Katie and son Sidney. Tom milked cows at Tremedda and carried the milk home across seven or eight fields. Later – Kate Sowdon from Ireland and her husband ran the Post Office. At one time there was a little shop in the cottage second from the top, where you could buy four toffee apples for a penny. During the Second World War years the Row became rather ramshackle and, including Treveglos Farm, was bought by Alec Brooks, a wealthy businessman who built himself a house, Carn Cobba, in the Zennor Valley, near the site of Steven's Mill. He refurbished the cottages and let them out at low rents to genteel folk of small means.
Bos Cres or Granny Griggs' House
Elizabeth (Bessie) Griggs (*née* Eddy) and children Maurice and Amy and later grand-daughter Alice Paynter. Here in the middle of the village, Granny provided lodgings for many an illustrious visitor.
The Tinners Arms
Early – William Nankervis and family including sons Tom (later of Carnellow) and Sam (later of Wicca). Later – among others Mr and Mrs Harfoot and sons Percy and Harold and home boy Reggie Wood. Harold

was killed in the Second World War serving in HMS *Gloucester* in the Mediterranean. Mrs Harfoot played the church organ for many years with Reggie in the background working the organ pump.

Chy-an-Eglos (House by the Church)

Early – Tom and Sarah White and family. Tom was a capital singer and used to garden at Tremedda for my mother. Later – Mr and Mrs Kliskey and daughter Marie. Mr Kliskey was at one time gardener to Mr Arnold Forster, also a full-time coast-guard at Gurnards Head. Mrs Kliskey was a clever seamstress and made long, yellow dresses with little mob caps for us four sisters when we were bridesmaids at Alice Paynter's wedding. The wedding service was in Zennor church with the reception in Granny Griggs' house, after which we all piled into a charabanc and went to Falmouth where the great treat was our first visit to Woolworths. Everything in Woolworths in those days cost no more than sixpence, and we each had sixpence to spend, a fortune indeed.

Bridge Cottage – once a mill house

Early – Eddy Trudgeon and family. He kept the blacksmith's shop in the village. Later – Mathew and Alma Osborne (*née* Thomas) and children Mathew James, Norman, Willie, Johnny, Robert and Alma. Mathew farmed at Trewey. The Osborne boys were great cricketers. Later – the musical family of Mr and Mrs Lloyd and children Mamie, George and Walter.

Inland from Churchtown – Foage Valley

Rose Cottage

Early – Tom (from the Tinners Arms) and Anne Nankervis and family (later of Carnellow). Later – Dick Stevens (carpenter and accumulator charger for wirelesses,) wife and son Dick.

Lower Carne

Early – Mr Lawrey and family.

Foage Farm

Early – the Stevens family from Eglosmeor Mill. Later – the Edwards family. Later – Harold and Clara Semmens and children Henry, Ivan, Eddy, Mary and Phillip. Harold was an excellent horseman and broke in many a wild steed.

Continuing west with the coastal farms:

The hamlet of Trewey

1. *Trewey Farm* – Willie and Elizabeth (*née* Edwards from Foage) Noy and children Eileen and Edward. Later – Harry and Elizabeth (*née* Berryman from Porthmeor) Mann (from Morvah) and children Jessie, Willie, Audrey, Arthur and Mary; Jessie and Willie had already left home.

2. *Higher Trewey Farm* – Early – Nankervis family (later of Wicca). Later

– Willie Bennetts, wife and son. Later – Rex and Renee (*née* Palmer from Chykembro Cottages) Whelan and children Caroline and Paul.

3. *Cottage and shop at the top of the Gurnick* – Miss Anne Hosking.

4. *Cottage* – Bob and Daniel Edwards, two old bachelors – who kept a horrible bulldog.

5. *Cottage* – 'Annie up Trewey's house'. Annie Thomas and her mother.

Pit Pry

Early – Mr Bevan the head teacher at Zennor school. Later – Mr and Mrs Greening (in publishing). At Christmas time, Mr Greening gave a party in Dicka's barn for the local children, bran tub and all.

Later – the workman's cottage for Kerrow. Garfield Hosking, wife Minnie (*née* Greening, niece of Mr Greening) and son Basil. Later – Mr and Mrs Poynter and daughter Minnie.

Hillside – smallholding

Early – Mr Pascoe (quarryman) and family. Early – the Botterell family who 'milked a dairy', i.e. milked cows belonging to someone else, made butter, etc. and sold the dairy produce. Milking a dairy was, hopefully, a step up the ladder to working one's own farm. Later – Jack Sampson and family. Jack had a licence to blast with dynamite and was employed by farmers to help with rock removals.

Kerrow Farm

Early – old Billy Nicholls, his wife 'Anne up Kerrow' (*née* Thomas from Bosporthenis) and children Beatie, Olive, Willie, Fanny, Charity and Janey. Later – son Willie and wife Ida (*née* Jelbert, sister to Charlie of Carnellow).

Tregraint Cottage

Colonel Hirst, antiquarian.

Pennance Farm

Early – Daniel and Annie (*née* Lawrey from Lower Carne) Edwards and son. Later – Mr and Mrs Tripp and daughters Eva and Margaret.

Chykembro Farm

Early – Berryman family. Later – Legg family. Later – William (Bill) (from Wicca) and Betty (an artist) Nankervis. Later – Willie Craze (from Trevega), wife Robina (*née* Griggs) and daughters Alannah, Catherine and Cherry.

Carnellow Farm

Early – Thomas family. Later – 1920, Tom and Anne (*née* Eddy, sister to Granny Griggs) Nankervis (from Rose Cottage) and daughters Hilda and Dorothy. Later – Daughter Hilda and husband Charlie Jelbert, and children Charles and Hazel. Charlie was a great singer, dancer and wrecker and Hilda sang and played the church organ. Later – son Charles and Pat and sons Grant and Sean.

Poniou

The Old Coastguards – Mrs Hosking and daughters Dorothy known as Dill Doll (a school teacher) and Gwen (later of Treen). Mr Hosking died in South Africa. Later – Dill Doll and friend.

Cottage – Miss Anne Hosking, after retiring from her shop at Trewey. Aunt to Dorothy and Gwen.

The Bungalow – Early – Annie Christopher and niece Nellie. Nellie married David Berryman from Chykembro. Later – Katie and Annie Quick Thomas, two spinsters from Treen. Katie was rather prim and proper and kept Annie under her thumb. When living at Treen, they provided cream teas for visitors.

The hamlet of Boswednack Farms

1. *Boswednack Farm* – Early – Tom and Mary Grace Osborne (*née* Eddy from Bosigran, sister to Robert) and children Jack, Bernard, Betty and Gordon. Jack was a powerful chap and always won the sheaf pitching competitions. Later – son Gordon, wife May and daughters Katherine and Anne.

2. *Boswednack Farm* – Early – Thomas family. Later – Leonard Berryman (from Gurnards Head Hotel), wife Janey (*née* Hollow, from Trevega) and daughters Joan and Joyce and workman Bert.

3. *Bungalow* and smallholding – Mr and Mrs Paynter.

4. *Gear Farm* – Early – William Quick Thomas (from Treen), wife (*née* Eddy from Bosigran, sister to Robert) and daughter Hilda. Later – daughter Hilda and husband Mr Nicholas from Pendeen, and son Eric.

Gurnard's Head Hotel

Among others, 'Dick Landlord' Berryman (home from South Africa), wife Jane (*née* Stevens) and children including Clara, Leonard and Lena.

The hamlet of Treen

1. *Treen Farm* – Early – Mr and Mrs Jim Quick Thomas and children Mary, William (later of Gear Farm), Katie and Annie. In later years Katie, Annie and their father went to live at Chy Barnett, a house nearby, before the two sisters retired to Poniou. Billy, known as Farmer and David, known as Racco, brothers of Mr Quick Thomas, worked on the farm and lived in a cottage. Later – 1915, Willie Berryman (from Treveglos), wife Gwen (*née* Hosking from Poniou) and children Enid, John and Ken. Later – son Ken, wife Sonia and daughters Sarah, Joanna and Alison.

2. *Small Farm* – Early – Jimmy Thomas (not a Quick Thomas), sister Mary and daughter Vera. Jimmy's wife (daughter of Mr Quick Thomas) died when Vera was a baby and his sister reared her. When Jimmy sold out, young John Berryman farmed the small farm. Eventually it was sold to the Trenbaths.

3. *Farm* – Early – Catherine and Ben Thomas and family. They moved to

Lanyon. Later – Mr and Mrs Pascoe (from Hillside), and son Willie. Granny Pascoe kept a small shop adjoining the farm. Later – son Willie and wife Katie. Later – yet another Thomas family from St Just. Later – John Curnow, wife Sylvia (*née* Carlyon from Higher Bosporthennis) and daughter Eleanor. Later – Basil and Beryl Olds. Later – Trenbath family.

4. *Cottage* – Early – old Mrs Kitty White and daughter Nanny, who was a teacher at Porthmeor school. Later – Nanny Johns (*née* White) and daughters Mabel and Katie (later Osborn of Tremeadow). When Nanny became Mrs Johns she went to live in Mousehole, and on soon becoming a widow, she returned to Treen with her children. She carried the post for many years.

5. *Cottage* – Early – Fred Carlyon and wife Martha and daughters Rachel, Sylvia and Maggie. The last two worked at Tremedda for my mother.

6. *Cottages* – Later – Vera Thomas (daughter of Jimmy Thomas) and Katie Pascoe.

The hamlet of Porthmeor Farms

1. *Farm* – Early – Will and Jess Berryman and family. Later – son Jim and wife Liza (*née* Craze) and sons William and Frank.

2. *Farm* – Arthur Berryman's family including Arthur, Betsy (a Zennor school teacher), Wilmot, and Arther's two daughters Ada and Annie.

Bosigran Farm

Early – Robert and Janey (*née* Berryman, sister to Jim of Porthmeor), Eddy and sons Claude, Jack and Cyril. Mrs Eddy played the old schoolroom piano with great gusto for parties, etc. Later – David Berryman (from Treveglos), wife Sybil and family.

Inland from Porthmeor

Higher Porthmeor – sometimes known as 'Little London' – Early – Mr Bassett and family. Later – Powel Noy and family.

Bosporthennis Farms – known locally as Sprennis

Higher Bosporthennis – Mathew and Alma Osborne (from Bridge Cottage) and their nine children. They moved here in 1913 when Mathie James, the eldest son, was eight years old. Six years later, in 1919, they moved to Lower Bosporthennis where they lived for a further six years, when they moved out of the parish to Brunyan in Towednack parish. Later – John and Sylvia (*née* Carlyon from Treen) Curnow.

The hamlet of Lower Bosporthennis

1. Mathew Eddy and family, including his sister Anne Eddy, the seamstress.

2. Tommy Thomas and family.

Inland from Foage

Home of the 'Mountainy People' or 'Downsers'

Mill Downs Farm

David and Mildred Osborn and daughters Rhona and Maureen.

The hamlet of Lady Downs

1. *Farm* – Early – Prowse family. Later – Bert James and family.
2. *Farm* – Andrew Lawrey, wife and son Andrew.

Higher Kerrow Farm

Early – Warren family; great chapel people. Later – Mr Lawrey and family. Later – son Donald and wife Stella and family.

An old open chimney, p. 16

APPENDIX 2

The Cornish Language, and a Vocabulary

ACCORDING to Hobson and Mathew's *History of St Ives, Lelant, Towednack and Zennor*, the parishes of Towednack and Zennor were very late in exchanging the Celtic speech of their inhabitants for the Saxon. The families of Stevens and Trewhella were among the last to keep up the Cornish language in the parish of Towednack. Old Dr Stevens of the middle to late nineteenth century said that his great-grandfather Andrew Stevens of Trevega used to take his (Dr Stevens') grandfather on his knee and say "Come here my little *kennack* [rush light]" and would make the youngster count after him in Cornish "*woanen, deau, tri, pedar, pemp*". He also used the exclamation "*scavel angow!*" meaning a pack of lies or gossip.

In the year 1890, one John Davey lived at Boswednack in Zennor parish. He still had some hereditary knowledge of the Cornish language and could converse on a few simple topics.

CORNISH DIALECT WORDS IN USE IN ZENNOR PARISH
AND FARMING AND TRADE TERMS

A

Adit	Tunnel to drain water from, or for entrance to, a mine
Arrish	Corn field after the harvest has been gathered in, stubble

B

Ballyrag	To Scold
Bester	Great one
Biddicks	Long-bladed turf digger
Broach	Stout stick, usually blackthorn, sharpened at one end tohammer into a rick when thatching.
Brandis	Three-legged iron trivet on which cooking pots are placed over an open fire.
Buddle	Small moat surrounded by a stone wall, in which crushed tin-stone was washed.

C

Chainer	Extra horse hitched by two chains to the front of a working horse to help with heavy loads.
Chislers	The short cutting shears on a scuffler
Count house	Mine offices
Clome	Earthenware
Croft	Rough land, usually between fields and higher moorland

D

Dram	Long thick line of cut hay
Draw	Flat wood or metal sheet on two iron runners

E

Eval	Five-pronged dung fork

F

Feather	Piece of curved metal, similar to a length from a bucket handle
Ferns	Bracken
Flasket	Oval basket for washing
Furze hitch	Long piece of cylindrical metal with a barb at one end and wooden handle at the other.

G

Gad	Iron chisel-like wedge
Gon	Hanging scales for weighing heavy goods in a shop

H

Hames	Two long metal pieces that fit into grooves on a

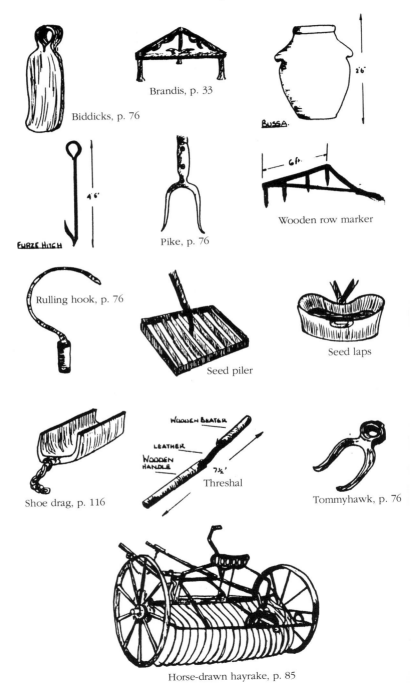

Biddicks, p. 76

Brandis, p. 33

2'6"

BUSSA.

4'6"

FURZE HITCH

Pike, p. 76

6 ft.

Wooden row marker

Rulling hook, p. 76

Seed piler

Seed laps

Shoe drag, p. 116

WOODEN BEATER

LEATHER

WOODEN HANDLE

7½'

Threshal

Tommyhawk, p. 76

Horse-drawn hayrake, p. 85

working horse's collar. These are fitted with rings through which the reins run, and hooks for the pulling chains.

Hipping stock   Stone mounting-block

J

Jouster   A man who buys fish from the boats and goes round the villages, usually with a horse and cart, selling them.

Jumper   Steel-nosed iron bar about five feet long used for making holes in rock.

K

Kitty bags   Pieces of sacking tied around trouser legs for protection

Kibble   Large bucket used in mines

L

Leasing   Picking up (stones)

Liner   Sheaf of corn threshed by a barn thresher

Ley   Land temporarily under grass

M

Mawn   Large basket with a handle on either side for farm good

Mops   Headgear for the working horse

Mow   Small round stack of corn

O

Opening up   The first cut of corn around the edge of a field, done with a scythe.

Ovice   The last ring of sheaves on a rick stem, laid with a slight overhang to shoot rainwater clear of the rick sides.

P

Pook   Small showerproof mound of hay

Q

Quillet   Very small field, paddock

R

Ragged sheaf   Sheaf partly threshed by a barn thresher, with some of the grain left on the stalk.

Riggers   Wooden frames erected at the front and rear of a wain to keep a load in place.

Rulling   Taking out a sufficient amount of corn for one sheaf with a rulling hook.

Rulling hook   Semi-circular hook of cylindrical iron with a wooden handle.

S

Scuffler   Implement for tearing up turf when breaking new ground.

Seal	Hedge trimmings, bracken, brambles, etc. used as a thick base for corn- and hayricks.
Seed-laps	A pan for seed sowing, curved to fit the body with two straps over the shoulders.
Shock	Small wigwam-like structure of eight sheaves, each s tanding on its butt with the ears leaning in to a point.
Slab	Cast-iron Cornish range or cooking stove
Stamps	Water-driven machine that lifts heavy pieces of iron and lets them fall onto tin stone, to break it up.
Stuggy	Short and rotund

T

Threshal	Two pieces of wood, leather-jointed, used as a flail for hand-threshing sheaves of corn.
Tommyhawk	A long-handled two-clawed iron digger with its points turned slightly inwards.
Touser	Coarse apron

V

Vor	Furrow

W

Whim	Horse-powered machine for raising kibbles of tin stone from mine shafts or for working a barn thresher
Whim round	Circular raised granite platform paved with rab around which a horse walked to work the whim
Whipsaderry	Horse-drawn contrivance with a back-and-forth movement, to raise kibbles of tin stone from mine shafts.

WORDS OF CORNISH DERIVATION STILL IN USE IN 1990

	Cornish	*English*
Bowly	Bulyen	Pebble
Browse	Brows	Crumb, fragment
Bussa	Bussa	Large earthenware salting pot
Bern	Bern	Heap, rick, stack (bundle)
Carn	Carn	Rockpile, hill
Carracks	Carreck	Rockmass, huge rock
Claws	Glos	Dried cow-dung fuel
Clydgy	Clyjjy	Toffee
Coose	Cows	Speech, talk, discourse
Croust	Crowst	Noon meat, meal taken to work
Crow	Crow	Shed, hut, sty

Dan	Den	Man
Fitty	Fyttya	To prepare, make fit or ready
Gavars	Gavar	Goat
Gleaner	Galliyna	Guinea fowl
Guldise	Gol	Parish Feast
Guldise	Goldhey's	Harvest Home
Ibbo	Ebol	Small *mow* – rock this shape off Gurnard's Head
Kibble	Kybel	Tub, mine or well bucket
Lias	Lys	Mud
Peath	Pyth	Sunk, stone-lined well
Piggywidden	Pyg-byghan	Smallest pig of the litter
Pygal	Pygal	Pick, mattock
Rab	Rabmen	Granite gravel and clay
(Seed) Piler	Pylya	To strip, peel, skin, make bare
Stank	Stank	Heavy tread
Stog	Stok	Stem, stump, stick
Tealing	Tewlel	To throw, toss, cast
Troy	Troghya	Wash, dip, plunge, or steep; wash-tub
Tubban	Tymmyn	Sods
Tubban	Tomen	Small tuft of turf
Ushan	Usyn	Chaff, husk of cereal

Place Names

Prefixes to place names

Bos	Abode, dwelling place
Chy	House, building
Nans	Valley, dale
Pen	Head, chief, top
Pol	Pool, pond
Porth	Port, harbour, cove
Tre (with v before a vowel)	Dwelling place, homestead, farm, village

Place Names

Chy-an-Eglos	Eglos = church		House by the Church
Chykembro	Kembro= Welshman		House of the Welshman
Poniou	Ponsow or Ponygow	Bridges little bridge	

Pitpry	Pyt = pit	Claypit
	Pry = clay	
St Budoc	Budoc	The drowned one
	Budhy	To drown .
Treveglos	Farm, etc., by the church	

Field Names

	Cornish	*English*
Castle Skudjack	1. Scos	Defence
	2. Skewyek	Sheltered
Cross Close	1. Crows	Cross
	2. Clos	Enclosure
Dalvins	Tal	End, top
	Veyn	Stones
Dormullion	Dor	Ground
	Mullyon	Clover
Druzel (Moor)	1. Dreyslon	Thicket of brambles
Gallalas	Goles	Bottom, lowest part
Park Leata	Park	Field
	Liyth	Moist
Shoot Field	Shuta	Water conduit

The Cornish language, from which these present day words and names have been derived, has been worked out from *An English Cornish and Cornish English Dictionary* edited by R. Morton Nance.